Invoking Empire

Manchester University Press

STUDIES IN IMPERIALISM

When the 'Studies in Imperialism' series was founded by Professor John M. MacKenzie more than thirty years ago, emphasis was laid upon the conviction that 'imperialism as a cultural phenomenon had as significant an effect on the dominant as on the subordinate societies'. With well over a hundred titles now published, this remains the prime concern of the series. Cross-disciplinary work has indeed appeared covering the full spectrum of cultural phenomena, as well as examining aspects of gender and sex, frontiers and law, science and the environment, language and literature, migration and patriotic societies, and much else. Moreover, the series has always wished to present comparative work on European and American imperialism, and particularly welcomes the submission of books in these areas. The fascination with imperialism, in all its aspects, shows no sign of abating, and this series will continue to lead the way in encouraging the widest possible range of studies in the field. 'Studies in Imperialism' is fully organic in its development, always seeking to be at the cutting edge, responding to the latest interests of scholars and the needs of this ever-expanding area of scholarship.

To buy or to find out more about the books currently available in this series, please go to: https://manchesteruniversitypress.co.uk/series/studies-in-imperialism/

Invoking Empire

Imperial citizenship and Indigenous rights across the British World, 1860–1900

Darren Reid

MANCHESTER UNIVERSITY PRESS

Published by Manchester University Press
Oxford Road, Manchester, M13 9PL

www.manchesteruniversitypress.co.uk

British Library Cataloguing-in-Publication Data
A catalogue record for this book is available from the British Library

ISBN 978 1 5261 8162 6 hardback

First published 2025

EU authorised representative for GPSR:
Easy Access System Europe, Mustamäe tee 50,
10621 Tallinn, Estonia
gpsr.requests@easproject.com

Typeset by Newgen Publishing UK

Contents

Maps

Introduction

The British Empire underwent an enormous change between 1848 and 1893. Previously, most British colonies were what are now known as Crown Colonies, administrated by imperial governors with varying levels of representative institutions that subordinated local input to imperial authority. In 1848, however, Britain granted responsible government to two Canadian colonies (Nova Scotia and the Province of Canada), so that, with new parliaments consisting entirely of locally elected politicians, they became the Empire's first self-governing colonies. The development was contagious: as Alan Lester, Kate Boehme, and Peter Michell put it, once Britain had "released the genie of responsible government, it proved impossible for the Colonial Office to put it back in its bottle."[1] Within eleven years, self-government had taken hold in Prince Edward Island (1851), New Zealand (1853), New Brunswick (1854), Newfoundland (1855), New South Wales (1855), Victoria (1855), Van Diemen's Land (1855), South Australia (1856), and Queensland (1859). Change came slower to regions such as British Columbia, the Cape Colony, and Western Australia, where the road to self-government commenced in the 1850s and 1860s with partially representative institutions but full responsibility was delayed until 1871, 1872, and 1890, respectively. Nevertheless, with the dawn of self-government in Natal in 1893, the British Empire had effectively been cleaved into dependent Crown Colonies and the independent settler colonies that would eventually become the nation-states of Canada, South Africa, Australia, and New Zealand. This book is about the cleavage of the self-governing settler states from the administrative authority of the British Empire and, more particularly, about how Indigenous peoples and settlers living in such colonies during the transitional decades between 1860 and 1900 adapted, resisted, and gave shape to the changes in sovereignty and jurisdiction that were happening around them.

Certainly, for many settlers, the dawn of self-government was the triumphant culmination of passionate campaigns against imperial mismanagement. These campaigns took on different aspects in each colonial location.

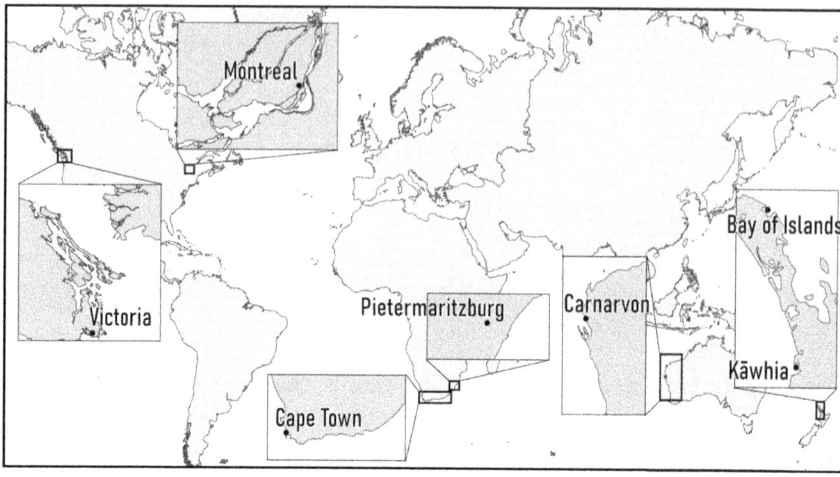

Map 0.1 Case studies in this book

In Canada, the Upper and Lower Canadian Rebellions of 1837–1838 became potent symbols of settler resistance against an imperial administration that had completely broken down because of gridlock between nominated imperial officials and elected settler officials.[2] Similar issues arose in the Cape Colony and Natal, where, in the face of economic recession in the 1860s, stalemates between nominated imperial officials pushing for higher taxes and elected settler officials demanding reduced government spending became emblematic of imperial maladministration.[3] In the Australian colonies, the continuation of convict transportation – Britain's practice of using the colonies as prisoner dumping grounds to relieve its own overcrowded jails – in the face of settler calls for its abolition was a particularly striking representation of the imperial government's disregard for colonists.[4] In New Zealand, Governor Sir George Grey's unilateral suspension in 1848 of an agreed-upon constitution that would have provided settlers with an elected House of Representatives served as evidence of the imperial government's autocracy.[5] For many of the settlers who witnessed these and more instances of ineffective and even hostile government by irresponsible imperial officials, self-government represented a victory over despotism and the winning of political rights (for propertied white men, at least; universal political rights were many decades away).

However, self-government was not a victory for everybody. In every settler colony, the realization of settler rights was contingent upon the denial of Indigenous rights. Historians today often refer to this as the settler colonial logic of elimination, in which settler demands for land, labour, and sovereignty required the extinguishment of Indigenous land rights, the destruction of Indigenous economic independence, and the denial of Indigenous sovereignty.[6] British administrators had acknowledged the antagonistic relationship between settler and Indigenous societies since the 1835 Parliamentary Select Committee on Aborigines, which recommended that the imperial government do more to regulate settler–Indigenous relations, to "civilize" Indigenous peoples, and to protect them from destruction and prepare them for assimilation into European society,[7] but these recommendations only contributed to settler perceptions of imperial despotism. Throughout the 1830s and 1840s, imperial policies of "humanitarian governance" such as the retrocession of Queen Adelaide's Province from the Cape Colony to Xhosa ownership in 1835, the execution of seven New South Wales settlers following the Myall Creek Massacre in 1838, and the exoneration of Te Rauparaha and Te Rangihaeata for killing twenty-two New Zealand settlers following the Wairau Incident of 1843, all became flashpoints of settler–imperial animosity that fuelled campaigns for self-government. Early-nineteenth-century imperial humanitarians lobbied hard to maintain imperial control over "native affairs" as a means of limiting colonial violence, and settler societies counter-lobbied just as hard to undermine humanitarian credibility and assert themselves as the true experts and rightful rulers of Indigenous populations. Settlers eventually overcame the imperial humanitarian lobby through a combination of their own efforts to change public opinion, the disillusionment of metropolitan humanitarians following the unprofitability of emancipation, and the British government's desire to offload administrative costs onto the colonies.[8] Winning self-government was thus a double victory over Indigenous sovereignty and imperial humanitarianism, with settlers, Indigenous peoples, and imperialists forming the triangular relationship of settler colonialism theorized by Lorenzo Veracini.[9]

Of course, contrary to widespread settler expectations that Indigenous peoples would inevitably vanish in the face of European civilization,[10] Indigenous peoples persisted and became critical elements within settler societies. Not only did Indigenous *peoples* not disappear, but Indigenous *sovereignty* persisted also. The traditional European interpretation of territorial sovereignty as the indivisible, supreme political power over a defined space, which Lisa Ford demonstrates was largely a settler invention of the early nineteenth century designed to undermine Indigenous rights,[11] is problematically applied to many Indigenous peoples who lived (and continue to live) within settler spaces where they lacked the economic, political, and judicial power to claim or perform territorial sovereignty. However, Goenpul scholar Aileen Moreton-Robinson reminds us that Indigenous sovereignty can also be interpreted as embodied ways of being, knowing, and relating to ancestors, people, and lands.[12] And as Mohawk scholar Audra

Simpson demonstrates, Indigenous peoples have continued such a form of sovereignty alongside settler territorial sovereignty through the everyday sovereign practice of deciding for themselves how to live their lives.[13] Such practice takes many forms, sometimes entailing armed resistance; sometimes making strategic adaptations; and other times making choices about how, in the words of Ojibwe/Dakota scholar Scott Lyons, to "live a new life" in changing circumstances that challenge the problematic binary of resistance/assimilation.[14] Consequently, from the very moment that settlers gained self-government, their claims to territorial sovereignty were compromised by the continuing embodied sovereignties of Indigenous nations.

Moreover, Indigenous peoples were not the only dissident members of the self-governing settler colonies. An important element of campaigns for self-government that national mythologies frequently ignore is the fact that many settlers did not want to be self-governing, so that winning responsible government was just as much about defeating other settlers as it was about defeating imperial humanitarians and Indigenous peoples. Deemed "anti-responsibles," they hailed from a range of backgrounds. Some derived from minority demographics such as anglophones in prevailingly French parts of Canada and British settlers in largely Afrikaner regions of the Cape Colony, whose feelings of precarity led anti-responsibles to see imperial administration as a bulwark against numerical domination by larger social groups. Some anti-responsibles simply believed that their fellow settlers were too corrupt, too divided, or too inexperienced to form an effective government. Yet others, especially those from upper-class backgrounds, feared the rise of democracy as "mob rule" and instead clung to the power and prestige they received from imperial nominations and preferences. In some colonies, anti-responsibles were able to successfully thwart campaigns for self-government for years and even decades. Even when colonies did finally receive responsible governments, the experiment of self-government was so new and unfamiliar that many anti-responsibles continued living as they had always done, assuming that the imperial authorities would step in and intervene in settler affairs when necessary.

Thus, in the decades after self-government, three groups occupied the settler colonies: a settler majority intent upon making settler sovereignty work, various settler minorities intent upon remaining under imperial sovereignty, and countless Indigenous peoples undermining the basis of self-government by asserting their own continuing sovereignties. This book is about the lived experiences of these overlapping and conflicting spheres of Indigenous, settler, and imperial sovereignty, focusing specifically on Indigenous peoples' and settlers' efforts to leverage imperial political authority for the fortification of their own competing interests. I demonstrate that imperial authority was a malleable concept, capable of being invoked to defeat responsible government as well as to support it; to undermine Indigenous rights as well as to protect them. Such invocations took three key forms: lobbying the British government through correspondence and personal connections, appealing to British public opinion through pamphlets and letters to the editor, and physically travelling to Britain to liaise with government officials. I have two overarching purposes in focusing on lived experiences of imperial sovereignty in this period of transition. First, I want to explore the ways in which Indigenous peoples and settlers conceptualized the role of the imperial government in their local environments following the official retreat of the Empire from the administration of self-governing colonies. How did the rise of settler self-government impact local understandings of and relationships with imperial authority? Second, I want to assess the consequences of local engagements with the imperial government on the historical trajectories of settler colonialism. What was the relationship between imperial authority and the settler power structures that took shape in the years leading up to and following the cession of self-government? Each chapter addresses these questions in different ways, and I return to these questions with a synthetical perspective in the concluding chapter.

Imperial humanitarianism

A central element running throughout this entire book is the concept and discourse of imperial humanitarianism, which has received growing scholarly attention in recent years. "Humanitarianism" is an anachronistic concept applied by historians to a range of activities variously termed by contemporaries as philanthropy, charity, friendship, and benevolence, all of which shared a basic commitment to improving the welfare of other people.[15] Humanitarian action took many forms in the British Empire, encompassing anti-slavery, anti-convict transportation, famine relief, mission work, war casualty relief, and more.[16] Indigenous rights activism was merely one small part of this broader humanitarian milieu, but its significance to the development of settler colonial politics has given it prominence in the historiography of imperial humanitarianism.

A major recent focus in this historiography is the concept of humanitarian governance. In their influential 2014 study, Alan Lester and Fae Dussart challenge the assumption that the British Empire was evenly divided into government officials and humanitarian critics of government. On the contrary, they argue that imperial government officials were always guided by humanitarian discourses that evolved over the course of the nineteenth century, becoming increasingly more oppressive in response to the on-the-ground difficulties of governing settlers and Indigenous peoples.[17] This argument has been further developed and nuanced by a range of historians in the intervening decade. Amanda Nettelbeck, for instance, proposes that imperial government administrators were not merely informed by humanitarian impulses, but that the notion of "protecting" Indigenous peoples and their rights was used as a pretence for remaking Indigenous peoples into "productive" and loyal British subjects.[18] Conversely, Richard Price challenges the idea that humanitarianism was *always* connected to imperial governance, instead arguing that it only morphed into a method of governing and controlling Indigenous peoples under the influence of settlers following representative and responsible government.[19] Together, such explorations of humanitarian governance reveal that considerations of Indigenous rights protection were wedded to government efforts at subjugating and controlling Indigenous bodies.

However, while this historiography has extensively examined the role of humanitarian discourses within imperial and colonial governments, less attention has been directed to the significance of humanitarian discourses for non-governmental subjects and citizens. Most of such work has been focused on Indigenous uses of humanitarian discourses for defending their own interests, emphasizing humanitarianism's mutability for both undermining and supporting Indigenous agendas.[20] Settler humanitarianism, on the other hand, remains severely understudied. The two most substantial works on the subject, both written more than twenty years ago, consist of collections of individual stories proving that settler humanitarians did exist, presenting such humanitarians as social outliers and offering little critical analysis of the societal significance of settler humanitarianism more broadly.[21] More recently, Jane Lydon refutes the idea that settler humanitarians were "obsessives and outsiders" and instead argues that humanitarianism was prominent in settler "everyday culture."[22] Lydon and Sam Hutchinson have each begun examining the role played by humanitarianism in Australian society, emphasizing its functionality for legitimizing colonial violence, while Kenton Storey has contributed a similar assessment regarding New Zealand and British Columbia.[23]

Invoking Empire contributes to this scholarship by providing a synthetical perspective combining insights from seven colonial sites and spanning four decades. I argue that there was an Empire-wide culture, shared by Indigenous peoples and settlers alike, of intercepting existing humanitarian discourses and networks in the pursuit of imperial intervention, using ideas of justice, honour, and humanity to lend moral weight and political capital to demands upon the imperial government. The Aborigines' Protection Society (APS), a voluntary lobbying group formed in the wake of the 1835 Select Parliament on Aborigines and continuing in some form until 1947, was a particularly useful resource, with its longstanding political and social capital providing a back door into the offices of British newspaper editors and government officials.[24] This book demonstrates the ubiquity of tapping into the APS's imperial humanitarian network in the pursuit of local objectives, including large agitations for and against responsible government as well as petty personal squabbles over perceived prejudices and persecutions. Moreover, by including Indigenous and settler usages of the APS within the same frame, the book reveals that there were significant structural barriers that hampered the use of humanitarian networks by colonial subjects. I argue that three such barriers existed: retribution by settlers hostile to imperial intervention, disinterest in Indigenous issues on the part of the British public, and imperial communication regimes that privileged settler government perspectives over those of Indigenous and settler individuals. Through an examination of correspondence between the colonies and the APS in combination with petitions from the colonies to the British government and letters from the colonies published in the British press, this book attends to how both supporters and dissidents of settler self-government in the late nineteenth century attempted, and eventually failed, to navigate the tensions between Indigenous, settler, and imperial sovereignties inherent within settler colonialism by performing imperial citizenship through a humanitarian lens.

Sources and methodology

In the pages that follow, you will meet a range of unique individuals. They include Māori and Xhosa chiefs, Canadian scientists and Australian preachers, Black journalists from the Cape Colony, and white politicians from Natal. Each of these very different persons had important things in common. They each witnessed or directly experienced violence or oppression at the hands of settler societies, ranging from the enslavement of Indigenous peoples in Western Australia to the destruction of an Indigenous church in Quebec to the disenfranchisement of Black Africans in the Cape. They each interpreted these acts of violence through a humanitarian discourse of violated rights, whether that be a right to freedom, a right to religious equality, or a right to vote. They each called for the British government to rectify their violated rights as imperial citizens when local settler governments proved unwilling or incapable, and they each also failed to have their rights vindicated by the Empire. The shared experiences of these individuals in the face of their extraordinary differences drive the main argument of this book: that in the immediate decades surrounding settler self-government, imperial citizenship performed through humanitarian discourses and networks afforded both Indigenous peoples and settlers a means of leveraging the power of the imperial government for the defence of their own interests.

Yet these individuals' differing experiences of imperial citizenship are no less important. They are revealing of the flexibility and nuances of imperial citizenship in diverse situations, and point to the many structures that incentivized colonial rather than imperial political subjectivities. I explore these nuances and structures by organizing this book into two stages of disaggregation. The first stage divides the book into three parts based on the relationship imperial subjects had with their local governing structures. Part I attends to settlers living under Crown and representative governments whereby they enjoyed only nominal political rights, for whom working through imperial authority was the primary means of participatory politics. Conversely, Part II attends to settlers living under responsible governments whereby they received political rights from their local governments, yet who continued to claim overarching rights from their imperial government. Moving beyond settler perspectives, Part III attends to Indigenous and colonized peoples living under responsible settler governments who were denied political rights, for whom imperial authority held the promise of keeping settler governments in check through upholding treaty obligations and vetoing unconstitutional legislation. By exploring how individuals performed and experienced imperial citizenship in each of these three contexts, *Invoking Empire* demonstrates the continuity and breadth of the concept of imperial citizenship while simultaneously emphasizing the specificity in which it was mobilized by different people in different circumstances.

The second stage of disaggregation occurs at the chapter level, where I contextualize the operation of imperial citizenship through nine case studies of Indigenous–settler conflicts spanning seven unique colonial spaces: Natal, Western Australia, the Cape Colony, New Zealand, Quebec, Bechuanaland, and British Columbia. I chose these case studies based on several criteria. The research underlying *Invoking Empire* is based on petitions (to the British government as well as to local colonial governments), newspaper materials (primarily letters to the editor of colonial and British newspapers), and personal correspondence (in the form of letters sent from the colonies to British politicians, the APS, and family members in Britain). Each of these types of primary sources was created with different audiences and objectives in mind and used different rhetorical strategies and evidence, so that a clear picture of imperial citizenship only arises when multiple types of sources are combined. Consequently, while imperial citizenship was widely practised in settler societies, this book is limited to a select group of individuals for whom multiple overlapping types of primary sources exist. Case studies were also chosen to avoid redundancy or repetition. Many individuals performed imperial citizenship for similar reasons and in similar ways, and to include all such examples would provide quantitative support as to popularity without offering new insights into its operation or historical significance. The nine case studies that make up this book were therefore chosen with as much an eye to their contradictions as to their similarities, so that when read in juxtaposition to one another they reveal the breadth and nuance of visions of imperial authority in late-nineteenth-century settler colonies as well as the structural obstacles in Britain and the colonies that hampered imperial intervention.

Problematically, two characteristics of my case studies that I could not satisfactorily control for were gender and class. All central figures of the case studies in this book were male, and although nearly all of them had wives who undoubtedly played a significant role in their political activities, none of their wives' voices appears in the archival record of the events discussed in this book. John Akerman's wife Emma Elizabet Brumby (Chapter 1) and John Tengo Jabavu's wife Elda Sakuba (Chapter 3) are entirely absent from their political writings. John Gribble (Chapter 2) and Philip Carpenter (Chapter 5) make passing references to their wives Mary Brown and Minna Meyer, but only as housekeepers and childminders. There is a surprisingly expansive archival record of Octavius Hadfield's wife Catherine Williams (Chapter 4), with twenty-five of her letters to family members surviving in the Wellington City Libraries to provide some insight into her role in Octavius's political activities. Unfortunately, these letters predate the events discussed in this book by many years, so we can only speculate on her direct involvement.

The invisibility of women in imperial and colonial politics is not an indication of their absence from political activity. Rather, it is the consequence of social norms that coded political work as inherently male, as well archival norms that failed to see value in recording women's labours, contributions, and voices.[25] I attend to women's voices throughout this book whenever possible, especially in Chapter 8's discussion of the British philanthropist Charlotte Weale. For the most part, however, the case studies in this book provide a decidedly male perspective, and further research is necessary to explore imperial citizenship through a gendered lens.

Moreover, all but one of the case studies hailed from middle- and upper-class backgrounds, highlighting the fact that performing imperial citizenship entailed significant class-based barriers. The most immediate barrier was monetary cost. Writing letters and petitions from the colonies to the metropole could be prohibitively expensive: in 1863, the cost of a letter from Cape Town to London was 1 shilling, roughly equivalent to 2 pounds of beef.[26] Newspapers by the late nineteenth century were relatively cheap, with a copy of the *Sydney Morning Herald* in 1880 costing only 2 pence, but that was still equivalent to around a pound of beef per newspaper, so that following prolonged conversations in letters to the editor could be an expensive hobby.[27] And travelling to England to liaise with government officials was exorbitantly costly for Indigenous groups, costing hundreds and sometimes thousands of pounds to transport, lodge, and feed multiple delegates over periods of several months. This forced delegations either to direct valuable community resources to a strategy with little chance of success, or else to fall under the influence of interested parties in Britain who offered them funding with political strings attached.[28]

Imperial citizens also faced significant knowledge barriers, of which English literacy was only the beginning. The act of writing letters and petitions in the nineteenth century was policed and informed by cultural norms illustrated by the massive proliferation of letter-writing manuals and textbooks in the eighteenth century, which disseminated standardized formats, styles of writing, and etiquette for different types of letters.[29] Knowledge about metropolitan society was also a significant factor. To lobby British politicians, submit letters to British newspapers, or organize a delegation to Britain, imperial citizens needed enough knowledge of metropolitan society to know that these actions could have an impact, along with the mailing addresses of relevant people. Imperial citizens also needed to appear sufficiently credible and respectable for people in England to take them seriously. As will be seen in Chapter 3, this was particularly challenging for David Carley from Western Australia, who was dismissed by British officials because he was an ex-convict. Yet Carley's ability to perform imperial citizenship in the face of class-based barriers is the exception, and it must be remembered that invoking imperial authority in the settler colonies was not a strategy that everybody could take advantage of.

Interpretating imperial citizenship

The fundamental characteristic that makes imperial citizenship such a fascinating and rich concept for historical analysis is that it never literally existed. Since the *Calvin v. Smith* case of 1608, all who lived within the sovereignty of the British monarch, and later the monarch-in-parliament, were automatically British subjects. Subjecthood was understood as a reciprocal relationship between subject and sovereign: in return for loyalty, the sovereign was obliged to protect their subjects by allowing them the right to access English law and to petition the Crown to redress personal grievances. Subjecthood was inherently apolitical: it was involuntary, could not be revoked, and united all subjects indiscriminately.[30] Conversely, citizenship was deeply political. It policed inclusion and exclusion from political units and thereby controlled access to political rights and responsibilities, among them the rights to vote, to stand for office, and to have a say in public affairs. The political rights of British citizens slowly developed through the Reform Acts of 1832, 1867, and 1884, with such rights coming from a combination of having a stake in the local environment, measured by property ownership or income, and meeting evolving social requirements such as age, religion, gender, and place of living.[31] Citizenship, and the political rights that came with it, were highly local, determined by the members of individual political units rather than an overarching imperial authority. It was not until the British Nationality Act of 1948 that there was any attempt to codify the citizenship rights of imperial subjects, and even then, inclusion as a "Commonwealth citizen" was dependent upon already being a citizen of either the United Kingdom or one of its dominions.[32] Citizenship, strictly speaking, was therefore never imperial.

As such, when historians use the term "imperial citizenship," they refer not to a singular concept, but to one of three interpretations. In the first interpretation, scholars of British political and intellectual history interpret imperial citizenship in reference to schemes of imperial federation that political theorists debated in the late nineteenth and early twentieth centuries but that never came to fruition.[33] These schemes were born from anxieties about international military and economic competition with Germany and the United States as well as fears of domestic social unrest. They varied widely in terms of structure, with some schemes envisioning a strict political hierarchy of states and others proposing a loose alliance of self-governing nations. Yet all failed to attract substantial popular support in the settler colonies, where nationalist citizenship predicated on racial exclusion represented, in the words of Marilyn Lake and Henry Reynolds, the "betrayal of the idea of imperial citizenship."[34] This is the most literal interpretation of imperial citizenship as well as the most limited in terms of contemporary popularity, and none of the case studies in this book focuses on the concept of imperial federation. The individuals under study believed imperial authority to be accessible through parliamentary lobbying, public opinion, and treaty relationships, but not through a formal structure of imperial federation.

Historians of popular imperial culture developed the second interpretation of imperial citizenship to capture settler attachment to an imperial community defined by a shared identity of Britishness. This approach is rooted in the dual nature of citizenship as both a political concept encompassing rights and responsibilities and a cultural concept denoting membership with a community, and contends that settler imperial citizenship consisted of only the latter by "rejecting subservience to the British *government*, but affirming equality with Britain as 'British peoples.'"[35] Various touchstones of Britishness as a cultural identifier sustained this notion of belonging, from the monarchy, liberalism, and Protestantism to the circulation of news, commodities, and familial letters, all of which contributed to multilayered settler identities as simultaneously British and Canadian,

Australian, South African, and New Zealander.[36] The now extensive scholarship of cultural Britishness as a bond of imperial belonging, developed within the British World historiographical approach, provides a crucial window into the operation and continuation of the British Empire following settler self-government. This feeling of belonging "reduc[ed] the imaginative distance between the former colonies and the metropole," and thereby enabled Britain and the future settler states to combine their resources and work together to maintain the economic, military, and cultural power of the "White Men's Countries" that still dominates global politics today.[37]

However, I argue that this bifurcation of imperial belonging into, as Andrew Thompson puts it, "being loyal to 'Downing Street' ... and being loyal to Britain" produces a prohibitively narrow cultural interpretation of imperial citizenship.[38] To be sure, it captures an important element of settler relationships with the wider Empire (and as well as those of many "respectable" people of colour, to use Charles Reed's phrasing), and it helps contextualize the worldviews of many of the individuals in this book by showing how they were able to maintain identities as belonging to a wider British community despite their growing distance from British governmental oversight.[39] However, the bifurcation of political and cultural citizenship fails to capture the form of imperial citizenship that is at the heart of this book, which, as will be seen, was consistently articulated as bound up with political rights and responsibilities guaranteed by the British government and enforceable through imperial interference in settler spaces.

The third interpretation, developed by historians of subaltern and Indigenous experiences of empire, proposes that imperial citizenship can be understood as a strategic performative claim by disenfranchised people to obtain political rights denied to them in the colonies. The denial of Indigenous political (and also property and cultural) rights, as well as the conditional granting of political rights pending assimilation to settler society and reformation into governable citizens, was fundamental to the development of Britain's settler colonies throughout the nineteenth century.[40] There were, and continue to be, countless responses to the denial of Indigenous rights, from resistance and accommodation to the refusal to recognize settler legitimacy or to court settler recognition.[41] For some, the cultural tropes of Britain as a bastion of freedom and tolerance in combination with the ambiguous rights of British subjecthood provided an avenue to pursue political rights through the strategic use of an imperial citizenship discourse. In light of their exclusion from settler political units, performative imperial citizens looked to imperial power to demand political rights through inclusion in a wider imperial unit.[42]

At the heart of the performative imperial citizenship concept is the recognition that citizenship is inherently claims-based. While it is convenient to make clean categorical borders between citizens as bearers of rights and subjects as rightless members of a political unit, in practice there has always been a grey area between the two where citizens and subjects alike debate its meaning. This has led to scholarly understandings of a claims-based citizenship that "has to be claimed, enacted, performed, and therefore is permanently subject to revision and considerable modification."[43] This allows people without formal citizenship to claim rights and sometimes have those claims recognized, just as people *with* formal citizenship can have their rights violated if not pursued and defended. In Britain, for example, women and working-class people were not originally included as British citizens, but by claiming rights through what Engin Isin calls "acts of citizenship" they altered the definition of citizenship,[44] and subaltern and Indigenous peoples made similar efforts to alter the definition of imperial citizenship. In Jared McDonald's study of Khoesan imperial citizenship, these performances occurred in petitions to colonial authorities, when petitioners strategically emphasized their loyalty to the British Empire to obtain the rights due to them in return.[45] Loyalty was particularly resonant in the context of early-nineteenth-century South Africa's violent frontier, where unrebelliousness was a marketable characteristic. Conversely, Sukanya Banerjee's study of Indian imperial citizenship in the late nineteenth and early twentieth centuries emphasizes various cultural characteristics that Indian petitioners strategically employed to demonstrate membership within an imperial British community and thus to claim rights as redefined British citizens. Such characteristics included cleanliness, creditworthiness, education, and professional experience, all of which "provided narrative frames sustaining the logic of what were unprecedented colonial articulations of formal equality."[46]

Performative imperial citizenship is the closest of the three historiographical interpretations to the version articulated by the individuals in this book, yet there remain two limitations. First, by assuming that imperial citizenship was only utilized by Indigenous peoples or "people otherwise pushed to the margins,"[47] the performative interpretation fails to capture the ways that settlers and Indigenous peoples alike used imperial citizenship both to challenge and to support settler colonial regimes. Second, by focusing on the ethereal nature of an imperial citizenship that existed largely in rhetoric alone, or what Jared Macdonald calls an "imagined subject-citizenship,"[48] the performative interpretation fails to acknowledge that imperial citizenship was sometimes entrenched in governmental and legal structures such as colonial constitutions protected by the imperial veto, treaty agreements with the Crown, and the rulings of the Privy Council. By addressing these limitations, *Invoking Empire* offers an expanded application of the performative citizenship model while simultaneously extending it to non-Indigenous subjects. Moving beyond a focus on subalternity and ethereality, I argue that the performance of imperial citizenship was a fundamental prism through which many diverse British subjects living in settler spaces experienced and negotiated the overlap between Indigenous, settler, and imperial sovereignties.

Sovereignty and the new colonial history

By bringing nine case studies together as a meta-analysis of the entanglement of imperial citizenship and settler colonialism, this book contributes to ongoing historiographical conversations about the role of empire in the histories of the settler colonies. Inspired by postcolonial scholarship of the mid-to-late twentieth century emphasizing the violent and oppressive impact of imperialism on colonized peoples, as well as by new imperial history's focus on the impact of empire and colonization on the metropole, a strand of research that Zoë Laidlaw tentatively refers to as a "new colonial history" has begun to examine the impact of empire on the formation of settler colonialism.[49]

Much of this scholarship focuses on the contingency of settler state development on imperial networks that enabled Canada, Australia, New Zealand, and South Africa to share news of local developments and build racialized power structures in collaboration with one another. Lisa Ford and Angela Woollacott, for instance, argue that settler territorial sovereignty and self-government were constructed collaboratively across the settler colonies in the early nineteenth century through the circulation of highly mobile people "with Vattel and Blackstone under their arms" who were "developing their political agendas in more than one metropolitan or colonial context, and bringing previous experience to new locations."[50] Another significant branch of new colonial history focuses on the importance of family and kinship connections in facilitating the diffusion of imperial power across colonial spaces. Adele Perry, Laura Ishiguro, and Elizabeth Elbourne each point to different ways that family networks knitted colonial and imperial power, ranging from metropolitan family members securing powerful and lucrative employment for their colonial relations to colonial family members constructing racialized narratives through correspondence with their metropolitan relations.[51] Yet another branch of new colonial historiography attends to the entanglement of imperial and colonial power through analyses of settler imperialism. In particular, William Matthew Kennedy developed the concept of "the settler colonial political cosmology of empire" to describe how self-government in the Australian colonies was "motivated by claims to fuller participation in empire rather than efforts to achieve emancipation from it," whereby Australian settlers believed that supporting Britain's imperial activities in Africa and Asia was fundamental to Australia's own interests.[52] Similar arguments have recently been applied to New Zealand's participation in Britain's colonization of the Pacific Islands and Canada's visions of colonizing Britain's former territories in the Caribbean, demonstrating that the development of the settler colonies and states was connected to and contingent upon their direct participation in the extension and maintenance of Britain's foreign empire.[53]

These new colonial histories have done much to excavate the contingencies of settler colonial power regimes upon imperial contexts, networks, and resources, yet they remain limited in various ways. Discussing the rise of postcolonialism and new imperial history, Jon Wilson and Andrew Dilley argue that an overcorrection took place whereby the traditional focus on politics and economics was replaced with a hyperattention to cultural categories such as race and gender "with little or only token reference to the diverse and specific political forms with which imperial authority was asserted."[54] I contend that a similar overcorrection has occurred within the new colonial histories discussed above, in that historians attend to the entanglement of cultural forms of settler and imperial power with little or only token reference to the entanglement of settler and imperial governmental bodies through which direct imperial authority flowed. Rather than wallowing in the messiness of the British Empire's plurality of overlapping, competing, and codependent Indigenous, settler, and imperial sovereignties, historians have constructed overly simplistic linear narratives of settler colonial administration – progressing from Crown government to representative government to responsible government – which do not capture the complex struggles between competing Indigenous, settler, and imperial political subjectivities. The idea of pluralistic sovereignty within European empires is, of course, nothing new. Lisa Ford and Lauren Benton in particular have written extensively on legal pluralism in the seventeenth, eighteenth, and early nineteenth centuries, exploring the complexity of overlapping imperial assemblages of jurisdictions, political communities, and forms of law.[55] Amanda Nettelbeck *et al.* continued this focus on imperfect and quasi-sovereignty into the late nineteenth century, demonstrating how policing and colonial law and order were used to claim settler sovereignty for the subjection of Indigenous societies in self-governing Canada and Australia.[56] Yet the bulk of this scholarship is focused on judicial understandings of sovereignty as it was exerted in court systems, ignoring contests over political sovereignty by competing claims to supreme authority by settler, imperial, or Indigenous governments.

Indeed, historians have long displayed a tendency to represent the winning of responsible government as a watershed in settler battles over Indigenous and imperial sovereignties. With the dawning of responsible government, settler societies radically recast the humanitarianism that had previously been an imperial project of ameliorating Indigenous–settler relations into a settler discourse for justifying control, assimilation, and exclusion, and from that moment, freed from the restraint of nominally humanitarian imperial oversight, a host of oppressive legislation poured forward.[57] To be sure, this watershed was not a complete disconnection from imperial power structures. Ann Curthoys and Jessie Mitchell point out that many of the coercive features associated with self-governing settler colonies such as child removal and forced assimilation were continuations of policies developed by imperial administrations. Moreover, economically and demographically inclined historians including John Darwin, James Belich, Philip Buckner, and Gary Magee and Andrew Thompson demonstrate that settler societies could not have thrived as they did without continuing injections of people, commodities, and capital from across the Empire, and New Zealand's first two decades of self-government were particularly dependent upon the continuing presence of the imperial military.[58] Yet most historians agree that from the point of self-government onwards, imperial interference in settler–Indigenous relations was highly unlikely if not effectively impossible, so that settler political sovereignty was effectively secured from competing claims by the imperial government.[59]

This narrative of responsible government as a watershed in the history of settler colonialism fits well with the contention held within settler colonial studies that imperial and settler colonialisms were different processes (the former designed to extract resources from Indigenous intermediaries and the latter designed to eliminate Indigenous peoples and replace them with permanent settler landholders),[60] providing a convenient and comprehensible point in time marking the official change from one colonialism to another and, with it, the shift from imperial to settler political sovereignty. Yet responsible government did not end imperial sovereignty over settler spaces. Lorenzo Veracini tries to sidestep this issue in his theoretical framework of settler colonialism by claiming that settler and imperial sovereignties could coexist because they were directed over different territories, with settler sovereignty directed over domestic territory and imperial sovereignty directed over foreign territory.[61] However, the British government did retain various powers over domestic settler affairs following self-government, from the power to amend and disallow legislation to the power to overturn judicial decisions through the Privy Council.[62] The continuation of imperial sovereignty over the top of settler self-government for a period ranging from several years to several decades (depending on the colony in question) highlights the importance of understanding how coexisting imperial and settler sovereignties interacted, complemented, and challenged one another. Indeed, if we are to follow the adage to consider settler colonialism as a structure rather than an event, then we must treat the winning of responsible government as only a singular event in a continuing relationship between two opposing yet overlapping structures.

Invoking Empire argues that Indigenous peoples and settlers maintained attachments to imperial authorities following responsible government because of the allure of imperial citizenship as a solution to local contests over conflicting Indigenous and settler sovereignties. For the Indigenous case studies in this book, dispossession of land and disenfranchisement from political self-determination represented the direct encroachment of settler over Indigenous sovereignties. In these instances, imperial citizens intercepted the political and social capital of imperial humanitarianism to strengthen their claims to sovereignty.[63] Conversely, the settler case studies in the book revolve around sectional disputes between settler groups with competing visions of the future of settler societies. Imperial citizens amidst these disputes used instances of injustice towards Indigenous peoples, alongside imperial humanitarian discourses and networks, as catalysts to invoke and channel imperial governmental authority against their opponents in ways that were nominally about Indigenous rights but were actually about settler rights. Imperial sovereignty was thus a mutable idea that intersected with Indigenous and settler sovereignties in multiple ways, supporting one or the other depending on who was the invoking party.

A major question that arose during the course of writing this book was how to approach the significance of failed endeavours. One of the reasons why imperial citizenship post responsible government has remained understudied is that it rarely "worked." Indeed, none of the case studies within this book obtained their objectives by invoking imperial power. Lobbying British politicians resulted in debates in the House of Commons that did not go anywhere. Publishing letters in the British press achieved some level of supportive public opinion in Britain but did not translate into local political change. Physically travelling to liaise with government officials produced some heated discussions between imperial and settler governments, but Britain always backed down. As storytellers and investigators of "significance," historians are drawn to study people, events, and concepts that did something rather than those that failed to do something. Yet failure *is* significant. As Antoinette Burton demonstrates, "the very character of imperial power was shaped by its challengers."[64] Rather than assuming that the modern settler nation-state was an inevitable progressive development from the nineteenth century to the present, Corey Snelgrove, Rita Dhamoon, and Jeff Corntassel remind historians that a host of contingent and conditional elements afforded settler colonialism the opportunity to become hegemonic.[65] By exploring how imperial subjects deployed lobbying, public opinion, and delegations to intercept imperial authority and observing how each strategy failed to fulfil expectations for various reasons, I suggest that the rise of the settler nation-state was not of an inevitable outcome of a hegemonic settler colonialism, but was partly the consequence of faltering methods for sustaining imperial citizenship.

Chapter overview

Part I surveys three unique experiences of settler imperial citizenship under representative governments in British Columbia, Natal, and Western Australia. Chapter 1 examines invocations of imperial authority during the campaign for responsible government in British Columbia in the late 1860s through the lens of a settler named William Sebright Green. Green was a strong supporter of responsible government, yet he faced successive governors who were adamantly opposed. Green therefore looked over the governor's head to imperial authorities in Britain to advocate for the necessity of responsible government, and this chapter explores how Green used humanitarian ideas around ameliorating smallpox outbreaks and compensating Indigenous peoples for their land to undermine his governor's authority and prove the necessity of constitutional reform to the Colonial Office. By locating Green's advocacy within the context of his campaign for responsible government, I argue that imperial humanitarianism provided settlers with both a language for justifying their right to self-government and a method of applying political pressure to imperial government administrations in which they had no direct input.

Whereas Green used imperial authority to support his campaign for responsible government, Chapter 2 examines an opposite case from Natal where imperial authority was used to circumvent the necessity for responsible institutions. My case study, John William Akerman, was a settler politician who was forced by public opinion to endorse responsible government, but who was secretly an anti-responsible. Just like Green in Chapter 1, Akerman too used humanitarian discourses around Indigenous rights to pursue his own agendas, in this case obtaining African land and undermining African economic independence. Yet rather than seeking to institute responsible government, Akerman hoped to remain under imperial jurisdiction, and he worked secretly through the British House of Commons by having the APS surreptitiously raise motions on his behalf. Through a juxtaposition of Akerman's public support for responsible government with his private efforts to make imperial authority work to his own interests, this chapter argues that imperial citizenship afforded settlers a means to bend imperial power to their own benefit. At the same time, backlash against

Akerman demonstrates the unsustainability of imperial citizenship as an acceptable subjectivity within settler societies.

Chapter 3 provides yet another unique perspective of imperial citizenship within representative governments, this time focusing on its entanglement with notions of legal corruption and the right to a fair trial in Western Australia. Western Australia's campaign for responsible government hit a roadblock in 1886 when four settlers became whistleblowers on the extensive enslavement of Indigenous peoples in the northern regions of the colony, convincing the Colonial Office that Western Australia was not yet ready to manage its own affairs. Yet it was not the intention of the whistleblowers to impede responsible government. All four were embroiled in local lawsuits in which imperial control over the colony's legal system had resulted in the proliferation of corrupt legal officials that inhibited their access to justice, and they consequently believed that responsible government was necessary to make legal officials answerable to the people. By exploring how these whistleblowers petitioned the imperial government against the enslavement of Indigenous peoples in pursuit of their own rights to a fair trial and to protect their own property and livelihoods, this chapter argues for the situational malleability of imperial citizenship in colonial life prior to responsible government. Petitioning the Colonial Office was not always about either supporting or opposing campaigns for responsible government, as in the cases of Green and Akerman. Rather, in the context in which imperial power was ubiquitous and access to justice was controlled by administrators thousands of kilometres away, petitioning the imperial government was also a commonplace means of responding to a wide variety of issues encountered in everyday life.

Moving beyond representative government contexts in which interacting with imperial authority was a necessary element of political life, Part II attends to performances of settler imperial citizenship within responsible government contexts where imperial authority became less directly relevant to daily life. Chapter 4 examines a series of pamphlets published in Britain by New Zealand settlers during the First Taranaki War from 1860 to 1861. Although New Zealand had gained responsible government in 1853, Britain retained control over both Māori affairs and military defence, so that the First Taranaki War was fought primarily by British forces and orchestrated by imperial officials. The pamphlets published during the war debated its legality and called upon the British government either to surrender in deference to Māori property rights or else to crush Māori forces in a demonstration of imperial power. By approaching these pamphlets as performances of imperial citizenship, this chapter argues that the continuation of imperial control over military affairs in New Zealand resulted in the continuing relevance of imperial authority to settlers following self-government, since the safety of their lives and property remained in the hands of irresponsible imperial military leaders.

Whereas the imperial government's control over military defence in New Zealand is an obvious and straightforward example of the continuing relevance of imperial authority after responsible government, Chapter 5 demonstrates that a much more nebulous situation arose when minority settler groups within self-governing colonies looked to imperial authority to protect their rights to civil equality. This chapter looks at the experiences of English settlers in Quebec in the 1870s, where a newly powerful Quebec provincial government repeatedly discriminated against the English Protestant minority in favour of the French Catholic majority. In 1875, a Protestant Defence Alliance was formed in Montreal, petitioning the British government to force Quebec to respect English rights. Yet unlike the New Zealand case, where the imperial government retained the authority to respond to petitions regarding military defence, there was little the imperial government could effectively do to interfere in Quebec's provincial affairs. Recognizing this, the purpose of the Protestant Defence Alliance's petition was not to achieve direct imperial intervention, but rather to shame the Canadian government into standing up to Quebec. Through an examination of the Protestant Defence Alliance's mobilization of Britishness as political leverage against both the British and the Canadian governments, this chapter argues that imperial citizenship provided settlers who found themselves in minority positions with a means of resisting perceived encroachments on their civil rights when local forms of citizenship failed.

While Chapters 4 and 5 both cover events that can easily be classified as either within imperial jurisdiction (in the case of defence in New Zealand) or outside it (in the case of minority rights in Quebec), such classification was not always so clear, and the operation of imperial citizenship in self-governing colonies could become even more complicated in moments where jurisdictions overlapped. Chapter 6 attends to one such moment in southern Africa known as the Bechuanaland Wars of 1882–1885. These wars took place outside the Cape Colony's boundaries, making it a matter of imperial concern, yet the wars also jeopardized trade and social stability in the Cape, making it a matter of immense colonial concern. Recognizing that domestic matters that should have been under colonial control were being influenced by imperial politics, settlers across the Cape Colony initiated waves of dozens of petitions to the Colonial Office in an attempt to assert their voting rights at an imperial scale. Through an analysis of these petitions, this chapter argues that settlers did not shift their perception of political subjectivity from the empire to the colony on a one-for-one basis, but rather combined their attachment to democratic responsible governance with their ongoing entanglement with imperial authority. Moreover, by emphasizing the importance of domestic concerns within their imperial petitions, the chapter demonstrates how domestic and imperial jurisdictions could become intimately interwoven despite efforts to establish strict jurisdictional boundaries.

A major element of all case studies from Parts I and II is backlashes against settler performances of imperial citizenship, yet the trials and tribulations of settlers who appealed to imperial authority paled in comparison to the hostility facing Indigenous imperial citizens. Part III is therefore dedicated to surveying the myriad challenges that Indigenous peoples faced when appealing to imperial authority. Chapter 7 examines Black political leader John Tengo Jabavu's lobbying efforts against the disenfranchisement of African voters in the Cape Colony. In 1887, the Cape government passed the Parliamentary Registration Act in a blatantly unconstitutional effort to deprive African people of their right to vote. The imperial government retained the power to overrule such unconstitutional legislation, but the distance between the Cape and London created an opportunity for the Cape government to exploit London's misunderstanding of African affairs and convince the Colonial Office that the new act was not unconstitutional at all. John Tengo Jabavu challenged these efforts by sending counter-petitions to the Colonial Office, but his counter-petitions never reached the Law Officers of the Crown, the Colonial Office's legal advisors who made final rulings about the constitutionality of colonial laws. His petitions were intercepted by the Secretary of State for the Colonies, so that the Law Officers ultimately determined the Parliamentary Registration Act to be constitutional based only on the reports of the Cape government. I therefore argue that Jabavu's access to imperial authority was undermined by the structure of imperial governmental communication, which enabled interested parties to suppress the voices of Indigenous and colonized peoples as they travelled the vast distances between colonies and metropole.

Even when Indigenous peoples travelled to Britain to sidestep governmental control over imperial communications, settler governments still retained substantial influence over the imperial government's perception of colonial affairs. Chapter 8 follows the 1882 Ngāpuhi delegation to London made up of Hirini Taiwhanga, Hakena Parore, and Wiremu Reweti Puhi Te Hihi from the Bay of Islands, New Zealand. Responding to rampant land dispossession and infringements on Māori sovereignty, the Ngāpuhi delegation met with the Secretary of State for the Colonies to demand the creation of a separate New Zealand parliament reserved for Māori members to govern Māori affairs. This was a request that the British government did retain the power to fulfil, but it was convinced not to do so by propaganda emanating from the New Zealand government that raised doubts about the delegation's credibility as a representative of the Ngāpuhi. Similar to the way the Cape government was able to undermine John Tengo Jabavu's lobbying through the privileged flow of information via official channels, the failure of the Ngāpuhi delegation reveals the significant influence that settler governments had over interpretations of imperial citizenship even when those citizens left settler borders.

But it was not only government agencies that worked to undermine Indigenous performances of imperial citizenship. Chapter 9 looks at the negative influence of British humanitarians on the 1884 Waikato delegation to London by Tāwhiao, Te Whēoro, Tōpia Tūroa, Hōri Rōpiha, Wiremu Pātara Te Tuhi, and George Skidmore from Kāwhia, New Zealand. Although the Waikato delegation benefited from the social connections and political capital of the APS, it also suffered interference and sabotage by "well-meaning" humanitarians, particularly a philanthropist named Charlotte Weale, who believed that it was more important for the Waikato to learn about British culture than to pursue political objectives. Focusing on how Charlotte Weale interfered in the Waikato delegation by asserting control over their choice of interpreter and sabotaging their efforts to obtain an audience with the royal family, this chapter argues that her refusal to recognize the delegation as political agents underscores the inherent limitation of imperial citizenship claims. The success of such claims depended on the concept of imperial citizenship being recognized as a source of rights by the very imperialists who had taken those rights away in the first place. Weale was only willing to recognize Māori rights to be educated and assimilated to European culture, and she did the best she could to convince the Waikato delegation that those were the only rights they had.

Notes

1 Alan Lester, Kate Boehme, and Peter Mitchell, *Ruling the World: Freedom, Civilisation and Liberalism in the Nineteenth-Century British Empire* (Cambridge: Cambridge University Press, 2021), 108.

2 Allan Greer, "1837–38: Rebellion Reconsidered," *The Canadian Historical Review* 76, no. 1 (1995): 1–18, www.muse.jhu.edu/article/574662 (accessed 11 March 2025).

3 J. L. McCracken, *The Cape Parliament, 1854–1910* (Oxford: Clarendon Press, 1967); John Lambert, "The Responsible Government Question in Natal, 1856–1893," *Kleio* 7, no. 1 (1975): 22–39, DOI: 10.1080/00232087585310021.

4 Peter Cochrane, *Colonial Ambition: Foundations of Australian Democracy* (Melbourne: Melbourne University Press, 2006).

5 Raewyn Dalziel, "Southern Islands: New Zealand and Polynesia," in Andrew Porter and William Roger Louis (eds), *The Oxford History of the British*

Empire, Vol. III, *The Nineteenth Century* (Oxford: Oxford University Press, 1999), 573–596.

6 For discussions of logics of elimination, see Patrick Wolfe, "Settler Colonialism and the Elimination of the Native," *Journal of Genocide Research* 8, no. 4 (2006): 387–409, DOI: 10.1080/14623520601056240; Neil Nunn, "Toxic Encounters, Settler Logics of Elimination, and the Future of a Continent," *Antipode* 50, no. 5 (2018): 1330–1348, DOI: 10.1111/anti.12403; and Lorenzo Veracini, "Containment, Elimination, Endogeneity: Settler Colonialism in the Global Present," *Rethinking Marxism* 31, no. 1 (2019): 118–140, DOI: 10.1080/08935696.2019.1577611.

7 Elizabeth Elbourne, "The Sin of the Settler: The 1835–36 Select Committee on Aborigines and Debates over Virtue and Conquest in the Early Nineteenth-Century British White Settler Empire," *Journal of Colonialism and Colonial History* 4, no. 3 (2003), DOI: 10.1353/cch.2004.0003.

8 Alan Lester has played a prominent role in constructing and sustaining this narrative. See Alan Lester and Fae Dussart, *Colonization and the Origins of Humanitarian Governance: Protecting Aborigines across the Nineteenth-Century British Empire* (Cambridge: Cambridge University Press, 2014); Alan Lester, "Race and Citizenship," in Martin Hewitt (ed.), *The Victorian World* (London: Routledge, 2012), 381–397, DOI: 10.4324/9780203718056; Alan Lester, "Humanitarians and White Settlers in the Nineteenth Century," in Norman Etherington (ed.), *Missions and Empire* (Oxford: Oxford University Press, 2005); Alan Lester, "British Settler Discourse and the Circuits of Empire," *History Workshop Journal* 54, no. 1 (2002): 24–48, DOI: 10.1093/hwj/54.1.24; Alan Lester, "Colonial Settlers and the Metropole: Racial Discourse in the Early 19th-Century Cape Colony, Australia and New Zealand," *Landscape Research* 27, no. 1 (2002): 39–49, DOI: 10.1080/01426390220110757; and Alan Lester, *Imperial Networks: Creating Identities in Nineteenth-Century South Africa and Britain* (New York: Routledge, 2001).

9 Lorenzo Veracini, *Settler Colonialism: A Theoretical Overview* (Cham: Palgrave Macmillan, 2010).

10 For a discussion of this "fatal impact theory," see Patrick Brantlinger, *Dark Vanishings: Discourse on the Extinction of Primitive Races, 1800–1930* (Ithaca: Cornell University Press, 2003).

11 Lisa Ford, *Settler Sovereignty: Jurisdiction and Indigenous People in America and Australia, 1788–1836* (Cambridge, MA: Harvard University Press, 2010).

12 Aileen Moreton-Robinson (ed.), *Sovereign Subjects: Indigenous Sovereignty Matters* (Crows Nest: Allen & Unwin, 2007), 2.

13 Audra Simpson, *Mohawk Interruptus: Political Life across the Borders of Settler States* (Durham, NC: Duke University Press, 2014), 2.

14 Scott Richard Lyons, *X-Marks: Native Signatures of Assent* (Minneapolis: University of Minnesota Press, 2010), 8–9.

15 Claire McLisky, "'Due Observance of Justice, and the Protection of Their Rights': Philanthropy, Humanitarianism and Moral Purpose in the Aborigines Protection Society circa 1837 and Its Portrayal in Australian Historiography,

1883–2003," *Limina: A Journal of Historical and Cultural Studies* 11 (2005): 57–66, DOI: 10.3316/informit.225751412200669.

16 Rebecca Gill, *Calculating Compassion: Humanity and Relief in War, Britain 1870–1914* (Manchester: Manchester University Press, 2013); Hilary Carey, *Empire of Hell: Religion and the Campaign to End Convict Transportation in the British Empire, 1788–1875* (Cambridge: Cambridge University Press, 2019); Richard Huzzey, *Freedom Burning: Anti-Slavery and Empire in Victorian Britain* (Ithaca: Cornell University Press, 2012); Andrew Porter, *Religion versus Empire? British Protestant Missionaries and Overseas Expansion, 1700–1914* (Manchester: Manchester University Press, 2004); Andrea Major, "British Humanitarian Political Economy and Famine in India, 1838–1842," *Journal of British Studies* 59, no. 2 (2020): 221–244, DOI: 10.1017/jbr.2019.293.

17 Lester and Dussart, *Colonization and the Origins of Humanitarian Governance*, 6–24.

18 Amanda Nettelbeck, *Indigenous Rights and Colonial Subjecthood: Protection and Reform in the Nineteenth-Century British Empire* (Cambridge: Cambridge University Press, 2019), 3–4.

19 Richard Price, *Empire and Indigeneity: Histories and Legacies* (London: Routledge, 2021), 52.

20 Elizabeth Elbourne, "Indigenous Peoples and Imperial Networks in the Early Nineteenth Century: The Politics of Knowledge," in Phillip Buckner and Douglas Francis (eds), *Rediscovering the British World* (Calgary: University of Calgary Press, 2005), 59–86; Zoë Laidlaw, *Protecting the Empire's Humanity: Thomas Hodgkin and British Colonial Activism 1830–1870* (Cambridge: Cambridge University Press, 2021), 239–279; Darren Reid, "The Aborigines' Protection Society as an Anticolonial Network: Rethinking the APS 'from the Bottom Up' through Letters Written by Black South Africans, 1883–87," *Journal of Colonialism and Colonial History* 22, no. 2 (2021), DOI: 10.1353/cch.2021.0028; Darren Reid, "Shadrach Boyce Mama and the 'Kaffir Depot': Navigating Imperial Networks to Agitate against the Forced Removal of Xhosa Women and Children from Cape Town, May–December 1879," *South African Historical Journal* 72, no. 4 (2020): 561–578, DOI: 10.1080/02582473.2020.1827018. For more on Indigenous uses of humanitarianism, see Amanda Nettelbeck, " 'We Are Sure of Your Sympathy': Indigenous Uses of the Politics of Protection in Nineteenth-Century Australia and Canada," *Journal of Colonialism and Colonial History* 17, no. 1 (2016), DOI: 10.1353/cch.2016.0009; and Ann Curthoys and Jessie Mitchell, "Bring This Paper to the Good Governor: Aboriginal Petitioning in Britain's Australia Colonies," in Saliha Belmessous (ed.), *Native Claims: Indigenous Law against Empire, 1500–1920* (Oxford: Oxford University Press, 2011), 182–198.

21 Henry Reynolds, *This Whispering in Our Hearts* (St Leonards: Allen & Unwin, 1998); Celia Haig-Brown and Daniel Nock (eds), *With Good Intentions: Euro-Canadian and Aboriginal Relations in Colonial Canada* (Vancouver: University of British Columbia Press, 2005).

22 Jane Lydon, *The Flash of Recognition: Photography and the Emergence of Indigenous Rights* (Sydney: University of New South Wales Press, 2013), 12–32.

23 Jane Lydon, *Imperial Emotions: The Politics of Empathy across the British Empire* (Cambridge: Cambridge University Press, 2020); Sam Hutchinson, *Settlers, War, and Empire in the Press: Unsettling News in Australia and Britain, 1863–1902* (London: Palgrave Macmillan, 2018); Kenton Storey, *Settler Anxiety at the Outposts of Empire: Colonial Relations, Humanitarian Discourses, and the Imperial Press* (Vancouver: University of British Columbia Press, 2016).

24 For a comprehensive overview of the APS, see James Heartfield, *The Aborigines' Protection Society: Humanitarian Imperialism in Australia, New Zealand, Fiji, Canada, South Africa, and the Congo, 1836–1909* (New York: Columbia University Press, 2011).

25 For explorations of women's participation in imperial and colonial politics, see Zoë Laidlaw, "'Aunt Anna's Report': The Buxton Women and the Aborigines Select Committee, 1835–37," *The Journal of Imperial and Commonwealth History* 32, no. 2 (2004): 1–28, DOI: 10.1080/0308653041000 1700381; Adele Perry, *Colonial Relations: The Douglas-Connolly Family and the Nineteenth-Century Imperial World* (Cambridge: Cambridge University Press, 2015); Elizabeth Elbourne, *Empire, Kinship and Violence: Family Histories, Indigenous Rights and the Making of Settler Colonialism, 1770–1842* (Cambridge: Cambridge University Press, 2023); and Laura Ishiguro, *Nothing to Write Home About: British Family Correspondence and the Settler Colonial Everyday in British Columbia* (Vancouver: University of British Columbia Press, 2019). For broader discussions of women and imperial history, see Philippa Levine (ed.), *Gender and Empire* (Oxford: Oxford University Press, 2004); Angela Woollacott, *Gender and Empire* (New York: Palgrave Macmillan, 2006); and Clare Midgley (ed.), *Gender and Imperialism* (Manchester: Manchester University Press, 1998).

26 Fred Melville, *The Postage Stamps of the Cape of Good Hope, with Mafeking and Vryburg* (London: The Melville Stamp Books, 1913); Pim de Zwart, "Cape Colony Price Index, 1835–1910," International Institute of Social History, www.iisg.nl/hpw/data.php#southafrica (accessed 11 March 2025).

27 John James Jones, *The Emigrants' Guide: Being a Statement Culled from Reliable Sources, as to the Relative Merits of the Dominion of Canada, New South Wales, Victoria, South Australia, Queensland, Western Australia, New Zealand, Tasmania, Cape of Good Hope, Natal, United States of America, etc., with Their Wages, Cost of Living, and Other Necessary Information for Those Seeking New Homes* (London: The International Employment & Emigration Agency, 1880), 43.

28 Gwilym Colenso, "Breaking with the Old Pattern of Control: African Deputations to Britain from Southern Africa in the Late Nineteenth and Early Twentieth Centuries," *South African Historical Journal* 69, no. 4 (2017): 501–547, DOI: 10.1080/02582473.2017.1398777.

29 Eve Tavor Bannet, *Empire of Letters: Letter Manuals and Transatlantic Correspondence, 1688–1820* (Cambridge: Cambridge University Press, 2005), 54–94.

30 Hannah Weiss Muller, *Subjects and Sovereign: Bonds of Belonging in the Eighteenth-Century British Empire* (Oxford: Oxford University Press, 2017); Jeremy Bierbach, *Frontiers of Equality in the Development of EU and US Citizenship* (The Hague: TMC Asser Press, 2017), 17–66.

31 Frederick Cooper, *Citizenship, Inequality, and Difference: Historical Perspectives* (Princeton: Princeton University Press, 2018); Rieko Karatani, *Defining British Citizenship: Empire, Commonwealth and Modern Britain* (London: Routledge, 2022).

32 Jatinder Mann, "The Evolution of Commonwealth Citizenship, 1945–1948 in Canada, Britain and Australia," *Commonwealth & Comparative Politics* 50, no. 3 (2012): 293–313, DOI: 10.1080/14662043.2012.692923.

33 Duncan Bell, *The Idea of Greater Britain: Empire and the Future of World Order, 1860–1900* (Princeton: Princeton University Press, 2007); Daniel Gorman, *Imperial Citizenship: Empire and the Question of Belonging* (Manchester: Manchester University Press, 2007).

34 Marilyn Lake and Henry Reynolds, *Drawing the Global Colour Line: White Men's Countries and the International Challenge of Racial Equality* (Cambridge: Cambridge University Press, 2008), 5.

35 John Darwin, *The Empire Project: The Rise and Fall of the British World-System, 1830–1970* (Cambridge: Cambridge University Press, 2009), 147 (my emphasis).

36 Simon Potter, *News and the British World: The Emergence of an Imperial Press System, 1876–1922* (Oxford: Clarendon Press, 2003); Hilary Carey, *God's Empire: Religion and Colonialism in the British World, c. 1801–1908* (Cambridge: Cambridge University Press, 2011); Charles Reed, *Royal Tourists, Colonial Subjects and the Making of a British World, 1860–1911* (Manchester: Manchester University Press, 2017); Cecilia Morgan, *Building Better Britains? Settler Societies in the British World, 1783–1920* (Toronto: University of Toronto Press, 2016); Felicity Barnes, *Selling Britishness: Commodity Culture, the Dominions, and Empire* (Montreal: McGill-Queen's University Press, 2022); Angela Woollacott, *Settler Society in the Australian Colonies: Self-Government and Imperial Culture* (Oxford: Oxford University Press, 2015).

37 Barnes, *Selling Britishness*, 6; Kynan Gentry, *History, Heritage, and Colonialism: Historical Consciousness, Britishness, and Cultural Identity in New Zealand, 1870–1940* (Manchester: Manchester University Press, 2015); Joseph Hardwick, *Prayer, Providence and Empire: Special Worship in the British World, 1783–1919* (Manchester: Manchester University Press, 2021); Stephen Jackson, *Religious Education and the Anglo-World: The Impact of Empire, Britishness, and Decolonization in Australia, Canada, and New Zealand* (Boston, MA: Brill, 2020); John Mitcham, *Race and Imperial Defence in the British World, 1870–1914* (Cambridge: Cambridge University Press, 2016).

38 Andrew Thompson, "The Languages of Loyalism in Southern Africa, c. 1870–1939," *The English Historical Review* 118, no. 477 (2003): 617–650 (620), www.jstor.org/stable/3489288 (accessed 11 March 2025).
39 Reed, Royal Tourists, pp. 124–161.
40 Julie Evans, Patricia Grimshaw, and David Phillips, *Equal Subjects, Unequal Rights: Indigenous People in British Settler Colonies, 1830–1910* (Manchester: Manchester University Press, 2003); Nettelbeck, *Indigenous Rights and Colonial Subjecthood*; Jodi Byrd, *The Transit of Empire: Indigenous Critiques of Colonialism* (Minneapolis: University of Minnesota Press, 2011).
41 Zoë Laidlaw and Alan Lester (eds), *Indigenous Communities and Settler Colonialism: Land Holding, Loss and Survival in an Interconnected World* (London: Palgrave Macmillan, 2015); Lyons, *X-Marks*; Simpson, *Mohawk Interruptus*; Glen Coulthard, *Red Skin, White Masks: Rejecting the Colonial Politics of Recognition* (Minneapolis: University of Minnesota Press, 2014).
42 Sukanya Banerjee, *Becoming Imperial Citizens: Indians in the Late-Victorian Empire* (Durham, NC: Duke University Press, 2010); Jared McDonald, *Khoesan and Imperial Citizenship in Nineteenth Century South Africa* (New York: Routledge, 2023); Zaki Nahaboo, "Rémy Ollier and Imperial Citizenship," *Interventions* 20, no. 5 (2018): 717–733, DOI: 10.1080/1369801X.2018.1487317; Khwezi Mkhize, " 'To See Us as We See Ourselves': John Tengo Jabavu and the Politics of the Black Periodical," *Journal of Southern African Studies* 44, no. 3 (2018): 413–430, DOI: 10.1080/03057070.2018.1462993.
43 Paula Hildebrandt and Sybille Peters, "Introduction," in Paula Hildebrandt, Kerstin Evert, Sibylle Peters, Mirjam Schaub, Kathrin Wildner, and Gesa Ziemer (eds), *Performing Citizenship: Bodies, Agencies, Limitations* (Cham: Palgrave Macmillan, 2019), 3; See also Cooper, *Citizenship, Inequality, and Difference*, 1–13.
44 Engin Isin, "Theorizing Acts of Citizenship," in Engin Isin and Greg Nielsen (eds), *Acts of Citizenship* (London: Palgrave Macmillan, 2008), 15–43.
45 McDonald, *Khoesan and Imperial Citizenship*.
46 Banerjee, *Becoming Imperial Citizens*, 8.
47 Jack Harrington, *The Uses of Imperial Citizenship: The British and French Empires* (Lanham: Rowman & Littlefield, 2020), 3.
48 McDonald, *Khoesan and Imperial Citizenship*, 74.
49 Zoë Laidlaw, "Breaking Britannia's Bounds? Law, Settlers, and Space in Britain's Imperial Historiography," *The Historical Journal* 55, no. 3 (2012): 807–830 (808), DOI: 10.1017/S0018246X12000313.
50 Ford, *Settler Sovereignty*, 4; Woollacott, *Settler Society*, 103–104.
51 Elbourne, *Empire, Kinship and Violence*; Laura Ishiguro, *Nothing to Write Home About*; Perry, *Colonial Relations*.
52 William Matthew Kennedy, *The Imperial Commonwealth: Australia and the Project of Empire, 1867–1914* (Manchester: University of Manchester Press, 2023), 2.

53 Katie Pickles and Catharine Coleborne (eds), *New Zealand's Empire* (Manchester: Manchester University Press, 2016); Paula Hastings, *Dominion over Palm and Pine: A History of Canadian Aspirations in the British Caribbean* (Montreal: McGill-Queen's University Press, 2022).

54 Jon Wilson and Andrew Dilley, "The Incoherence of Empire; or, The Pitfalls of Ignoring Sovereignty in the History of the British Empire," *Transactions of the Royal Historical Society* 1 (2023): 191–217 (199), DOI: 10.1017/S0080440123000063.

55 Lauren Benton and Richard Ross (eds), *Legal Pluralism and Empires, 1500–1850* (New York: New York University Press, 2013); Lauren Benton, *A Search for Sovereignty: Law and Geography in European Empires, 1400–1900* (Cambridge: Cambridge University Press, 2009); Lauren Benton and Lisa Ford, *Rage for Order: The British Empire and the Origins of International Law* (Cambridge, MA: Harvard University Press, 2016); Ford, *Settler Sovereignty.*

56 Amanda Nettelbeck, Russell Smandych, Louis A. Knafla, and Robert Foster, *Fragile Settlements: Aboriginal Peoples, Law, and Resistance in South-West Australia and Prairie Canada* (Vancouver: University of British Columbia Press, 2016).

57 Nettelbeck, *Indigenous Rights and Colonial Subjecthood*; Ann Curthoys and Jessie Mitchell, *Taking Liberty: Indigenous Rights and Settler Self-Government in Colonial Australia, 1830–1890* (Cambridge: Cambridge University Press, 2018); Price, *Empire and Indigeneity*; Edward Cavanaugh and Lorenzo Veracini (eds), *The Routledge Handbook of the History of Settler Colonialism* (Oxford: Routledge, 2017).

58 Darwin, *The Empire Project*, 9; Gary Magee and Andrew Thompson, *Empire and Globalisation: Networks of People, Goods and Capital in the British World, c. 1850–1914* (Cambridge: Cambridge University Press, 2010), 3–6; James Belich, *Replenishing the Earth: The Settler Revolution and the Rise of the Anglo-World, 1783–1939* (Oxford: Oxford University Press, 2011), 9; Phillip Buckner, "The Creation of the Dominion of Canada, 1860–1901," in Phillip Buckner (ed.), *Canada and the British Empire* (Oxford: Oxford University Press, 2010), 66–86 (68–70); Charlotte Macdonald, "Woolwich to Wellington: From Settler Colony to Garrisoned Sovereignty," *New Zealand Journal of History* 53, no. 1 (2019): 50–76, https://muse.jhu.edu/pub/426/article/883327 (accessed 11 March 2025).

59 Paul McHugh and Lisa Ford, "Settler Sovereignty and the Shapeshifting Crown," in Lisa Ford and Tim Rowse (eds), *Between Indigenous and Settler Governance* (London: Taylor & Francis, 2012), 23–34; J. R. Miller, "Petitioning the Great White Mother: First Nations' Organizations and Lobbying in London," in *Reflections on Native–Newcomer Relations: Selected Essays* (Toronto: University of Toronto Press, 2004), 217–241; Sarah Carter and Maria Nugent (eds), *Mistress of Everything: Queen Victoria in Indigenous Worlds* (Manchester: Manchester University Press, 2017); Buckner, "The Creation of the Dominion of Canada, 1860–1901," 66–86; Ann Curthoys, "The Dog that Didn't Bark: The Durham Report, Indigenous Dispossession,

and Self-Government for Britain's Settler Colonies," in Karen Dubinsky, Adele Perry, and Henry Yu (eds), *Within and without the Nation: Canadian History as Transnational History* (Toronto: University of Toronto Press, 2015), 25–48.

60 Veracini, *Settler Colonialism*; Wolfe, "Settler Colonialism and the Elimination of the Native"; Donald Denoon, "Understanding Settler Societies," *Historical Studies* 18, no. 73 (1979): 511–527, DOI: 10.1080/10314617908595611.

61 Veracini, *Settler Colonialism*, 53–74.

62 John Martin, "Refusal of Assent: A Hidden Element of Constitutional History in New Zealand," *Victoria University of Wellington Law Review* 41, no. 1 (2010): 51–84, DOI: 10.26686/vuwlr.v41i1.5245; Thomas Mohr, "A British Empire Court: A Brief Appraisal of the History of the Judicial Committee of the Privy Council," in Anthony McElligott, Liam Chambers, Ciara Breathnach, and Catherine Lawless (eds), *Power in History: From Medieval Ireland to the Post-Modern World* (Dublin: Irish Academic Press, 2011); Alpheus Todd, *Parliamentary Government in the British Colonies*, 2nd edn (London: Longmans, Green, 1894).

63 For more on the use of humanitarianism by Indigenous peoples, see Nettelbeck, "We Are Sure of Your Sympathy."

64 Antoinette Burton, *The Trouble with Empire: Challenges to Modern British Imperialism* (Oxford: Oxford University Press, 2015), 1.

65 Corey Snelgrove, Rita Dhamoon, and Jeff Corntassel, "Unsettling Settler Colonialism: The Discourse and Politics of Settlers, and Solidarity with Indigenous Nations," *Decolonization: Indigeneity, Education & Society* 3, no. 2 (2014): 1–32, https://jps.library.utoronto.ca/index.php/des/article/view/21166/17970 (accessed 11 March 2025).

Part I

Settler imperial citizenship within representative governments

1

Undermining imperial maladministration: British Columbia, 1869–1870

The decade 1861–1871 contained some of the most turbulent years in the history of British Columbia, witnessing the massive Cariboo Gold Rush as well as the colony's rapid development from a Crown Colony with limited representative institutions to a responsible government within a confederated Canada.[1] Coincidentally, these years also marked the presence in British Columbia of a settler named William Sebright Green (1829–1906), who, in those ten years, in addition to working as a solicitor, tried his hand at farming, journalism, liquor selling, and railway building, before running unsuccessfully for a seat in the Legislative Council and then returning to England. Green was, in many ways, representative of many upper-middle-class settlers in the colony. Although he lost the 1868 Legislative Council election, his platform was essentially identical to that of all the candidates, who universally called for responsible government, retrenchment of government spending, and delaying confederation until British Columbia was powerful enough to resist domination by the eastern provinces.

Where Green seemingly differed from his fellow candidates was in his attitude towards Indigenous peoples. This manifested in various ways. Whereas many settlers viewed intermittent smallpox outbreaks as a means of reducing the Indigenous population and even threatened to spread smallpox on purpose,[2] Green championed improved vaccination and medical programmes for Indigenous communities. More prominent, however, was Green's approach to land rights. Prior to the merger of Vancouver Island and British Columbia in 1866, many politicians and newspaper editors in Victoria had advocated recognizing Indigenous land rights as a method of conciliation to prevent an Indigenous uprising.[3] But as successive gold rushes and smallpox outbreaks shifted the balance of power between Indigenous and settler populations, support for Indigenous land rights virtually disappeared from popular discourse. Green's contemporary political candidates, such as John Helmcken, who would later help negotiate the terms of British Columbia's confederation, and Amor de Cosmos, who would become the second premier of a confederated British Columbia, both vocally opposed recognizing Indigenous land rights, believing that such rights stood in the way of settler expansion. This is not to say that Green's fellow settlers were devoid of any humanitarian feeling whatsoever, but simply that most settlers carefully defined humanitarianism in terms of assimilation rather than land rights. Helmcken, for example, insisted that "the question of 'Indian title' and the question of the duty of the government to civilize the aborigines of the country, are two separate and distinct questions."[4] He argued that "the sooner they are taught the valueless nature of their roving title, and, indeed, that they have no title whatever the better for them," for only then would Indigenous peoples abandon their attempts at self-determination and submit to becoming "fitting members of the body politic."[5]

Green, on the other hand, not only supported recognizing Indigenous land rights, he was also an informant for the Aborigines' Protection Society (APS) in Britain and even tried to establish a local branch of the APS in Victoria. Green was far from the only settler to stand up boldly for Indigenous land rights against the greater animosity of their settler societies. Joanna Cruickshank and Patricia Grimshaw, for example, point to the common trope of settler humanitarians advocating to temporarily recognize Indigenous land rights as a token comfort for Indigenous populations that were believed to be on the brink of extinction.[6] Green, however, did not support recognizing Indigenous land rights for this reason. To some extent, his support for Indigenous land rights was partially rooted in fear of uprising and concern for his family's safety. But he also used the language of Indigenous rights to undermine the efficacy of imperial administration and justify the necessity of settler self-government. Green worked through the APS to place political pressure on the Colonial Office during British Columbia's campaign for responsible government, pointing to his colony's poor treatment of Indigenous peoples as evidence that a change in government was needed. He therefore provides a useful window into the interconnections between imperial authority, humanitarianism, and settler self-government in the late nineteenth century.

This chapter examines how Green intertwined his Indigenous rights activism with his concurrent demands for responsible government. As outlined in his correspondence with the APS, Green was principally concerned about three Indigenous issues: recognition of land rights, equality before the law, and the prevention and treatment of smallpox. Historians of British Columbia demonstrate that land dispossession, legal inequality, and the rampant spread of smallpox were intimately connected to the settler colonial project of eradicating Indigenous peoples from the land.[7] According to Green, however, these issues were the fault of the imperial government, not of settlers who had no political authority in a Crown Colony. Moreover, he asserted that the imperial government's failure to recognize Indigenous

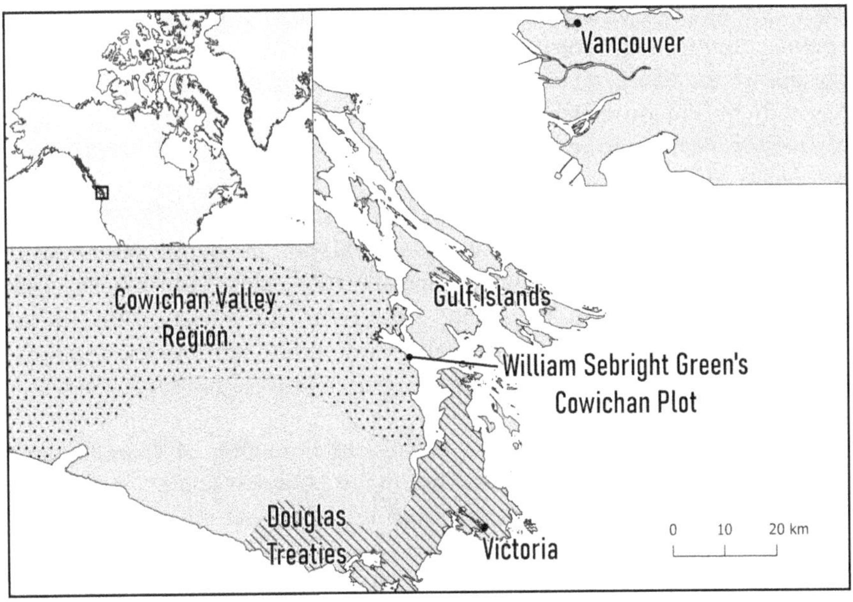

Map 1.1 Southern Vancouver Island

rights in British Columbia was a direct threat to settler society, with frustrated and smallpox-ridden Indigenous peoples liable to attack and infect settlers. By attending to how Green's version of Indigenous rights activism revolved around his concerns about imperial despotism, this chapter argues that humanitarianism provided settlers with both a language for justifying their right to self-government and a method of applying political pressure to imperial government administrations in which they had little direct input.

The responsible government campaign in British Columbia

British Columbian politics in the late 1860s revolved around two key and interrelated issues: responsible government and confederation. Both issues responded to the fact that British Columbia was suffering from crippling debt that seemed impossible to get out of. The main problem was that government officials were extremely overpaid as well as too powerful to allow their salaries to be reduced. This had not been a problem while the Fraser and Cariboo Gold Rushes produced inflated revenue, but when gold profits dried up in 1865, high government salaries and low alternative income quickly plunged the two colonies of Vancouver Island and British Columbia into a debt of more than $1.3 million. Problematically, however, the majority of these government officials were appointed rather than elected, with both colonies governed autocratically by imperial governors with no responsibility to local constituents. This meant that only the governor had the power to reduce salaries or remove appointed officials, but Governor Kennedy of Vancouver Island and Governor Seymour of British Columbia clashed over where to make the necessary cuts. In 1866, the two colonies were merged under Governor Seymour in the hope that one strong governor could straighten out the budget but, as Walter Sage observed, "Seymour was not strong enough ruthlessly to use the pruning knife. Some officials were dismissed but the establishment remained far too heavy."[8] Further measures were thus needed to save the colony from ruin. Annexation to the United States was proposed by some, primarily Americans, but it failed to obtain a significant following. The only two alternatives were responsible government or confederation, or both.

Confederation with the newly established dominion of Canada came with significant economic benefits that many believed would solve British Columbia's debt problem without requiring a change in government structure. At a Legislative Council debate on confederation on 9 March 1870, Attorney General Henry Crease argued that British Columbia's debt crisis "is not, as some allege, because of the particular form of Government we at present enjoy," meaning irresponsible government, but rather "that policy of isolation which has kept us aloof from the assistance and sympathy of a kindred race."[9] Confederation would end that isolation, and in so doing would allow the Canadian government to assume the public debt, enable British Columbia to borrow money using Canada's public credit, lead to transcontinental railways that would expand British Columbia's market eastwards, and bolster internal immigration.

Others, however, argued that confederation was akin to switching one imperial overlord for another, and that only obtaining responsible government would free British Columbia from mismanagement. At a public meeting held to debate the benefits of responsible government, one attendant proclaimed that confederation without responsible government would "make this a colony of a colony, and the officials would still finger the finances and bring us again, as they had already done, to absolute ruin."[10] Yet confederation without responsible government was the only version of confederation that the majority of British Columbia's appointed officials were willing to consider, given that responsible government would inevitably lead to the loss of their exorbitant salaries. When the Legislative Council crafted their terms for confederation with Canada, they included a demand that "the Constitution of the Executive authority and of the Legislature of British Columbia shall ... continue as existing at the time of Union."[11] This led some reformers to combine their demands for confederation with those for responsible government. Amor de Cosmos, for example, was the leading proponent of confederation on Vancouver Island and has become known as the father of British Columbia's entry into confederation, yet even he held that "the uppermost and most important" issue of his day was to "change from the existing Despotic one-man Government to the Free Constitution of a Self-governing people,"[12] and he openly proclaimed that "the questions were Confederation with Responsible Government or Irresponsible Government and no Confederation."[13]

Others, particularly those with ties to agriculture, called for responsible government without confederation on the grounds that the tariffs that protected British Columbia agricultural industries would be removed under confederation to the detriment of its farmers. While Vancouver Island had historically been a free port, British Columbia possessed a relatively high protectionist tariff policy. In 1869, for example, Canadian tariffs on the importation of British Columbia products including eggs, fish, flour, vegetables, and lumber were all "free goods" exempt from taxation, whereas British Columbia tariffs on these products were $0.125 per dozen, 15 per cent, $1.50 per barrel, $0.02 per pound, and between $1 and $5 per 1,000 feet, respectively.[14] Even the Canadian butter tariff, which was $0.04 per pound, was more than double in British Columbia at $0.10 per pound. The Canadian tariff therefore became one of the principal arguments against confederation, with John Helmcken, member of the Legislative Council for Victoria, arguing that "if Confederation should come, bringing with it the Tariff of Canada, not only will the farmers be ruined, but our independence will be taken away ... I am opposed to Confederation, because it will not serve to promote the industrial interests of this Colony."[15] But Helmcken nevertheless believed that responsible government was necessary without confederation, reiterating that "I have ever advocated a change in the Constitution of the Legislative and Executive Councils,"[16] and this is precisely what Green advocated as well. When running for a seat on the Legislative Council in 1868, Green campaigned on the idea of responsible government "without having recourse to Confederation. I believe that the two questions of Confederation with Canada and Free Trade are dead and buried."[17]

Green lost his campaign for a seat in the Legislative Council, but so did all those who advocated agitating for reform. Governor Seymour and the Legislative Council of 1868–1869 were unanimously against both confederation and responsible government. Green was therefore half victorious: his desire for representative institutions was foiled, but he at least was guaranteed the continuation of the British Columbia tariff system. This changed with the sudden death of Governor Seymour on 10 June 1869 and the appointment of Governor Musgrave in his stead. Musgrave had previously acted as governor of Newfoundland and had played a large part in bringing

Newfoundland into confederation, and on 17 June the *British Colonist* excitedly printed excerpts from one of Musgrave's pro-confederation speeches as evidence that his arrival heralded the dawn of confederation in British Columbia.[18] Indeed, Musgrave was specially instructed by the Colonial Office to bring about confederation as quickly as possible, a task he carried out effectively by promising the existing appointed government officials generous pensions or lucrative postings in other colonies should they lose their jobs following confederation.[19] But while Musgrave supported confederation, he was adamantly opposed to responsible government, proclaiming in the Legislative Council that "I have no hesitation in stating my opinion that the form commonly called 'Responsible Government' would not be found at present suited to a community so young and so constituted as this."[20] Thus, with the arrival of Governor Musgrave, Green went from half a loaf to no loaf at all, and it was only a week after the *British Colonist* printed its celebration of Musgrave's confederationist leanings that Green began writing to the APS. He used these letters to emphasize to the imperial government the importance of granting British Columbia responsible government, using his government's maladministration of Indigenous affairs as evidence of its inefficacy, starting with public health responses to smallpox.

Imperial ineptitude in fighting smallpox

Green lived through two smallpox epidemics in his ten years' residence on Vancouver Island, and those experiences significantly shaped his perceptions of imperial administration. The first lasted from 1862 to 1863, killing over 14,000 Indigenous peoples along the coast of British Columbia, and has received extensive historiographical attention because, according to Robert Boyd, it "served as a final blow to the Native peoples of British Columbia and paved the way for the colonization of their lands."[21] Conversely, the 1868 epidemic lasted only a couple months, probably killed in the hundreds rather than the thousands, and has gone completely unmentioned in the historical literature. Both epidemics, however, were plagued by governmental mismanagement that led to inflated mortality rates. Effective vaccines were available and knowledge of quarantine was widespread at the time. Indeed, mass vaccination and quarantine had been effectively employed by the Hudson's Bay Company during an 1837 smallpox epidemic as well as by the Canadian government in an 1876 smallpox epidemic to save thousands of lives.[22] In the 1862–1863 British Columbia epidemic, however, infected Indigenous peoples were evicted from cities rather than quarantined, spreading the disease across the entire province, and vaccination was handled almost completely by independent missionaries, leaving select groups protected but the bulk of the province completely vulnerable.[23] A similar pattern emerged during the 1868 epidemic. The outbreak started in Victoria, and rather than quarantining those affected, the British Columbia government advised all Indigenous peoples in Victoria to leave the city.[24] A quarantine of incoming trading vessels and a coordinated vaccination campaign were initiated by the mayor of Victoria in November,[25] but the epidemic had already been spreading through Indigenous communities since August, resulting in hundreds of deaths in Indigenous communities around the island.

Green was not alone in showing concern for Indigenous peoples' suffering: his language of pity for "the poor creatures" had been a common feature of settler responses to the 1862–1863 smallpox epidemic. Kiran van Rijn argues that these settler discourses of pity, as opposed to empathy or compassion, were little more than a token expression of distress that "frees the individual from an emotional commitment to the sufferer and absolves him of responsibility, thereby enabling him to turn his back on suffering."[26] Such a perspective echoes broader arguments around imperial humanitarianism that affective language by colonizers towards victims of colonization served to maintain racial hierarchies by defining the Indigenous peoples solely in terms of subservience to colonizers. For example, in relation to anti-slavery discourses, Lynn Festa argues that "the subject produced by sentimental antislavery is granted only a diluted form of humanity grounded in pain and victimhood, a humanity that lasts only as long as the recognition of the metropolitan subject who bestows it."[27] Humanitarian discourses of pity also established clean boundaries between victims, perpetrators, and humanitarians, absolving the last of responsibility by situating themselves as activists and pointing the blame elsewhere. This is precisely what Green did in his letter to the APS and his article in the *British Colonist*: by clearly allocating blame for the spread of smallpox to his government and situating himself as a concerned citizen trying to hold his government accountable, he utilized a humanitarian framework to distance his own complicity as a settler benefiting from the destruction of Indigenous societies.

However, there is an additional focus in his writing about the impact of Indigenous sickness on settler livelihoods that suggests that his humanitarianism was about more than simply clearing his own conscience. For example, Green criticized the government's policy of evicting infected Indigenous people, not because it spread disease to other Indigenous communities, but because it led to "the extension of the disease to our young and thriving agricultural settlements at Saanich, Cowichan and Comox."[28] He went on to proclaim that "it is impossible to neglect the interests of those around us without the great law of compensation stepping in; and to tolerate a people living alongside of us in a state of barbarism, is attendant by not only moral but physical retribution."[29] These statements indicate that the spread of smallpox in Indigenous communities was much more than just a cause for pity; it also threatened the health and safety of settler communities. This sense of self-preservation had been a major element of government responses to the 1862–1863 epidemic, when settlers were vaccinated and Indigenous peoples driven out of cities to protect settler lives. Yet, as Green argued, simply vaccinating settlers and expelling Indigenous peoples was not without danger to settlers, particularly because vaccinations were not always reliable. It was not yet understood in the mid-to-late nineteenth century how exactly smallpox vaccination worked, why immunity sometimes faded over time, or why vaccinated people could still contract mild cases of smallpox.[30] Green observed that many settlers who had been vaccinated were still getting sick, and he believed this was because of a faulty batch of vaccines, with "vaccinations having been performed with lymph affording no protection."[31] As such, he argued that smallpox could not be controlled within settler communities independently of Indigenous communities, so that humanitarianism towards Indigenous peoples was inherently humanitarianism towards settlers as well.

But even if concern for his and his family's health was top of mind during the epidemic of 1868, this does not explain why Green was writing to the APS about smallpox at the end of 1869, when there was no public health threat to settler lives. Green was not writing to the APS to lobby for a better public health policy, he was using the government's bungling of the smallpox epidemic to underscore its inability to meet the administrative needs of the colony. For while pity for Indigenous suffering was a major rhetorical tool in his writing, his overarching emphasis was on maladministration. Green had been working as an editor for the *British Colonist* during the 1868 epidemic, and at that time he wrote a scathing critique of the government's failure to contain the outbreak. "The inhumanity and gross neglect of the welfare of the Indian population that have characterized the proceedings of the authorities during the present epidemic are beyond anything we can find words to express."[32] Green highlighted the government's failure to quarantine infected people, its use of ineffective vaccines, and its failure to shut down an "Indian Dance House" that had allegedly become a superspreader hotspot. In his letter to the APS he continued this emphasis on maladministration. He informed them that

> the provisions made by the authorities for the protection of the Indians during the prevalence of this frightful scourge were infamously bad. After numbers of deaths had occurred, the sum of ten dollars was expended in the erection of a tent, open at the sides, to which the poor creatures were taken from the town in carts, and left to die ... Hundreds of bodies were left on the rocks outside the harbour unburied, and you can imagine how disease was fostered by such a course of proceeding.[33]

This emphasis on the imperial government's maladministration shows that while displacing personal responsibility and protecting settler health and security were certainly integral to Green's perception of humanitarianism and Indigenous rights, the more immediate motivation for his writing was to prove to imperial authorities that the current model of government was not working. Indeed, Green's first letter to the APS was written only ten days after the death of Governor Seymour and the appointment of Governor Musgrave in his place, a move that had spelled doom for Green's vision of a self-governing British Columbia unattached to the Canadian confederation. Green had written previously that "the Colonial Office is not so firmly attached to the present system of Government, as to withstand the steady pressure of the people."[34] It is therefore likely that Green hoped sufficient pressure from the APS regarding the failures of the British Columbia government might convince the Colonial Office that a change in government system was necessary. But he did not rely on public health measures alone. In addition to critiquing responses to smallpox, Green also stressed the inadequacy and inhumanity of the government's land policies.

The duplicity of the imperial land regime

While the dispossession of Indigenous land is the foundation of settler colonialism in all parts of Canada, British Columbia's legacy of dispossession differs from the other Canadian colonies and provinces. Whereas Indigenous land title in the eastern provinces was typically "extinguished" through treaties, British Columbia's land policy, similarly to that of the Australian colonies, hinged upon the doctrine of *terra nullius*, whereby Indigenous ownership of the land was resolutely denied.[35] Fourteen small-scale treaties were initially negotiated in the early 1850s with a few select nations on Vancouver Island, but this process ended in 1854. Only one more historic treaty would be signed in 1899, called Treaty 8, which only eight British Columbian First Nations signed, so that around 95 per cent of the land in modern British Columbia remained unceded. From 1854 onwards, rather than creating reserves through treaty negotiations, the colonies of Vancouver Island and British Columbia (and the united Colony of British Columbia from 1868) created reserves unilaterally. Government agents travelled throughout the countryside, asking First Nations to mark out village sites and cultivated areas that would be protected from settler intrusion. These sites became reserves, while all land not marked as protected was opened for settlement. And while some consultation did take place lending this process a façade of consent, government agents regularly ignored the boundaries set out by Indigenous nations, visited their territories while community members were out hunting, or in other ways avoided consultation.[36]

Green witnessed first-hand the British Columbia government's duplicitous methods of stealing Indigenous land, and it significantly informed his perception of colonial land regimes. Green pre-empted land in the Cowichan Valley in 1862 as part of a government-sponsored settlement scheme dubbed the "Cowichan Expedition." The government promised potential settlers 150 acres of land (plus 50 acres for wives and 10 acres per child), transportation on the HMS *Hecate*, and protection in the form of a gunboat and "a competent party to deal with the Indians."[37] As this last would suggest, safety from attack by Indigenous neighbours was a primary concern for would-be settlers, and the government went to great lengths to make reassurances. At a public meeting to address settler concerns, one audience member "spoke very forcibly on the necessity of cultivating friendly relations with the Indians. He liked the project, but Indians were treacherous, and the settlers should be protected."[38] In response, surveyor general Joseph Pemberton explained that "the Indians were anxious to have the whites come among them as soon as they were settled with for the land ... government would no doubt compensate them reasonably for the land; 100 might settle there, and there was no danger of a fight."[39] The House of Assembly moved unanimously for "the extinguishment by His Excellency the Governor of the Indian Title at Cowichan, from the proceeds of land sales,"[40] and settlers also had to sign a contract stating that "any person desirous of selecting land in the Districts of Cowichan or Quamichan may do so on condition that the Surveyor General certifies that the land selected is situated in such a manner as is not likely to lead to any misunderstanding of difficulty with the Indians."[41] Settlers in Cowichan, including Green, were thus given full assurances by the government that Indigenous landowners would be compensated for their land and would bear no resentment or anger towards them.

As it turned out, however, the government was lying through its teeth. The Cowichan peoples had no interest in allowing settlers onto their territory. Land speculators had been attempting to purchase land in the Cowichan Valley for over ten years, and the government had attempted to conduct surveys, but the Cowichan peoples repeatedly destroyed survey instruments and removed survey posts.[42] Indeed, the very same year that the surveyor general claimed "the Indians were anxious to have whites come among them," the Royal Navy commander Richard Charles Mayne admitted that the Cowichan people "have shown no favour to those settlers who have visited their valley. Although it has been surveyed it cannot yet be settled, as the Indians are unwilling to sell, still less to be ousted from their land."[43] The government therefore landed the Cowichan Expedition during fishing season, when the majority of the Cowichan people were on the mainland, so as to avoid any initial resistance. Monetary compensation was then pledged to take the sting out of the land theft, and $9,700 was set aside in the government's 1863 and 1864 budget expressly for the purpose of compensating Cowichan First Nations for their land.[44] But such compensation was never made. Indeed, the Cowichan First Nations did not want it, instead asserting their continuing and unceded sovereignty over their territory. The Cowichan First Nations would continue to petition the colonial and imperial governments long into the twentieth century for recognition of their unceded land rights, and are currently (April 2024) in negotiations with the British Columbia government to establish a new treaty.

But the Cowichan First Nations were not the only ones lied to. The government had expressly promised the Cowichan Expedition settlers that there would be no trouble with the local Indigenous peoples because they would be treated fairly, and when this promise was broken the settlers found themselves in a dangerous situation. On 2 March 1863, just a few months after the Cowichan Expedition had landed, one of the settlers wrote to the *British Colonist* that "previous to our settling here and taking up land, we were promised everything, all we could wish, and now we are left almost isolated and forgotten" with not even "a semblance of security and law … We have not even a constable now, and the Indians knew it."[45] A month later, the *British Colonist* reported a series of "horrible murder[s] by Indians" in the Cowichan and Gulf Islands area, deeming it a "reign of terror" that "seriously affects the security of settlers in the outlying districts."[46] One of these murders had taken place just across the water from Green's estate. Two weeks later, when a gunboat (the HMS *Forward*) was sent to the area to apprehend suspects in these murder cases, the Cowichan First Nations resisted the assertion of colonial authority and fired upon the gunboat, killing one seaman and withstanding hours of heavy retaliatory bombardment with grape and canister shot, artillery shells, and rockets.[47]

Newspaper records did not connect these events to animosity about stolen land, but Green certainly did. He complained to the APS that "after some months' experience" at in the Cowichan Valley he had "been forced to throw up my land rather than expose my wife to what I considered danger from the proximity of Indians, burning under an acute sense of unfair treatment on the part of the Colonial Government."[48] The problem, he explained, was that "the district of Cowichan was thrown open for settlement, and the Indians were promised remuneration in money, or blankets for the land which was taken from them, a reserve was set apart for them, and every sort of assistance and protection was promised them. They have *never* been paid for their land."[49] But not only had the government failed to conciliate Indigenous peoples with payment, they had also failed to punish subsequent outbreaks of violence. He complained to the APS that the government allowed Indigenous peoples "to shoot and kill one another within rifle-shot of the city, without interference."[50] Green was referring to one specific instance in 1864 when a Cowichan man known as How-A-Matcha was accused of murdering another Indigenous person. One of Green's Cowichan Valley neighbours had asked him to bring the case before Governor James Douglas, which he agreed to do "in the belief that if the tribes commenced a system of retributive justice between themselves, there would be no security for the settlers."[51] But Governor Douglas had refused to get involved, indicating to Green either the unwillingness or the inability of the government to maintain law and order and protect settler lives.

Green's concerns about Indigenous reprisals for mistreatment and his government's inability to control Indigenous violence was shared by many of his neighbours. Kenton Storey shows that, at least prior to 1866, settlers regularly called for their government to provide compensation for Indigenous land in order to avoid reprisals, while Jane Sampson argues that many settlers interpreted their government's inability to police Indigenous crime as a disgrace to national and cultural prestige.[52] These twin themes – fear of Indigenous violence and pride in British cultural prestige – reappear in Chapter 4's discussion of settler responses to the First Taranaki War in New Zealand. Indeed, as the growing historiography of the rule of law in settler colonies demonstrates, settler insecurities and fantasies of controlling colonial spaces played a major role in the development of oppressive policing, legal regimes, and colonial violence.[53]

Green was certainly influenced by, and part of, this larger culture of settler insecurity, and his criticisms of the British Columbia government's failures in this area were to some extent written out of concern for his and his family's safety. But, once again, the timing of his complaints to the APS is strange. His decision to flee the Cowichan Valley, along with the How-A-Matcha affair, took place years before he wrote to the APS. There is no smoking gun directly tying Green's complaints about Britisih Columbia land policy with his opposition to Governor Musgrave and his campaign for responsible government without confederation, but there are many circumstantial pieces of evidence indicating the connection.

First is the emphasis Green placed upon the governor's responsibility for Indigenous rights issues in his letters to the APS. When outlining the context of British Columbia's Indigenous policies, Green was careful to explain that it was governed by an irresponsible executive and legislature "of whom two-thirds are nominated by the Governor."[54] He went on to criticize the despotic power of individual governors for failing to implement a stable government policy towards Indigenous peoples, writing that "each Governor has, in turn, treated Indians differently" so that "we have, I regret to say, no Indian policy whatever."[55] Green then suggested that the British Columbia government's neglect of Indigenous rights was purposeful, charging that "to judge from the policy adopted of letting Indian affairs take their chance, it would seem that our Government was following the example of America, and trying to exterminate the Indian race."[56] Finally, he directly questioned Governor Musgrave's capacity to govern by suggesting that locals knew better how to govern themselves than outsiders, writing that "I fully expect that the governor will report that he considers my statements somewhat exaggerated, he has not been here long enough himself to judge of the real state of affairs amongst the Indians."[57] All of these language cues demonstrate that Green's ideas about Indigenous rights to land, health, and legal protection were intimately connected to his opposition to Governor Musgrave and British Columbia's lack of input into government policy making.

Another important piece of circumstantial evidence connecting Green's humanitarianism and political ideals is the timing of his letters to the APS. Not only was his first letter written only days after the appointment of a pro-confederation and anti-responsible governor, his second letter was also written just days after the electoral defeat of an anti-confederation candidate for the Legislative Council. A vote took place on 3 December 1869 between two opposing candidates for the Victoria District seat, the same seat that Green had campaigned unsuccessfully for in 1868. The defeated member, James Lowe, campaigned on an anti-confederation platform, while the victorious member was Amor de Cosmos, the celebrated father of British Columbian confederation. The victory of de Cosmos over Lowe signalled "a pure and unadulterated verdict in favor of Confederation hot and strong,"[58] and the timing of Green's next letter to the APS just days later further suggests correlation between his political defeats and his critiques of British Columbia's Indigenous policy.

Perhaps even more telling than when he wrote his letters is when he *stopped* writing his letters. On 12 April 1870, Green acted as secretary of a public meeting called to rally support for responsible government, and the next day he served as a delegate of a meeting to petition Governor Musgrave to ensure that "Responsible Government be made an indispensable condition" for any confederation agreement.[59] At this meeting, Governor Musgrave finally capitulated. He reiterated his personal opinion that "Responsible Government would not be suitable to this colony," but he nevertheless conceded that following the upcoming elections, "if, through a return of a majority of representatives, the people said unmistakably that they desired Responsible Government, they would get it ... he would not throw himself into the breach single handed to oppose it."[60]

Following this outcome, Green wrote no more letters to the APS. Indeed, the sudden deep interest in Indigenous peoples that he developed following Governor Musgrave's appointment seems to have vanished entirely. Green moved back to England shortly after British Columbia joined confederation, and became a regular speaker at the Royal Colonial Institute on matters relating to British Columbia, but he never once made even a passing reference to Indigenous peoples. On the contrary, he raved about the abundance of great (stolen Indigenous) land that was available for such low prices. He proclaimed that "there is still abundance left for sturdy British families who desire a new outlet for their energies and wish to remain under the old flag; and with its good climate and vast mineral resources it is probably one of the most promising places for British settlers. Land can still be acquired on very easy terms."[61] Gone were any of his previous reservations about who actually owned the land. Gone also were any criticisms of Governor Musgrave, whom he now called "the ablest governor that British Columbia ever had."[62] With his political campaign for responsible government accomplished, Indigenous rights discourses were no longer useful.

Conclusion

Green's correspondence with the APS is not unknown to historians of British Columbia, appearing in many footnotes and bibliographies over the past century, yet historians have done little to unpack the significance behind his humanitarianism. Jane Samson, for example, mentions him only in a footnote as a concerned humanitarian who "became so incensed by the unfair treatment of Indians that he contacted the Aborigines Protection Society in London in 1869."[63] Kenton Storey and Robin Fisher, on the other hand, both bypass Green's letters entirely and focus on the response his letters generated from Joseph Trutch, the chief commissioner of lands and works.[64] They emphasize that for Trutch it was more humanitarian to treat Indigenous peoples with equality than with favouritism, and that since settlers had no inherent land rights, neither did Indigenous peoples. They then explain that Trutch went on to list all of the ways that colonization had benefited Indigenous peoples with roads, jobs, and scientific knowledge, arguing that it was more humanitarian to forcefully extend these benefits onto Indigenous territory than it was to recognize Indigenous sovereignty. Storey and Fisher therefore use Trutch's reply to Green as evidence of the use of humanitarian discourses by government officials to justify the colonization of Indigenous territory, and they largely dismiss Green as a solitary activist with outdated ideas about Indigenous rights.

Storey's and Fisher's narrative of the British Columbia government's malevolent use of humanitarian discourses aligns with the treatment of settler humanitarianism more broadly. Beginning with Alan Lester and Fae Dussart's *Colonization and the Origins of Humanitarian Governance* (2014) and built upon by Ann Curthoys and Jessie Mitchell, Amanda Nettelbeck, and Richard Price, the concept of humanitarian governance has come to dominate scholarly treatment of humanitarianism in settler colonies.[65] In this context, humanitarian governance holds that efforts by settler governments to "protect" Indigenous peoples were intrinsically designed to facilitate the administration, control, and ultimately either the assimilation or eradication of Indigenous societies. Trutch's response to Green's correspondence with the APS certainly displays such humanitarian governance, using the language of benevolence and equality to justify administering sovereign Indigenous nations as wards of the state.

But Green's own letters reveal a different side of settler humanitarianism. As Alan Lester and others have argued for the past two decades, the advent of settler self-government in the 1850s was founded upon settlers defeating critiques from imperial humanitarians and then bending the discourse of humanitarianism to their own ends.[66] Within this argument is a necessarily antagonistic relationship between colony and metropole, with colonists challenging metropolitan concerns about their capacity to govern Indigenous peoples justly by asserting the Indigenous peoples' inherent inferiority and their need to be surveilled, coerced, and controlled. Green's case study is so fascinating because he flipped this argument on its head. Rather than basing his demands for self-government upon refutations of imperial humanitarianism, Green contended that the imperial administration was not humanitarian *enough*, and he located settler self-government as a solution to the inhumanity of imperial rule.

This also throws a new light upon Trutch's response to Green. Trutch was one of the appointed imperial officials who was standing in the way of responsible government for fear of losing his position. Thus, not only was he justifying colonization with a defence of his administration's humanitarian initiatives, he was also defending imperial rule against Green's demands for responsible government. Humanitarianism, therefore, was more than just a discourse for justifying colonization. Within liminal periods between imperial and settler administration such as that of British Columbia in the late 1860s, where the imperial government still maintained significant power, humanitarianism was a mutable language for measuring the relative value of competing visions for the future of colonial administration.

This mutability of humanitarianism is in line with Richard Price's argument that settler societies of the late nineteenth century not only challenged the authority of missionary philanthropists but also had to "clothe themselves in the garb of the humanitarian mission ... testimony of the power that humanitarian discourse carried in the British world of the nineteenth century."[67] More than that, however, Green's case reminds us that there was not *a* settler mutation of humanitarianism. Indeed, every chapter in this book explores a different way in which humanitarian discourses were used in settler and Indigenous politics in this period, demonstrating the depth and variety of humanitarianism as a political concept. As such, rather than speaking of humanitarian governance as a singular manifestation of humanitarian discourses in settler societies, this book is about the many ways that, and purposes to which, humanitarian rhetoric was employed and undermined by settlers, Indigenous peoples, and metropolitans alike to navigate the nebulous intersections between imperial, settler, and Indigenous sovereignties.

Notes

1 For an overview of the responsible government campaign in British Columbia, see Walter Sage, "The Critical Period of British Columbia History, 1866–1871," *Pacific Historical Review* 1, no. 4 (1932): 424–443, DOI: 10.2307/3633112.

2 Kiran van Rijn, "'Lo! The Poor Indian!' Colonial Responses to the 1862–63 Smallpox Epidemic in British Columbia and Vancouver Island," *Canadian Bulletin of Medical History* 23, no. 2 (2006): 541–560, DOI: 10.3138/cbmh.23.2.541; John Lutz and Keith Carlson, "The Smallpox Chiefs: Bioterrorism and the Exercise of Power in the Pacific Northwest," *Western Historical Quarterly* 55, no. 2 (2024): 87–104, DOI: 10.1093/whq/whae001.

3 Kenton Storey, *Settler Anxiety at the Outposts of Empire: Colonial Relations, Humanitarian Discourses, and the Imperial Press* (Vancouver: University of British Columbia Press, 2016), 102–128.

4 John Helmcken, "Indian Title," *British Colonist*, 5 November 1886.

5 *Ibid.*

6 Joanna Cruickshank and Patricia Grimshaw, "Indigenous Land Loss, Justice and Race: Ann Bon and the Contradictions of Settler Humanitarianism," in Zoë Laidlaw and Alan Lester (eds), *Indigenous Communities and Settler Colonialism: Land Holding, Loss and Survival in an Interconnected World* (Cham: Palgrave Macmillan, 2015), 54–55.

7 See Robert Boyd, *The Coming of the Spirit of Pestilence: Introduced Infectious Diseases and Population Decline among Northwest Coast Indians, 1774–1874* (Vancouver/Seattle: University of British Columbia Press/University of Washington Press, 1999); Cole Harris, *Making Native Space: Colonialism, Resistance, and Reserves in British Columbia* (Vancouver: University of British Columbia Press, 2002); and Jane Sampson, "British Authority or 'Mere Theory'?: Colonial Law and Native People on Vancouver Island," *Western Legal History* 39 (1998): 39–63.

8 Sage, "The Critical Period," 427–428.
9 British Columbia, *Debate on the Subject of Confederation with Canada: Reprinted from the Government Gazette Extraordinary of March, 1870* (Victoria: William H. Cullin, 1912), 2.
10 "Confederation, Responsible Government and the Delegates," *British Colonist*, 12 April 1870.
11 British Columbia, *Journals of the Legislative Council of British Columbia from the 15th February to the 23rd April, 1870* (Victoria: Government Printing Office, 1870), 33.
12 "To the Electors of Victoria City and Esquimalt Town," *British Colonist*, 3 November 1868.
13 "Confederation, Responsible Government and the Delegates."
14 Arthur Harvey (ed.), *The Year Book and Almanac of Canada for 1869: Being an Annual Statistical Abstract for the Dominion, and a Record of Legislation and of Public Men in British North America* (Montreal: Montreal Printing and Publishing Company, 1869), 116–118 (120).
15 J. S. Helmcken, "Debate on the Subject of Confederation with Canada," British Columbia Legislative Council, 9 March 1870, in James E. Hendrickson (ed.), *Journals of the Colonial Legislatures of the Colonies of Vancouver Island and British Columbia, 1851–1871*, Vol. V (Victoria: Provincial Archives of British Columbia, 1980), 449.
16 "To the Electors of Victoria and Esquimalt Towns," *British Colonist*, 24 October 1868.
17 "To the Electors of Victoria District," *British Colonist*, 31 October 1868.
18 "Governor Musgrave," *British Colonist*, 17 June 1869.
19 Sage, "The Critical Period," 439–441.
20 British Columbia, *Journals of the Legislative Council of British Columbia*, 4.
21 Boyd, *The Coming of the Spirit of Pestilence*, 172.
22 Paul Hackett, "Averting Disaster: The Hudson's Bay Company and Smallpox in Western Canada during the Late Eighteenth and Early Nineteenth Centuries," *Bulletin of the History of Medicine* 78, no. 3 (2004): 757–609, www.jstor.org/stable/44448061 (accessed 11 March 2025); Ryan Eyford, "Quarantined within a New Colonial Order: The 1876–1877 Lake Winnipeg Smallpox Epidemic," *Journal of the Canadian Historical Association* 17, no. 1 (2006): 55–78, DOI: 10.7202/016102ar.
23 Boyd, *The Coming of the Spirit of Pestilence*, 172–201.
24 "The Indians of Vancouver Island," *The Aborigines' Friend*, October 1870.
25 "Municipal Council," *British Colonist*, 19 November 1868.
26 Van Rijn, "'Lo! The Poor Indian!,' 544.
27 Lynn Festa, "Humanity without Feathers," *Humanity: An International Journal of Human Rights, Humanitarianism, and Development* 1, no. 1 (2010): 3–27 (9), DOI: 10.1353/hum.2010.0007.
28 Leader, *British Colonist*, 17 November 1868.
29 *Ibid.*
30 Derrick Baxby, "Smallpox Vaccine: Ahead of Its Time," *Interdisciplinary Science Reviews* 26, no. 2 (2001): 125–138 (130–132), DOI: 10.1179/isr.2001.26.2.125.

31 *Ibid.*
32 *Ibid.*
33 William Sebright Green to Frederick Chesson, 24 June 1869, quoted in "The Indians of Vancouver Island," *The Aborigines' Friend*, December 1869.
34 "The Unholy Alliance," *British Colonist*, 29 October 1868.
35 Stuart Banner, *Possessing the Pacific: Land, Settlers, and Indigenous People from Australia to Alaska* (Cambridge, MA: Harvard University Press, 2007), 195–230. See also Harris, *Making Native Space*.
36 Kenneth Brealey, "Travels from Point Ellice: Peter O'Reilly and the Indian Reserve System in British Columbia," *The British Columbian Quarterly* 115, no. 6 (1997): 181–236.
37 "The Meeting Last Night," *British Colonist*, 30 July 1862.
38 *Ibid.*
39 *Ibid.*
40 "House of Assembly," *British Colonist*, 1 April 1862.
41 "Public Notice: Cowichan Settlement," *British Colonist*, 15 August 1862.
42 Daniel Marshall, *Those who Fell From the Sky: A History of the Cowichan Peoples* (Duncan: Cowichan Tribes, 1999), 109–113.
43 Richard Charles Mayne, *Four Years in British Columbia* (London: John Murray, 1862), 152.
44 Marshall, *Those who Fell From the Sky*, 116–122.
45 "Cowichan Settlement," *British Colonist*, 6 March 1863.
46 "Horrible Murder by Indians," *British Colonist*, 9 April 1863; "Another Atrocious Murder!," *British Colonist*, 10 April 1863.
47 "Seven Indians and a Man-o'-Warsman Killed!," *British Colonist*, 27 April 1863.
48 Green to Chesson, 24 June 1869.
49 *Ibid.*
50 William Sebright Green to Frederick Chesson, 10 December 1869, Oxford, Bodleian Libraries (BodL), APS papers, Frederick Chesson files, MS Brit. Emp. s. 18 C137/9.
51 William Sebright Green to Henry Wakeford, 1 August 1864, enclosed in Arthur Kennedy to Edward Cardwell, 23 August 1864, The National Archives, London, Vancouver Island Original Correspondence, CO 305/23, no. 9624.
52 Storey, *Settler Anxiety*, 102–128; Sampson, "British Authority or 'Mere Theory'?," 48–49.
53 Amanda Nettelbeck, Russell Smandych, Louis A. Knafla, and Robert Foster, *Fragile Settlements: Aboriginal Peoples, Law, and Resistance in South-West Australia and Prairie Canada* (Vancouver: University of British Columbia Press, 2016); Heather Douglas and Mark Finnane, *Indigenous Crime and Settler Law: White Sovereignty after Empire* (New York: Palgrave Macmillan, 2012); Elizabeth Elbourne, *Empire, Kinship and Violence: Family Histories, Indigenous Rights and the Making of Settler Colonialism, 1770–1842* (Cambridge: Cambridge University Press, 2023), 189–231.
54 Green to Chesson, 24 June 1869.

55 *Ibid.*
56 *Ibid.*
57 William Sebright Green to Frederick Chesson, 22 January 1870, BodL, MS Brit. Emp. s. 18 C137/10.
58 "The Election," *British Colonist*, 3 December 1869.
59 "The Responsible Government Deputation and His Excellency the Governor," *British Colonist*, 14 April 1870.
60 *Ibid.*
61 William Sebright Green, "British Columbia," in *British America, with Two Maps* (London: Kegan Paul, Trench, Trübner, 1900), 169.
62 *Ibid.*, 164.
63 Sampson, "British Authority or 'Mere Theory'?," 58.
64 Storey, *Settler Anxiety*, 126–128; Robin Fisher, "Joseph Trutch and Indian Land Policy," in J. Friesen and H. K. Ralston (eds), *Historical Essays on British Columbia* (Ottawa: The Carleton Library, 1980), 269–271.
65 Alan Lester and Fae Dussart, *Colonization and the Origins of Humanitarian Governance: Protecting Aborigines across the Nineteenth-Century British Empire* (Cambridge: Cambridge University Press, 2014); Ann Curthoys and Jessie Mitchell, *Taking Liberty: Indigenous Rights and Settler Self-Government in Colonial Australia, 1830–1890* (Cambridge: Cambridge University Press, 2018); Amanda Nettelbeck, *Indigenous Rights and Colonial Subjecthood: Protection and Reform in the Nineteenth-Century British Empire* (Cambridge: Cambridge University Press, 2019); Richard Price, *Empire and Indigeneity: Histories and Legacies* (London: Routledge, 2021).
66 Alan Lester, *Imperial Networks: Creating Identities in Nineteenth-Century South Africa and Britain* (New York: Routledge, 2001), 138–175; Alan Lester, Kate Boehme, and Peter Mitchell, *Ruling the World: Freedom, Civilisation and Liberalism in the Nineteenth-Century British Empire* (Cambridge: Cambridge University Press, 2021), 108–143.
67 Price, *Empire and Indigeneity*, 249.

2

Influencing native policy through the British House of Commons: Natal, 1875–1880

The year 1875 marked a low point in Natal's campaign for self-government.[1] Only one year after Natal's first application for responsible government, the 1875 Constitutional Amendment Act hamstrung the elected members of its Legislative Council and rendered moot any possibility of passing a second application for responsible government until at least 1880. The dominant historiographical narrative of the past century holds that this "Jamaica reform," so called because it resembled the curtailment of Jamaican liberties following the Morant Bay rebellion,[2] became a turning point in convincing the majority of Natalians that responsible government was the only sensible choice for the future. There had never been universal support for responsible government in Natal, with farmers in the interior generally supporting more independence and merchants on the coast preferring close political ties with Britain. The Constitutional Amendment Act of 1875 played an important role in radicalizing settlers and pushing the responsible government movement into the mainstream, so much so that in the elections of 1880 every contestant for a seat in the Legislative Council ran on a responsible government platform. According to Sir John Robinson, then a member of the Legislative Council and later the first prime minister of a self-governing Natal, giving off the faintest hint of subservience to the imperial administration was enough to ruin any chance of re-election.[3]

Yet, as this chapter demonstrates, the road to responsible government in 1893 was much less linear than the existing narrative allows for. While some, like Robinson, became radicalised in 1875 to the responsible government cause, others searched for alternative pathways to self-determination through imperial citizenship, hoping to work *with* imperial sovereignty rather than against it. This chapter follows the efforts of one particularly prominent settler, Sir John Akerman (1825–1905), who secretly lobbied the British House of Commons to intervene in Natal affairs between 1875 and 1878. Akerman's lobbying blurs the line between settler and imperial interests. On one hand, he echoed settler demands for more African land and labour and championed the transfer of power from nominated imperial officials to elected settler politicians. He did so, however, by working through the British House of Commons in cooperation with the Aborigines' Protection Society (APS). This was perceived by most Natalians as an unacceptable fraternization with the enemy of colonial independence, and Akerman was forced to give up imperial lobbying in the face of local outrage against imperial sympathizers. As such, this chapter highlights some of the tensions inherent between imperial citizenship and settler colonialism. Imperial lobbying afforded settlers a means to bend imperial power to their own benefit, and was a necessary element of political participation prior to responsible government. Yet even when imperial authority was appealed to for the benefit of settler societies, the zeitgeist of the responsible government era – the contemporary knowledge that settlers in other parts of the empire were thriving under self-government – contributed to the unsustainability of imperial citizenship as an acceptable subjectivity.

A champion of popular rights

One of the factors making Sir John Akerman such a fascinating case study of imperial citizenship is the contrast between his public and private personae. Publicly, Akerman was a settler *par excellence*. Born in Plymouth in 1825

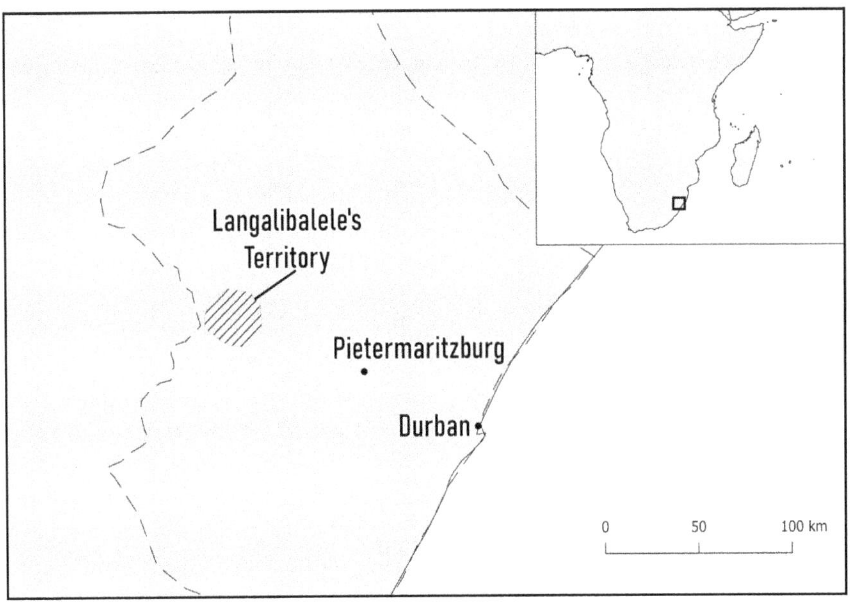

Map 2.1 Natal

and trained as a chemist, he travelled to Natal under the catastrophic Byrne emigration scheme, one of around 4,000 Britons who were deceived about the great promise of cotton farming in territory that was entirely unsuited to cotton.[4] Rather than giving up and moving elsewhere, as many did, Akerman studied farming with local Afrikaners and extracted a living from inhospitable terrain, leading him later to refer to himself as one of the real founders of Natal who "chose to fight it out with nature and the blacks."[5] After losing his son, Akerman opened a pharmacy in Pietermaritzburg and got involved in politics, serving variously as city councillor, mayor, member of the Legislative Council, and Speaker of the Legislative Council. He made a name for himself as a defender of settler rights during a constitutional crisis between 1869 and 1872 when Governor Robert Keate refused to recognize the Legislative Council's constitutional right to control financial policy. He feared the constant possibility of an African uprising, despised African culture, and coveted African land, leading him to advocate harsher assimilation and dispossession policies.[6] In 1880 he proclaimed that "the present form of Government is unsatisfactory and a failure ... it is the duty of everyone to try and obtain Responsible Government."[7] He would not always remain dedicated to the responsible government movement, writing in 1891 that "the freedom, that much-abused word, supposed to be inherent in Responsible Government, would in Natal be attended by serious risk and insecurity."[8] But in the 1870s and early 1880s Akerman remained firmly in the self-government camp, and he was hailed at the time as "a champion of popular rights in the Colony."[9]

However, at the same time that Akerman was gaining popularity by fighting for settler rights, he was maintaining a secret correspondence with the APS, the epitome of telescopic humanitarianism that was hated across setter societies as the enemy of settler rights. The APS's name was poisonous in the Natal public sphere. John Colenso, bishop of Natal and one of the most vocal APS collaborators in Natal, was branded "a traitor to his religion, his friends and his adopted country."[10] Just the suggestion that someone was in league with the APS was enough to tarnish their reputation. For example, when one Mr Brooks ran for a seat in the Legislative Council in 1878, the *Natal Witness* argued that an alleged connection with the APS disqualified him from holding office, and the accusation was serious enough that Mr Brooks had to hold a press conference at which he "disclaimed any connection with the Aborigines Protection Society."[11] This was not true, and the need to lie to distance oneself from any connection to the APS illustrates how risky corresponding with the society was for public figures, and yet Akerman wrote twenty letters to that body between December 1875 and August 1878.

Considering it took several months for a letter and a reply to travel from Natal to London and back, twenty letters in thirty-five months represents a close and active relationship with imperial humanitarians that would seem to contradict Akerman's public image as a champion of settler rights. Indeed, this is exactly how Natalians would interpret Akerman's correspondence with the APS when it was eventually discovered. Considered through the lens of performative imperial citizenship, however, it becomes obvious that Akerman was merely capitalizing on the APS's political connections to lobby the House of Commons in the pursuit of greater access to African land and labour. In order to align his appeals to imperial authority with the goals of settler colonialism, Akerman had to find ways of bridging the significant gap between settler and imperial humanitarian interests. His correspondence with the APS, the questions that he proposed they raise in the House of Commons, and the influence that he requested they exercise over British Members of Parliament (MPs) on his behalf therefore offer a valuable window into how imperial citizenship was reconciled and integrated into settler colonialism.

Debating Natal's native policy in the House of Commons

On 26 July 1878, a lively debate over the future of Natal's native administration took place in the British House of Commons. William McArthur, MP for Lambeth and committee member of the APS, proposed a compelling motion:

> That this House strongly condemns the policy of the Local Government of Natal in employing the machinery of British Courts in that Colony for the purpose of legalising polygamy and validating and enforcing native usages which recognise rights of property in women and children; and this House is of opinion that measures should at once be taken to promote the civilization of the native tribes, and to facilitate their withdrawal from the savage state, and recommends the appointment of a Commission to inquire into the subject.[12]

Legalizing polygamy and recognizing rights of property in women were the key foci of the motion, reflecting the prominence of gender in many elements of imperial discourses.[13] According to McArthur, "all the Native female population of Natal lived in a state of unquestionable slavery" because of the continuing operation of "native law,"[14] an uncodified body of Zulu law that included the customs of *isithembu* (polygynous marriage) and *ilobolo* (the offering of cattle from a groom to a bride's family). McArthur claimed that through these two legal processes, women were "being bought, sold, inherited, and their price recovered by law, like any other property," and he pointed to legal cases where fixed values for wives, daughters, mothers, "and even of grandmothers" were recognized by the courts of Natal as financial assets.[15] Worse still, McArthur alleged that the government of Natal was actively working to perpetuate the operation of native law and to secure the loyalty of the Zulu kingdom, not through a respect for "civilized" law, but solely through deference to a single man, the imperially appointed Secretary of Native Affairs, Sir Theophilus Shepstone. Such a state of affairs was not only a blight on Britain's identity as an empire of liberty, but also a threat to peace if that one man should fail to control Zulu hostility. For these reasons, McArthur declared that "it was of such vital importance that our relations with the Zulus should be placed on a permanently satisfactory footing."[16]

Complaints about *isithembu* and *ilobolo* were common in Natal society and traced back to a decades-long struggle between Natal settlers and Theophilus Shepstone. Shepstone had held the post of Secretary for Native Affairs since 1856, and his unique brand of native administration, later dubbed the "Shepstone system," played an important part in shaping the apartheid system of segregation in the twentieth century.[17] The context behind the Shepstone system was a tension between settler desires to possess African land and shape Africans into "civilized" and "productive" labourers on the one hand, and the impossibility of forcing this desire upon an African population that outnumbered settlers by twenty to one on the other. Shepstone determined that Africans could not be civilized too quickly without sparking revolt, and so his policy was designed to conciliate Africans in the short term while working towards civilization in the long term. Conciliation took the form of reserved "locations" on which Africans were segregated from white society and allowed to live according to their own customs, laws, and traditions. To work towards long-term civilization, European magistrates were placed in the locations as role models, in the hope that observing them would slowly entice Africans away from "barbarism." The Shepstone system therefore revolved around the simple principle that Africans would not be forced to abandon their lands, laws, and customs until they voluntarily decided to do so.

For the most part, settlers of Natal hated Shepstone's native policy. To start with, his reservation of large amounts of land for Africans directly conflicted with settler land hunger. Compounding the land issue was the protection of native laws enshrining practices that settlers deemed immoral, particularly the practices of *isithembu* and *ilobolo*, or what settlers called woman slavery and polygamy. As T. J. Tallie explains, the word "polygamy" does not capture the cultural significance of *ilobolo* in Zulu society at the time.[18] Socially, *ilobolo* provided a hierarchy for elite men to establish their power and status. Economically, it facilitated a system of production that had been adapted to the veldt over a very long period of time, and also functioned as an investment in the labour and productivity of the household. To settlers, however, *ilobolo* was a source of various anxieties. It demonstrated the inability of European culture to replace African culture. It threatened to corrupt Europeans into "going native" by taking multiple wives. It demonstrated the reproductive power of the Zulu, which threatened to overtake settler reproductive power. And, more materially, *ilobolo* provided Africans with a source of income that made it hard to induce them to became wage labourers for settler society. Shepstone, by protecting African land along with the practices of *isithembu* and *ilobolo*, made himself an enemy of Natalian settler society, and the concepts of polygamy and woman slavery became symbols of the tyranny of imperial rule.

It is therefore curious that William McArthur, a British MP and a member of the executive committee of the APS, should be found using settler talking points in the House of Commons. McArthur's motion appears on first glace to be based upon telescopic humanitarian concerns to, in his own words, "raise, educate, and confer upon [Indigenous peoples] the blessings of freedom and Christianity, and thus to make them happy and prosperous."[19] Indeed, the APS was the most vocal advocate in Britain for amending Natal's native policy, publishing various articles and pamphlets and sending numerous memorials to the Colonial Office on the subject. However, the impetus behind McArthur's question, and the reason why a telescopic philanthropist was spouting anti-imperial propaganda, lay in settler efforts to participate in imperial politics.

In addition to Akerman, a Natalian teacher named William Adams and his family played a significant role in raising awareness of Natal native policy in Britain. They wrote a lengthy letter to the APS detailing the experiences of various Zulu men and women who wanted to be exempted from native law but faced obstruction from Natal's native department, and this letter was then published by the APS in pamphlet and periodical formats. Adams also found himself under censure by Natalian society for daring to work with the APS, being castigated in the *Natal Witness* and defending himself by asserting that "I did not do so until I had tried all methods open to me in the colony."[20] Yet Adams did not make any specific demands of the imperial government, instead merely encouraging "every Christian man and Christian woman in the Realm of Britannia ... to lend their aid in rescuing our sisters in the Lord and his free women from the foul chains of heathen and savage laws."[21] As such, their efforts would be problematically labelled as imperial citizenship, given the definition established in the introduction as inherently claims-based. Conversely, Akerman made repeated and explicit claims upon the imperial government, and for this reason receives the bulk of attention in this chapter. It was his performance of a claims-based imperial citizenship that directly led to the House of Commons debate of 26 July 1878, and it was his anxieties about *isithembu* and *ilobolo* that informed McArthur's speech about polygamy and "woman slavery."

Overturning the Native Administration Act of 1875

Akerman's first act of imperial citizenship, and the first step in a three-year campaign to spark a debate on Natal native administration in the House of Commons, was to pressure the Colonial Office through the APS to amend the Native Administration Act passed by the Natal Legislative Council on 9 December 1875. The Native Administration Act was the Colonial Office's response to Natal's show trial of Langalibalele, chief of the AmaHlubi tribe, following his "uprising" in 1873. In that year the Natal government, led particularly by Shepstone and Governor Benjamin Pine, oversaw a brutal attack on the AmaHlubi people in a show of disproportionate retaliation.[22] Langalibalele had defied orders to surrender unregistered firearms, and had fled when confronted by a colonial militia on 3 November 1873. Four members of the colonial militia were killed in the ensuing chase and the rest initially retreated, only to return burning with racialized hate and fury. Governor Pine declared martial law on 11 November 1873, and for nearly two months the Natal militia and its African levies raped, murdered, and pillaged their way through AmaHlubi territory, selling off captured land, cattle, and women and children along the way, until Langalibalele was captured on 11 December. A month later he was put through a show trial headed by Governor Pine and Shepstone, who created the legal fiction that, as Supreme Chief, the governor could pick and choose from English law and the uncodified Native law to do whatever he wanted. Denied legal representation, witnesses, or appeal, Langalibalele was summarily exiled to life imprisonment on Robben Island, and hundreds of his followers were likewise banished or jailed.

The Colonial Office was horrified by these atrocities and took immediate action to assert greater control over Natal to rein in the excesses of settler colonialism. The inhumane violence was shocking enough, but more importantly, the publicity of the attacks posed a problem for plans to confederate the South African colonies. The Secretary of State for the Colonies, Lord Carnarvon, envisioned confederation partially as a means of normalizing native policy across the colonies, and the Langalibalele affair revealed the incompatibility of Cape Colony and Natal native policies. In the Cape Colony, in the interest of "civilizing" and, more accurately, controlling African bodies, extensive efforts had been made beginning with the first volume of the *Compendium of Kafir Laws and Customs* in 1858 to codify native law, and since 1865 all Black Africans were considered British subjects answerable to Cape laws.[23] Yet Governor Pine and Shepstone's piecemeal application of native and English law revealed that not only was native law in Natal uncodified, but it was still actively practised at the highest levels of the justice system and there had apparently been no efforts made to assimilate Africans into English law.

Natal's native policies needed to be completely reformed and placed under stricter imperial control for confederation to have a chance at becoming a reality, but the Colonial Office could not carry out these reforms unilaterally. Through the representative government established by the 1856 Charter of Natal, Britain retained the power to disallow and veto bills passed by the Legislative Council, but it could not enact legislation without a majority vote in the Legislative Council. Britain could, to some extent, rely on its nominated members of the Legislative Council (MLCs) to vote against those MLCs elected by and answerable to settler constituencies, yet the Electoral Divisions Act of 1873 had set the ratio of nominated to elected MLCs at 5 to 15. Given the widespread desire amongst settlers to exert more control over native policy, it was unlikely that the outnumbered nominated MLCs would be able to pass any legislation facilitating imperial interference in native policy. Thus, before native policy could be reformed, Lord Carnarvon sent Major General Sir Garnet Wolseley to reform the Legislative Council. Wolseley wined, dined, bribed, and seduced the Natalian elite into passing the Constitutional Amendment Act on 31 May, adding eight additional nominated MLCs to the Legislative Council in what became known as the "Jamaica reform." With elected MLCs no longer in a clear majority, the way to native policy reform was now clear, and a Native Administration Bill was tabled in August 1875.

Ironically, however, many settlers welcomed reforming native policy if it meant restricting the hegemony of Theophilus Shepstone and thereby leading to more African land and labour, and it was rather the imperial element in the form of Shepstone himself who stood in the way of real change. Shepstone had been given the task of drafting a bill to carry out Carnarvon's reforms, and when he submitted his Native Administration Bill to the Legislative Council, it was roundly criticized for failing to change anything and actually reinforcing Shepstone's position. The critical issue was that the bill purported to reduce Shepstone's monopoly over native law by creating a Native High Court, but this was rendered useless by making Shepstone the appellate authority to the High Court. Settler MLCs moved the bill into a Select Committee which transferred the appellate authority from Shepstone to the supreme court. This was enough to win a majority vote and the bill was passed on 9 December 1875, but two days later, on the last day of session when fewer than half of the members were in attendance (and only one member who opposed the bill), Shepstone sneaked in a "minor amendment" that placed himself on the appellate board of the supreme court, and so the Native Administration Act of 1875 enshrined the very thing it had intended to reform, and infuriated settler society.[24] It became yet another example of the imperial government intervening in things it did not understand and only making things worse.

In response to Shepstone's sabotaging of the Act, John Akerman drafted a long letter to the APS detailing settler criticisms and requesting that they forward them "to the notice of your influential parliamentary directors, so that they may prevail on the Secretary of State to remit it back to the colony for restoration to the form in which it was brought up by the select committee."[25] He had himself been part of the select committee that had altered the bill to suit settler interests, so that by seeking to convince the Colonial Office to remit the bill in the form determined by the select committee, Akerman was effectively trying to use imperial power to reinforce and consolidate his own power derived from the settler electorate. He tried to convince the Colonial Office that the Act's failure to break Shepstone's stranglehold over native administration would "in no way whatever break down in practice the power of chieftainship" that kept Africans "relegate[d] to fossilized barbarism," and he insisted that placing so much power in Shepstone as "lawgiver, lawmaker and judge" would only perpetuate the mismanagement of native affairs witnessed during the Langalibalele affair.[26] He closed his letter with a pointed question for the Secretary of State for the Colonies: "I ask is it safe expedient or proper that one person should have all this power, especially in giving decisions on Political questions?"[27]

As it turned out, the Colonial Office's answer was a tentative "yes." The APS dutifully forwarded the letter as Akerman had requested, and it received a mixed response. On the one hand, Lord Carnarvon remarked that "this is certainly an able letter, one in facts on which I own I feel disposed to concur."[28] On the other hand, internal notes on Akerman's letter reveal that the Colonial Office saw nothing wrong with empowering Shepstone. Pointing to his "extraordinary influence" over African chiefs, coupled with "the weakness of our military force there," the Colonial Office believed that making Shepstone the centrepiece of Natal's native administration was the best way to minimize the likelihood of an expensive war.[29] Lord Carnarvon forwarded Akerman's letter to Governor Bulwer, who provided Carnarvon with the Votes and Proceedings of the Legislative Council. Upon consulting these, Carnarvon determined that everything was to his liking and he refused to remit the Act in the manner requested. Carnarvon's refusal to intervene usefully captures that dissonance between imperial interests in cheap administration and settler interests in obtaining African land and labour. Yet Akerman did not acquiesce. He perceived his imperial citizenship as giving him the right not only to directly lobby the Colonial Office, but also to participate in debates within the House of Commons, and he looked to the House as a forum to convince Lord Carnarvon of the need to alter the Native Administration Act.

Akerman continued using the APS as a conduit for his imperial citizenship, providing them with the specific questions he wanted to be raised in parliament. The first question was intended to prove that the Colonial Office did not properly understand the implications of the Act because it was relying on information from Shepstone himself.

> Let an M.P. first obtain an official reply as to what was the date of receipt by the colonial office of copies of the votes and proceedings of the Natal legislative council for 1875. Should it be found, as I suspect is the truth, that this receipt was long posterior to Lord Carnarvon's reply to you on my opinions, then it follows that the pretended research into these matters was not made in England at all as the reply, I understand, imparts; but is but the endorsement of a report made from the colony and necessarily of a partisan character.[30]

This question referenced the Colonial Office's response to his first letter. Akerman believed that Carnarvon had not seen the actual Votes and Proceedings of the debate but only a report of the debate "of a partisan character," that is, written by Shepstone. By raising this question, Akerman hoped to convince the House of Commons to read the actual debate and reconsider remitting the Act. But the APS's go-to MP, William McArthur, was unwilling to ask such a question. Akerman was able to meet with McArthur personally when in London in 1877 and found McArthur hesitant to call for imperial intervention in Natal's native affairs because Shepstone insisted that meddling in native affairs could result in rebellion.[31] McArthur's hesitation frustrated Akerman, "as if England's mission in the world were to build up a wrong and never reform for fear of consequences!!"[32] Thus encountering the dissonance between imperial and settler interests, Akerman needed to develop a language that could span that gap, and he looked to the language of humanitarianism to do this.

Akerman adapted to McArthur's hesitation and offered him two more parliamentary questions that focused on revealing the immorality of the Act's failure to reform native law without explicitly calling for imperial intervention. One question focused on the immorality of effectively legalizing polygamy.

> Mr. McArthur M.P. to ask Mr. Lowther, whether it is true that a bill introduced into the newly constituted legislative council of Natal by the Secretary for Native Affairs and passed by the council and which enacts that the "customs and usages" of the natives shall be administered in the courts of law in that colony, has received the assent of the Crown. And whether HM government

> is aware that within this term "customs and usages" is included woman purchase and sale under and in the guise of marriage, that cattle unpaid for her at marriage can be recovered as a common debt in courts of law presided over by paid British magistrates and that polygamy is also freely practised by law. Is HM government aware that such Bill contains no provision to relieve natives when becoming Christians from native law; does not recognize a marriage between natives even when performed by a clergyman as legal, and that the paid official staff of the colony prevented those necessary previsions from being inserted in the bill?[33]

The other question emphasized the immorality of failing to "civilize" Africans within British territory: "Is not the ratification by special statute of the 'customs and usages' of the natives at this late period in the government of Natal a departure from the original intention which was the elevation of the native races and but a temporary toleration of their objectional practices[?]"[34] McArthur found such moralistic questions about civilization versus savagery much more acceptable than political questions about meddling with the government of Natal. First, on 23 April 1877, he asked the Undersecretary of State for the Colonies whether he was aware that the Native Administration Act failed to reform Natal's native law and thereby essentially legalized polygamy, and the Undersecretary replied that he could not go into the requisite detail and that the question was better if put to the House as a motion.[35] McArthur obliged, and he used Akerman's provided questions to form the structure of his motion in the House of Commons on 26 July 1878.

The ensuing debate meandered widely according to MP knowledge of and interest in the subject. For instance, William Cotton (MP for London) tried pivoting into a discussion of developing South Africa's railways and mineral industries, while Walter James (MP for Gateshead) went on a tirade about building more industrial schools for Black Africans. Conversely, those associated with the Colonial Office and who were the most well-informed on South African issues closed ranks around McArthur. Sir Michael Hicks Beach, Secretary of State for the Colonies, countered that it was unfair to blame the Natal government for upholding polygamy and bride prices since "it must be remembered that over a large portion of our Indian Empire laws are recognized of the precise character of those which are deprecated in the Motion."[36] Sir Henry Holland, future Secretary of State for the Colonies, agreed that McArthur was "extremely unfair to the Colony of Natal,"[37] and argued that outlawing ancient African customs would do nothing but push the Zulu into rebellion. Finally, Evelyn Ashley, future Undersecretary of State for the Colonies, called for McArthur to be patient. It was true that "all such laws and customs would have to be much modified," but "it could not be done immediately."[38] Faced with meandering interest from fellow

MPs on the one hand and stonewalling Colonial Office compatriots on the other, McArthur withdrew his motion, and so ended the last ever discussion of Natal's native administration in the House of Commons.

Akerman's appeals to the imperial government did not result in the amendment of the Act, yet it is striking that his strategy of gaining representation in the House of Commons through the APS actually worked. That the APS brought his case to the House of Commons demonstrates not only that Akerman perceived the APS to be a link between two very entangled and concomitant metropolitan and colonial spaces, but that this perception reflected reality. This is rendered even more significant in light of Akerman's earlier attempts to participate in imperial politics from Natal. Akerman had twice before called for imperial intervention, once in 1870 and again in 1873, both times seeking to use imperial sovereignty to override political decisions made by his local government, and both times sent in the form of letters directly to the Colonial Office.[39] The Colonial Office dismissed the first letter out of hand because it had not been sanctioned by the lieutenant governor of Natal,[40] and the second letter was largely ignored.[41] We can therefore observe that moving between the imperial networks of the Colonial Office and the APS was not just a way of performing imperial citizenship, but more specifically was a strategy of utilizing alternative overlapping networks as a means of circumventing barriers to imperial citizenship.

As an imperial subject but not a British citizen, Akerman was not entitled to raise these questions in the House of Commons. He could not vote for British MPs, and McArthur was not his parliamentary representative. And Akerman clearly did not care. He acted *as if* he had a right to representation in the House of Commons, and thereby manifested what Engin Isin calls "enacted citizenship."[42] Approaching Akerman's attempts to raise questions in the British House of Commons as a performance of imperial citizenship sheds light on Akerman's perception of the metropole–colony relationship. Akerman did not consider the imperial metropole to be spatially external to his colonial context, even though they were geographically distant. Rather, he was personally debating in his colonial parliament and – by proxy of the APS – debating in the imperial parliament *at the same time*, collapsing the apparent separation of metropole and colony into one singular imperial space.

Beyond the performance itself, the motivation behind Akerman's movement between imperial and colonial jurisdictions also reveals his perception of imperial and settler sovereignties. By raising questions in the British House of Commons to support settler responsibility for native policy, Akerman weaved together imperial and colonial sovereignty and made them codependent and coproductive. Sukanya Banerjee notes in the case of late-nineteenth-century Indian anti-colonialism that removing India from British sovereignty was not within the conceptual horizon of the time,[43] and the same argument can be applied to Akerman's concept of self-government. To him, self-government was not a rejection of British sovereignty, but a development of British sovereignty that would funnel imperial power into settler political agendas.

Despite Akerman's belief that imperial citizenship conferred upon him the right to participate in imperial politics, he also recognized that performing imperial citizenship was not acceptable to the majority of Natal's settler society. He explicitly demanded that the APS protect his identity and that his questions to parliament remain anonymous. Akerman marked his letters as "private," and he remonstrated with the APS when they did send one of his letters to the Colonial Office without his permission, complaining that "I did not quite intend for my name to have appeared so conspicuously before Lord Carnarvon and am not sure that I have escaped persecution in consequence."[44] Such persecution came from two directions. From above, Akerman feared reprisals from imperial officials should they learn that he was trying to mobilize against them, telling the APS that a settler's position "is never safe if he moves against the policy of fixed officials."[45] From below, Akerman feared alienating the public by appearing to side with the hated APS, and indeed this is precisely what happened.

When the *Natal Witness* learned that Akerman had been in communication with the despised APS, it ran an editorial calling him an "apologist for the Secretary of State" who had "allowed himself, independently of the interests and wishes of his constituents, to become the faithful servant of the Aborigines' Protection Society," and thus was "very seriously compromised."[46] He abandoned working with the APS as a result of the public criticism, writing that "I must not however say anymore or I shall again be branded as a conspirator,"[47] but the accusation of treachery to the colony continued to follow him for several months regardless. He tried to distance himself from identification with the APS, at one point criticizing a bill for restricting liquor sales to Africans as "more the outcome of the Aborigines' Protection Society than any measure of this session,"[48] but to little effect. In September 1878, the *Natal Witness* was still asserting that Akerman was "disabled from adequately representing the interests of the Colonists of Natal" because of his unacceptable attitudes towards the Empire.[49] He was later able to regain his reputation as a champion of settler rights by running on a platform of responsible government, but he never again tried lobbying the British government. He may have perceived imperial and settler sovereignties as entangled and co-constitutive, but he nevertheless found that imperial citizenship and settler colonialism were incompatible for public figures dependent on support from wider settler constituencies

Conclusion

The context surrounding Akerman's efforts at political participation through the British House of Commons makes it difficult for historians to assess the intentions and motivations behind his performance of imperial citizenship. On the one hand, appealing to imperial authority may have simply been a means to an end. Akerman experienced first-hand the dysfunctionality of representative government. He was an elected member of the Legislative Council who, prior to lobbying the British House of Commons, did his best to achieve change locally. On 28 October 1875, seven weeks before his letter to the APS, Akerman gave a lengthy speech in the Council against the Act, making the same arguments that he made in his letter.[50] He then sat on the select committee that was appointed to review the Act and, as he told the Legislative Council, "had done his utmost to make the best of the measure before him" by fighting to have the appellate authority moved from the Secretary of Native Affairs to a board of the supreme court.[51] Working through imperial authority was thus, in some ways, an act of desperation by someone who would have preferred not having to appeal to the House of Commons, and did so only out of necessity. Moreover, given that his correspondence with the APS overlapped temporally with the Colonial Office's five-year moratorium on applications for responsible government between 1875 and 1880, it is possible that working through the British House of Commons was something like a pressure-valve for his suppressed desire for self-determination.

Additionally, Akerman's appeals to British sovereignty could also be explained through the historical traditions of British loyalism in Natal. Natal was historically reliant on imperial defence. Where an African population outnumbered whites by around twenty to one in the 1870s, settler insecurity and desire to maintain control depended upon imperial military support.[52] Being dependent on the British government continuing to fund their defences, and on a British public continuing to sanction that expense, Natal settlers had a vested interest in maintaining the appearance of their loyalty and Britishness, and were in this way more connected to Empire than other groups in South Africa.[53] Akerman's actions could therefore have been informed by a concern to maintain Natal's imperial connections in addition to his own personal desire for African land and labour.

Yet the secrecy of Akerman's actions, and the backlash he experienced from Natal society, indicate that something deeper was going on. Akerman is not the only individual in this book who suffered for his appeals to imperial authority. The Indigenous leaders in Chapters 7 through 9 in particular were persecuted by their local governments for attempting to undermine their authority, and the Western Australian whistleblowers discussed in the next chapter also suffered boycotts and physical assaults by retaliatory settlers.

Akerman is, however, the only case study in this book who operated in secrecy. If imperial citizenship was just a means to either obtaining greater self-determination in the face of dysfunctional representative institutions or strengthening Natal's claims to imperial defence and commerce, there is no reason why it should have been so offensive to Akerman's constituents. On the contrary, Akerman's secrecy suggests that imperial authority was meaningful to him in a way that was incompatible with popular demands for responsible self-government. This was elaborated on in Akerman's 1891 petition against responsible government.[54] He explained that party politics brought with it a zero-sum element of winners and losers, whereas imperial supervision created a middle ground where win-win compromises were possible. Imperial supervision also ensured a continuity across governments that Akerman preferred to the temporary swings of party politics. This petition demonstrates that Akerman's imperial citizenship was not just a means to greater self-determination, but was a manifestation of his belief in the preferability of remaining under imperial sovereignty. And, importantly, this petition was sent anonymously, continuing the secrecy with which he lobbied the British House of Commons.

This secrecy has significant historiographical implications, for it raises questions about how far primary sources designed for public audiences reflect contemporary attitudes. This is certainly not a new issue. Douglas Lorimer, for example, broached this topic in his 1978 book *Colour, Class, and the Victorians*. He argues that the newspaper sources typically used to assess public attitudes towards race are necessarily sensationalized, so that only private sources such as diaries and personal correspondence can reveal what people actually believed.[55] And yet, nearly fifty years later, the dominant studies of settler imperial citizens by Daniel Gorman and Charles Reed continue to be based almost entirely on newspapers, political manifestos, government debates, and other public sources.[56] Thus, whereas the other settler case studies in this book can all be potentially dismissed as outliers who did not represent popular attitudes to imperial authority, Akerman's secrecy raises the possibility that what we currently think of as "popular attitudes" merely reflect the sensationalism of public sources. Historians including Laura Ishiguro and Angela Woollacott have shown how personal correspondence can be used to explore personal and private engagements with and attitudes towards empire,[57] but more work remains to be done to explore the dissonance between private and public ideas of imperial citizenship.

Yet while Akerman's secrecy raises the possibility that settler preferences for imperial supervision were more common than public sources can capture, the backlash he experienced, and the very necessity of secrecy, illustrate the momentum that responsible government had obtained by the late nineteenth century. This book contends, through an agglomeration of individual case studies, that attachments to imperial authority continued to exist in the decades before and after responsible government. But what Akerman's case highlights is that even when these attachments were used in support of widely accepted settler interests, their dissonance with the ideals of democracy rendered them antiquated and seemingly destined to disappear. Disincentivized from publicly acknowledging his preference for continuing under imperial sovereignty by the animosity of his fellow settlers, Akerman's experience of imperial citizenship shows that while support for the consolidation of settler sovereignties was not necessarily monolithic in the late nineteenth century, it was indeed too late to put the genie back in bottle.

Notes

1 For an overview of the responsible government movement in Natal, see John Lambert, "The Responsible Government Question in Natal, 1856–1893," *Kleio* 7, no. 1 (1975): 22–39, DOI: 10.1080/00232087585310021.

2 Jeff Guy, *Theophilus Shepstone and the Forging of Natal: African Autonomy and Settler Colonialism in the Making of Traditional Authority* (Scottsville: University of KwaZulu-Natal Press, 2013), 436; see also Ann Curthoys and Jeremy Martens, "Serious Collisions: Settlers, Indigenous People, and Imperial Policy in Western Australia and Natal," *Journal of Australian Colonial History* 15 (2013): 121–144.

3 T. R. H. Davenport, "The Responsible Government Issue in Natal, 1880–1882," *Butterworths South African Law Review* (1957): 84–133 (87).

4 Matthew A. Schnurr, "Cotton as Calamitous Commodity: The Politics of Agricultural Failure in Natal and Zululand, 1844–1933," *Canadian Journal of African Studies* 47, no. 1 (2013): 115–32, DOI: 10.1080/00083968.2013.771423.

5 "A Builder of Empire: Sir John Akerman, K.C.M.G.," Durban, University of KwaZulu-Natal Libraries, Papers of Sir John Ackerman, KCM 44690-44710.

6 John Akerman, *Native Government in Natal* (London: 17 King William Street, 1877).

7 "The Elections," *Natal Witness*, 26 August 1880.

8 Anonymous letter enclosed in J. Liege Hulett to Colonial Office, 16 March 1891, in British House of Commons, *Correspondence Relating to the Proposal to Establish Responsible Government in Natal, Presented to Both Houses of Parliament by Command of Her Majesty, July 1891* (London: Eyre and Spottiswoode, 1891), 60–66.

9 Leader, *Natal Witness*, 23 July 1878.

10 Quoted in Jeff Guy, *The Heretic: A Study of the Life of John William Colenso, 1814–1883* (Johannesburg: Ravan Press, 1983), 231.
11 Leader, *Natal Witness*, 12 December 1878; "Postscript," *Natal Witness*, 14 December 1878.
12 "Colony of Natal – Administration of Native Affairs," HC Deb., 26 July 1878, Vol. CCXLII, cols 451–476 (col. 451).
13 In particular, see Anne McClintock, *Imperial Leather: Race, Gender, and Sexuality in the Colonial Contest* (New York: Routledge, 1995).
14 "Colony of Natal – Administration of Native Affairs," col. 454.
15 *Ibid.*
16 *Ibid.*, col. 456.
17 See Guy, *Theophilus Shepstone and the Forging of Natal*; David Welsh, *The Roots of Segregation: Native Policy in Colonial Natal, 1845–1910* (Oxford: Oxford University Press, 1971).
18 T. J. Tallie, *Queering Colonial Natal: Indigeneity and the Violence of Belonging in Southern Africa* (Minneapolis: University of Minnesota Press, 2019), 18–30.
19 "Colony of Natal – Administration of Native Affairs," col. 456.
20 Leader, *Natal Witness*, 23 May 1878; John Adams, "Woman Slavery in Natal," *Natal Witness*, 1 June 1878.
21 William Adams, Ellen Martha Adams, Ellen Brooks, and Samuel Gibbs to Frederick Chesson, 18 December 1877, Oxford, Bodleian Libraries (BodL), MS Brit. Emp. s. 18 C123/57.
22 The Langalibalele Affair has generated an extensive historiography. See Welsh, *The Roots of Segregation*; Thomas V. McClendon, *White Chief, Black Lords: Shepstone and the Colonial State in Natal, South Africa, 1845–1878* (Rochester, NY: Boydell & Brewer, 2010); Jacob Ivey, "'The Same Effort and the Same Death': The Memory of the Langalibalele Incident of 1873," in Katherine Haldane Grenier and Amanda R. Mushal (eds), *Cultures of Memory in the Nineteenth Century: Consuming Commemoration* (Cham: Palgrave Macmillan, 2020), 165–181; Norman Herd, *The Bent Pine: The Trial of Chief Langalibalele* (Johannesburg: Ravan Press, 1976); and Guy, *Theophilus Shepstone and the Forging of Natal.*
23 Cape of Good Hope Commission on Native Laws and Customs, *Report and Proceedings: With Appendices of the Government Commission on Native Laws and Customs. Presented to Both Houses of Parliament by His Excellency the Governor, January, 1883* (Cape Town: W. A. Richards and Sons, 1883); John Maclean, *A Compendium of Kafir Laws and Customs: Including Genealogical Tables of Kafir Chiefs and Various Tribal Census Returns* (Mount Coke: Wesleyan Mission Press, 1858).
24 Guy, *Theophilus Shepstone and the Forging of Natal*, 446–450.
25 John Akerman to Frederick Chesson, 18 December 1875, BodL, MS Brit. Emp. s. 18 C123/69.
26 Akerman to Chesson, 18 December 1875.
27 *Ibid.*

28 Colonial Office minutes, "Native Administration Bill, Forwards Letter from Mr Akerman, a Member of Council Setting Forth His Objections Thereto," 25 February 1876, The National Archives, London (TNA), CO 179–122, no. 2289.
29 *Ibid.*
30 John William Akerman to Frederick Chesson, 25 September 1876, BodL, MS Brit. Emp. s. 18 C123/70.
31 For instance, Shepstone had said in 1864 that native law was a system "which only time can abrogate, because both men and women would equally oppose any violent attempt to destroy it." Quoted in Welsh, *The Roots of Segregation*, 71–72.
32 John William Akerman to Frederick Chesson, 7 March 1877, BodL, MS Brit. Emp. s. 18 C123/82.
33 *Ibid.*
34 *Ibid.*
35 "Native Customs and Colonial Legislation – Question," HC Deb., 23 April 1877, Vol. CCXXXIII, col. 1669.
36 "Colony of Natal – Administration of Native Affairs," col. 468.
37 *Ibid.*, col. 462.
38 *Ibid.*, col. 464.
39 John William Akerman to earl of Kimberley, 17 September 1870, TNA, CO 179–100, no. 12169; John William Akerman to earl of Kimberley, 28 November 1873, TNA, CO 179–113, no. 12879.
40 Colonial Office minutes, "Minute Paper," 18 November 1870, TNA, CO 179–100, no. 12169.
41 Colonial Office minutes, "Mr Shepstone's Mission to Zulu, on Occasion of Cetewayo's Assumption of Chieftainship," 28 November 1873, TNA, CO 179–113, no. 12879.
42 Engin Isin, *Citizens without Frontiers* (New York: Continuum International, 2012), 108–146.
43 Sukanya Banerjee, *Becoming Imperial Citizens: Indians in the Late-Victorian Empire* (Durham, NC: Duke University Press, 2010), 26.
44 John William Akerman to Frederick Chesson, 14 June 1876, BodL, MS Brit. Emp. s. 18 C123/71.
45 *Ibid.*
46 Leader, *Natal Witness*, 23 July 1878.
47 John Akerman to Frederick Chesson, 2 August 1878, BodL, MS Brit. Emp. s. 18 C123/94.
48 "Legislative Council," *Natal Witness*, 15 August 1878.
49 Leader, *Natal Witness*, 3 September 1878.
50 "Legislative Council," *Natal Witness*, 2 November 1875.
51 "Legislative Council," *Natal Witness*, 14 December 1875.
52 An imperial garrison was stationed in Pietermaritzburg, and while a colonial militia did develop over time, up until responsible government in 1893 the imperial garrison was greatly superior and the main assurance of security in

Natal. Paul Thompson, "The Natal Militia: Defence of the Colony, 1893–1910," *Journal of Natal and Zulu History* 29, no. 1 (2011): 20–65 (21), DOI: 10.1080/02590123.2011.11964164.

53 Andrew Thompson, "The Languages of Loyalism in Southern Africa, c. 1870–1939," *The English Historical Review* 118, no. 477 (2003): 617–623 (623), https://www.jstor.org/stable/3489288 (accessed 11 March 2025).

54 Anonymous letter enclosed in J. Liege Hulett to Colonial Office, 16 March 1891.

55 Douglas Lorimer, *Colour, Class, and the Victorians: English Attitudes to the Negro in the Mid-Nineteenth Century* (Leicester: Leicester University Press, 1978), 14–19.

56 Daniel Gorman, *Imperial Citizenship: Empire and the Question of Belonging* (Manchester: Manchester University Press, 2007); Charles Reed, *Royal Tourists, Colonial Subjects and the Making of a British World, 1860–1911* (Manchester: Manchester University Press, 2017).

57 Laura Ishiguro, *Nothing to Write Home About: British Family Correspondence and the Settler Colonial Everyday in British Columbia* (Vancouver: University of British Columbia Press, 2019); Angela Woollacott, *Settler Society in the Australian Colonies: Self-Government and Imperial Culture* (Oxford: Oxford University Press, 2015).

3

Opposing a corrupt colonial legal system: Western Australia, 1886

Western Australia's campaign for responsible government faced a crisis in the mid-1880s.[1] The colony had received representative government in 1870 in the form of a Legislative Council of twelve elected and six nominated Members (MLCs), but the governor was not responsible to the Council. A handful of radical MLCs throughout the 1870s proposed petitioning for responsible government as a means of speeding up economic development, but most MLCs opposed the idea. They believed that administration costs would be too expensive, and they feared that democratic elections would give too much power to working and middle classes. It was not until the Kimberly Gold Rush of 1885 that responsible government began to gain traction, largely in reaction to the rapid growth of the working and middle classes, whom MLCs hoped to prevent from obtaining too much power by setting the terms of their enfranchisement.

That same year, news broke in England of the extensive enslavement of Indigenous peoples in the northern regions of Western Australia. Four colonists – John Brown Gribble, David Carley, Edward Fox Angelo, and John Walkinshaw Cowan – became whistleblowers, lobbying the imperial government to expose the slavery system and gain stronger protections for Indigenous labour rights. Convinced that Western Australia could not be trusted with the administration of Indigenous affairs, the Colonial Office refused to consider any version of responsible government that would place Indigenous peoples under settler authority. When responsible government was finally granted in 1890, Section 70 of the Constitution required that Indigenous affairs be overseen directly by the governor through an independent Aborigines' Protection Board, funded by 1 per cent of the colony's revenue.

However, despite the fact that exposure of the slavery system hindered the responsible government campaign and enraged settlers who were embarrassed on an imperial scale, that was not the intention behind exposing the slavery system. Indeed, the four whistleblowers responsible for exposing the slavery system in Britain lobbied the imperial government, not to control settler violence, but to oppose imperial corruption. Gribble, Carley, Angelo, and Cowan each found themselves involved in lawsuits against enslavers or those invested in the slavery economy, and each discovered that the nominated imperial officials in control of the legal system were too corrupted by slavery interests to provide fair trials. These whistleblowers believed that, in the long term, responsible government would solve the slavery problem by making legal practitioners accountable to the people and consequently keeping enslavers accountable to the law. In the short term, however, they believed that imperial intervention was necessary to ensure that cases against enslavers were given fair trials, and they lobbied the Colonial Office to obtain justice in their own legal proceedings.

This chapter examines the whistleblowing activities of Gribble, Carley, Angelo, and Cowan as performances of imperial citizenship in the pursuit of their right to a fair trial. By lobbying the Colonial Office, these whistleblowers sought to invoke imperial governmental authority against legal decisions made by local legal officers. By emphasizing the corruption and inoperability of the legal system under the existing form of government, their performances of imperial citizenship used imperial authority to support the settler campaign for responsible government. Yet most settlers did not see it like this. Perceiving their whistleblowing as attacks on colonial morality and ways of life, settlers responded with physical assaults, legal counter-suits, and public boycotts. These cases thus provide valuable windows into the mutable and contradictory nature of imperial citizenship. Capable of using humanitarian discourses of Indigenous labour rights for the protection of settler legal rights, imperial citizenship could be simultaneously perceived by some as supportive of settler rights and by others as a betrayal of settler solidarity. Moreover, the backlash against these whistleblowers reveals the high stakes of displaying imperial or colonial subjecthood. Livelihoods and bodily security were on the line. Imperial citizenship was not an abstract principle for these whistleblowers, but the means of prosecuting those who assaulted them, restoring property stolen from them, and obtaining payment of debts owed to them.

The Western Australian slave system

From the beginnings of the pearling industry in 1867 until the Pilbara Strike of 1946, when Indigenous labourers protested unfair payment and working conditions, pearlers maintained a work force of both low-paid and enslaved Indigenous labourers.[2] The system arose from the combination of Western Australia's lengthy dependence on convict labour, which lasted until 1868 and contributed to "a culture of imprisonment,"[3] and the dangerous and

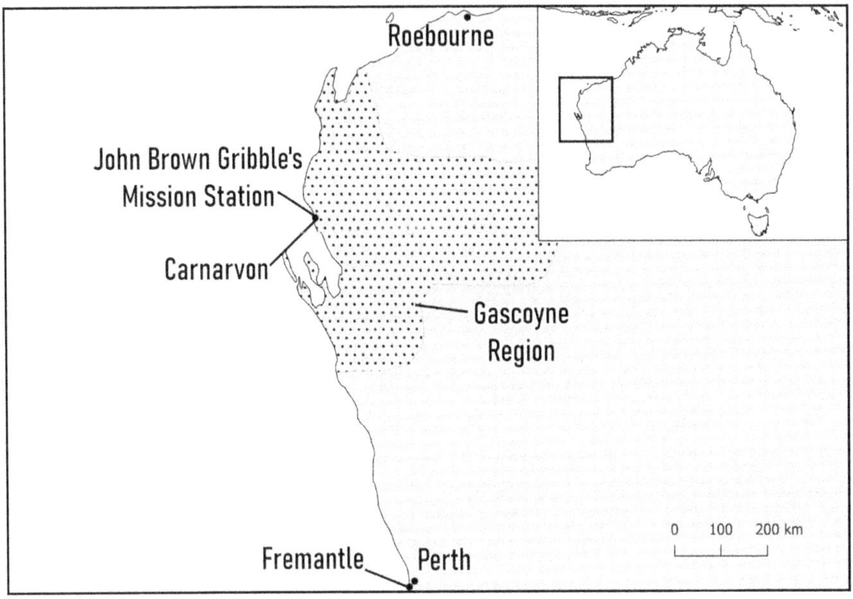

Map 3.1 Western Australia

harsh conditions of diving for pearl shells that failed to attract a steady flow of voluntary workers. The solution adopted was to force or trick Indigenous workers into labour contracts. "Blackbirders" also kidnapped Indigenous peoples from as far afield as the South Sea Islands and brought them to work in Western Australia. Pearling companies compelled contracted labourers to dive in the pearling season and then assigned them to local households as domestic labourers or pastoralists in the off season, so that forced labour became enmeshed within all parts of the economy around the northern coastal regions. Many labourers were abused, and running away was a criminal offence met with corporal punishment or transportation to the infamous Rottnest Prison.[4] The Western Australian government nominally opposed the use of forced labour and made several half-hearted attempts to regulate the pearling industry, but the seat of government at Perth in the far south and the pearling waters in the far north were so far removed that settlers were able to operate with little concern for government policies.[5]

There is a substantial scholarship on Gribble, Carley, and Angelo as whistleblowers on the Western Australian slavery system, although Gribble has received the most attention by far.[6] Each man came to Western Australia under very different circumstances. Gribble, an Anglican minister and missionary well known for his work with Indigenous peoples in Victoria and

New South Wales, was invited by the bishop of Perth to the Gascoyne region of Western Australia to establish a mission station in 1885. Angelo was a retired British soldier appointed as Government Resident at Roebourne in 1886. Carley was a general labourer who had been transported to Western Australia as a convict in 1861 and moved to Roebourne after being pardoned in 1872. Despite their differences, all three reacted with similar outrage at the slavery system operating in the north of the colony. They made complaints to local government officials, wrote letters to the Colonial Office and Aborigines Protection Society in England, and published pamphlets and letters in local newspapers denouncing the system and calling for more honorable and humane treatment of Indigenous peoples. They all suffered persecution for their humanitarianism. Gribble and Carley were both physically assaulted by angry northern pearlers. Angelo was withheld from promotion by Colonial Office officials who believed he had "lost his head." Gribble lost a libel suit against a local newspaper in which he was found guilty of being a "lying, canting humbug." And they all eventually gave up after finding that there was too much collusion between the pearling industry and the Western Australian government to permit any meaningful change. Gribble abandoned the colony to work in New South Wales. Angelo left the north to work in Bunbury in the south. Carley disappears from the record, but there is some evidence that he left for Victoria.

The existing scholarship provides detailed narratives of Gribble's, Carley's, and Angelo's activism and reveals important elements such as the role of religious literary traditions in Gribble's self-construction as a martyr and the contingency of the Church of Western Australia's complicity in Indigenous labour exploitation on the failure of Gribble's campaign.[7] However, while the existing scholarship acknowledges that Gribble, Carley, and Angelo worked with imperial bodies such as the Colonial Office and the Aborigines' Protection Society (APS) in their campaigns against the slavery system, no account has bothered asking crucial questions about why these men turned to such imperial bodies. What did they think these bodies could do for them? How did they attempt to convince theme that they were deserving of their help? And how did they relate their expectation of assistance from imperial bodies with their colony's ongoing movements for responsible government? By asking these questions (and including the perspective of a pearler, John Walkinshaw Cowan), this chapter contributes to assessments of whistleblowing on the slavery system by looking at it, not as act of humanitarian activism, but as a performance of imperial citizenship. Doing so reveals that, in addition to concerns about Indigenous labour rights, the whistleblowing of Gribble, Carley, Angelo, and Cowan was also fundamentally about protecting the income, property, and safety of white British subjects.

Four lawsuits

On 22 February 1886, after only two weeks on the job as Secretary of State for the Colonies, Granville Leveson-Gower, 2nd Earl Granville, received an angry letter from David Carley. The letter proclaimed that "the North West Coast of Western Australia is steeped to its neck with rapine, slavery, and murder," but more than this, it named specific government officials who were involved in covering it up.[8] Carley identified Chief of the Police Constabulary Captain Smith, Chief Justice Wrenfordsley, Attorney General Hensman, and three local magistrates and justices of the peace: R. Stoll, Frederick Pearce, and J. Lawrence. Carley claimed that he had made reports on instances of slavery to each of these men, and had even tried to get Pearce tried in court for using his authority to profit from the sale of enslaved Indigenous people. But no matter how hard he tried to bring a case against enslavers, Carley found that no government official was willing to allow such a case into a courtroom, and he told Lord Granville that "the law for the punishment of slavery is a dead letter in West Australia."[9]

Interestingly, however, Carley did not ask Lord Granville to intervene in the slavery system or protect Indigenous labourers. Rather, Carley's purpose in writing to the Secretary of State for the Colonies was to obtain legal protection and financial compensation *for himself*. Carley claimed that "on account of the writer [Carley] making these reports he has been swindled out of large sums of money, his life and liberty in danger, through the Magistrates and police, naming R. Stoll and Frederick Pearce, and denied any remedy at law in Perth for such for many years."[10] He does not elaborate in this letter as to what this means. However, in other letters to the APS, Carley claimed that he had lost over £1,400 in legal fees and had lost his business while attempting to bring a case against Frederick Pearce.[11] He further alleged that three police constables in Roebourne had beaten him up and arrested him when he tried to stop them from "tampering with a native woman" who was a witness in a case against the pearling company McRae & Co.[12] It was these grievances that Carley wanted Lord Granville to remedy. He explained that "as the writer [Carley] can get neither law nor justice for himself, in the city of Perth, on account of protecting the natives, he desires a full investigation of the charges he has made … and a compensation made to the writer for the losses he has sustained unlawfully."[13]

Lord Granville was annoyed at receiving such a letter directly from a colonial subject, and he instructed Governor Frederick Napier Broome to inform Carley that any future communications must come through the governor. Nevertheless, Granville asked Broome to investigate Carley's statements, and Broome responded with predictable results. Broome attacked Carley's credibility by producing a list of allegations that Carley was a thief, a bootlegger, had been fined for indecent exposure, and "lived in debauchery with several native girls of very tender age."[14] Broome also claimed that he had "caused search to be made for the reports which Carley states ... he has made to the Governor and different officials in times past," but that "such reports cannot now be produced to me."[15] Interestingly, Broome did admit finding one relevant report from 1881 in which Carley accused the Roebourne police of accepting bribes in return for allowing enslavement to continue. The report (which was written by the Magistrate J. Lawrence, whom Carley accused of corruption) admitted that "this is not by any means the first time that charges of accepting bribes have been brought against the police on the North West Coast," and even acknowledged that the accused officer did receive a bribe.[16] Nevertheless, the report argued that "knowing how ready such men as Carley are to make statements about the police ... it is highly improper and imprudent ... to give them an opportunity of doing so."[17] Broome therefore concluded that Carley was "a very disreputable person" and his accusations "simply preposterous nonsense."[18] As a consequence, the Secretary of State for the Colonies, the position by this time having transitioned from Lord Granville to Edward Stanhope, determined that the request for legal aid was unfounded, and no assistance was forthcoming for the beaten, indebted, and now defamed Carley.

As much as the Secretaries of State could ignore Carley on account of his character, they were prevented from ignoring his allegations of slavery in Western Australia by the arrival of another letter requesting imperial intervention, this time from John Brown Gribble.[19] Dated 25 May 1886, Gribble's letter arrived on Lord Granville's desk before the publication of his tell-all pamphlet *Dark Deeds in a Sunny Land; or, Blacks and Whites in North-West Australia* in July of that year, but after he had aroused settler animosity by publishing his diary of "My First Three Months on the Gascoyne" in the *Daily News* in early January. Unlike his letter to the *Daily News*, Gribble's letter to the Secretary of State for the Colonies was not designed to raise awareness of the slavery system or protect Indigenous labour rights. To be sure, Gribble did call Lord Granville's attention to "what is in my opinion an unpardonable miscarriage of justice," but it was not slavery.[20] On the contrary, the miscarriage of justice he wrote of was that committed against himself by the Western Australian government.

Gribble's grievance against the government began with a series of abuses he suffered at the hands of northern settlers who were angry that Gribble was criticizing their morality as well as their source of labour. The people of Gascoyne first boycotted Gribble, his family, and all those who supported him, refusing to sell them food or supplies. Then, as Gribble was travelling to Perth onboard a steamship, he was accosted by a mob of angry settlers who forced him to barricade himself in his cabin "with my back to the door and my feet to the wash stand ... from about half past one o'clock in the morning till after three o'clock."[21] Gribble told his bishop and superiors in the Church of England in Western Australia, who recommended that he pursue legal action against his attackers.[22] Gribble quickly discovered, however, just as Carley had, that the Western Australian government was composed of people invested in the slavery system who would not allow any legal proceeding to take place.

First, while in Perth, Gribble approached Attorney General Septimus Burt to file a suit against his attackers, but learned that the Attorney General "would not entertain my case."[23] Next, he went to the Police Court to issues summonses to detain witnesses to back him up, but found that the clerks at the Police Court avoided him, so that he "could not find any person to issue such summonses although I applied for them within prescribed office hours."[24] On his way back to the north, he approached the magistrate at Freemantle to file his suit, but there he was given the runaround: the magistrate referred the request to the Crown Law Officer, who referred it to the Attorney General, who referred it back to the magistrate. Gribble suspected that the magistrate was waiting for him to go back to the Gascoyne before filing his case. Whether or not that was the intention, Gribble had left the north by the time his case was finally processed, so that "practically the case had lapsed for I could not return again for the hearing."[25] His case against his attackers thus being continually refused, delayed, and finally closed in his absence, Gribble turned to the Secretary of State for the Colonies, "trusting that I shall receive from the Imperial Authorities ... that justice which is my due but which has been denied me in this Colony."[26] Just like Carley, Gribble demanded financial compensation for the "pecuniary loss and professional indignity" he had been subjected to.[27] More than that, however, he demanded recognition of his rights to "liberty and justice which I claim to be my birthright as an Englishman."[28]

Edward Stanhope, who was Secretary of State for the Colonies by the time a response to Gribble was forthcoming, could not reject his claim for legal intervention the same way Carley's had been rejected. Gribble was a respected missionary and a published author, and he provided the Secretary of State with the legal documents proving his efforts to initiate legal proceedings. However, Governor Broome had accompanied Gribble's petition with a cover letter indicating that "a concatenation of circumstances, partly favoured by Mr Gribble's ignorance of procedure or by that of his solicitor, but in no way the fault of the Govt, caused the case to be delayed."[29] Convinced, the Colonial Office determined that "there is no case for appeal to the Secretary of State," since "it is clear that the Government had nothing to do with the matter."[30] And so Gribble, like Carley before him, was rebuffed by the imperial government and left to see to his own legal problems, which would only multiply during his libel case against the *West Australian* later that year.

Stanhope sent his response to Gribble's petition on 6 September 1886, but was allowed only three months of peace before yet another letter about the Western Australian slavery system landed on his desk, this time from the Government Resident in Roebourne himself, Colonel Edward Fox Angelo. Angelo described a ring of corrupt government officials, including "several members of the legislature, leading bankers and lawyers, and all the local Justices of the Peace," who prevented him from prosecuting cases against enslavers.[31] He mentioned several specific court cases in which he had been forced to dismiss charges against enslavers. For example, on 27 October 1886, Angelo tried to convict a pearling company called McRae & Co. for coercing three Indigenous individuals into working on his pearling ship. According to Angelo, two of the five justices of the peace he had in the district were also defendants in the case and dismissed from sitting on the bench. Meanwhile, one of the justices who sat on the bench with him, J. B. Percy, was a banker for McRae and "throughout the proceedings has acted as advocate to McRae," while both of the justices dismissed intimidated witnesses from hidden positions around the court.[32] Angelo determined that McRae was guilty, but the three remaining justices on the bench called for the case to be dismissed, and Angelo was forced to concede. Unable to cope with being a party to "a state of things which I know to be repugnant to the sentiments of the Queen and the views of Her Majesty's Imperial Government,"[33] Angelo petitioned either to be granted further powers to override corrupt officials, or else to be granted a posting somewhere else.

Given Angelo's long record as a respected imperial soldier and civil servant, the Secretary of State could not dismiss his claims as easily as he had dismissed Carley's and Gribble's. He requested Governor Broome to make a report on all the cases mentioned in Angelo's letter. However, the Colonial Office lost their faith in Angelo's credibility when he wrote a follow-up letter on 11 November 1886. Fearing that there was a conspiracy "to get me out of the way somehow or another," Angelo asked that if he were to be assassinated, the imperial government would "provide handsomely for my large family."[34] The Colonial Office noted that it was "rather a wild letter" and that "the man is apparently off his head."[35] On 6 December, Angelo went so far as to accuse Governor Broome of being complicit in the conspiracy against him, the Colonial Office concluding that "the man can hardly be treated as serious" and "is, I fear, mad."[36] When Angelo continued to send letter after letter into 1887, the Colonial Office reflected that "we are only encouraging him" and told him to stop writing.[37] Angelo was eventually reassigned to Bunbury (to the south of Perth) in 1889.

Only a month after receiving Angelo's first letter, Edward Stanhope received a petition from yet another Western Australian colonist, this time a pearler and employer of Indigenous labourers named John Walkinshaw Cowan. Cowan reiterated many of the same themes as Carley, Gribble, and Angelo. He stated that "a shameful state of slavery and oppression has existed for years past, and is still carried out."[38] He alleged that the slavery system was "under the protection of the Western Australian Government ... which is rotten and corrupt from top to toe."[39] And he demanded from the imperial government "a fair and impartial investigation" for the purpose of "doing justice to her subjects black and white."[40] This last statement alludes to Cowan's interest in preserving his own rights in addition to those of Indigenous labourers, which he expanded upon in an enclosed document listing the various ways he personally suffered from the slavery system.

Cowan recounted several instances of his own Indigenous labourers being kidnapped and forcibly removed from his service. On one such instance, Cowan claimed that the young of two of his employees was taken away on horseback, "the boy shrieking with fright and his father and mother crying."[41] Upon reporting the incident to the local Government Resident, however, the Resident's response was "that he had been informed that the boy had come away willingly with the party, and that he had seen the boy, and that he appeared to be quite happy."[42] On another occasion, Cowan claimed that forty-four of his Indigenous labourers had been stolen from him at once. According to Cowan, he had sold one of his sheep stations to the firm of Wittenoom & Co., and expected to bring his Indigenous labourers – already under twelve-month contracts – to work on another station. Cowan later discovered that Wittenoom & Co. had believed that the sale of the station included the sale of its labourers, and they had signed new contracts with the forty-four workers. Cowan believed that the new contracts had either been forged or signed under intimidation, and he sued Wittenoom & Co. for the return of his workers. His case was dismissed, but Cowan remained adamant that "although the law has been decided against me, I do not relinquish my right to the native servants."[43]

He therefore turned to the Secretary of State for the Colonies to better protect Indigenous peoples' ability to choose whom they wanted to work for, and thereby enable him to regain those workers "whose services I have been deprived of by a trick."[44] The Colonial Office was sceptical of Cowan's claims, considering them to be "proved from hear-say" and revolving around "a good deal of party politics."[45] Moreover, an investigation into Cowan and Angelo's accusations had already been launched by the Western Australian government. Consequently, the Colonial Office, believing that the colonial investigation "seems to contain some promise," determined that "nothing can be done" for Cowan from the imperial end.[46]

Fighting imperial corruption and dysfunction

The history of criticism against the Western Australian slavery system has too often been reduced to a simplistic contest over frontier morality, with humanitarians condemning labour abuses and employers defending their way of life. Henry Reynolds, for instance, focuses on the actions of Gribble, Carley, and Angelo actions as rooted in concerns about Indigenous rights. Malcolm Allbrook and Reynolds both make passing reference to the men's legal troubles, noting that the lapse of Gribble's charges "caused him to refer his complaints to the Secretary of State for the Colonies," that Carley "attempted, unsuccessfully, to take legal action against the pearlers who openly bought and sold Aboriginal divers," and that Angelo was unable to effect change because of "the complicity of the leading men in business, the professions and the magistracy."[47] But for Reynolds and Allbrook these are minor details in a story of humanitarian critiques of settler violence that were silenced by settler society. Jane Lydon provides an alternative interpretation. Rather than approaching Gribble as an advocate and an activist, Lydon argues that Gribble is more appropriately understood as a martyr. She observes that the bulk of Gribble's publications about Indigenous slavery were actually "personal justifications of his behaviour" driven by "a need to show himself as wronged and yet steadfast," resulting in a portrayal of himself as "a Christian hero who had sacrificed himself for his ideals."[48] I agree with Lydon's assessment that Gribble's publications on Indigenous slavery were connected to other concerns around missionary martyrdom and Christian manliness. By applying a similar approach to the correspondence of Gribble, Carley, Angelo, and Cowan with the Colonial Office, this chapter shows that their critiques of settler violence were intimately bound up with larger issues around the accountability of the legal system to the people and the (dys)functionality of imperial administration.

Experiences of a corrupt and dysfunctional legal system connected all four applications to the Colonial Office. Historians have attended to the important role that dysfunction played in responsible government campaigns, although focus has been on political rather than legal systems. For example, in Canada, Natal, and the Cape Colony, gridlock between nominated and elected politicians demonstrated the ineffectiveness of representative government and evinced the need for elected officials to be given more authority.[49] In some respects, such political dysfunctionality rooted in the irresponsibility of nominated politicians was the same issue that plagued the Western Australian legal system, given that the Chief Justice was a nominated executive official. Indeed, the corrupt magistrates and justices of the peace that Carley, Gribble, Angelo, and Cowan complained about were appointed by the Chief Justice, an agent of the imperial government, and it was only through the imperial government that reforms could be achieved. Unlike political gridlock, however, which was largely only experienced by elite MLCs, legal corruption brought the dysfunctionality of imperial governance into the lives of everyday people. For this reason, Gribble perceived responsible government as the ultimate solution to corruption in the legal system. He wrote to the APS that "I hope the day will soon come when Responsible Government will be adopted and then may we hope to see a better state of things."[50]

Allbrook argues that the Gribble Affair "had the effect of unifying resistance in Western Australia to what was believed to be external interference in Aboriginal affairs," implying that Gribble, Carey, Angelo, and Cowan represented imperial intervention in settler affairs.[51] Ann Curthoys and Jessie Mitchell similarly argue that critiques of Indigenous slavery undermined the campaign for responsible government by revealing "a backward social and economic system that stood against everything colonists wanted to proclaim about themselves."[52] As this chapter demonstrates, however, their calls for imperial intervention were rooted in the dysfunctionality of imperial administration, not in the violence of settler colonialism. Those who defended the slavery system did not defend settler self-government, but did the opposite. It was the irresponsibility and capacity for corruption within imperial administration that enabled the slavery system to operate and, according to Gribble and Cowan, it was settler self-government that was the solution.

It may seem odd that Gribble longed for settlers to have more legislative power given that, according to Henry Reynolds, it was settlers who were responsible for the creation of the slavery system, and only through imperial administration were the more overt systems of genocide in other Australian colonies avoided.[53] However, while it is true that there was less overt genocide in Western Australia than in other Australian colonies, this chapter has shown that the dysfunctionality of imperial administration was directly connected to the oppression of Indigenous labourers. Indeed, Richard Haynes, the lawyer who would later defend the *Western Australian* in Gribble's libel case against the newspaper, adopted the slavery issue as a talking point in favour of responsible government. Haynes was a fervent supporter of self-government, becoming chairman of the Central Reform League, which lobbied for democratic reforms. Haynes became Cowan's legal representative, perceiving that Cowan's case against corruption in the legal system could be used to expose the dysfunction of imperial governance. This was not lost on Governor Broome when Haynes forwarded Cowan's letter to the Colonial Office. Broome informed the Secretary of State for the Colonies that Haynes advocated "the immediate adoption of Responsible Government for this Colony. It is, perhaps, partly to this end that he is one of a small band who attack myself and my government."[54] As Curthoys and Mitchell point out, the Colonial Office, too, understood that if slavery was conducted in Western Australia, it was a blemish both on settlers and on Britain itself. Because of the continuation of imperial administration in Western Australia, "while Queensland brought dishonour on the British Empire generally, Western Australia was bringing dishonour also directly to Britain itself."[55]

Conclusion

The letters from Carley, Gribble, Angelo, and Cowan to the Secretary of State for the Colonies show that imperial citizenship performed within a representative government context could just as easily be directed in support of settler self-government as against it. On one level, these whistle-blowers were working through the system that was available to them. The Chief Justice was an imperial agent, and so invoking imperial authority was necessary for reforming the legal system. On another level, they were confronting the imperial government with its own backwardness, and hoping to convince the Colonial Office that settler democracy was a necessary solution to legal corruption, and thus to leverage imperial power against itself. Consequently, in addition to interpreting the "Gribble Affair" as a battle between abusive settlers and humanitarians attempting to control settler violence, we can also read the affair as a battle between settlers who benefited from the corruption afforded by imperial governance and settlers who did not, who perceived responsible government as a key to undermining that corruption. It is true that, as Curthoys and Mitchell demonstrate, control over Indigenous affairs was withheld from settlers in the 1890 Constitution partially as a result of the Colonial Office becoming aware of the slavery system in the northern districts of Western Australia.[56] At the same time, however, the operation of the slavery system under the nose of imperial agents played an important role in convincing the Colonial Office that settler democracy was necessary for the better protection of Indigenous rights.

In addition to offering a new perspective on the relationship between imperial citizenship and responsible government, approaching the Gribble Affair through letters to the Colonial Office also provides insight into the range of different rights that the concept of imperial citizenship could be mapped on to. Scholars have not so far examined any cases where imperial citizenship was used to lay claim to a right to a fair trial. Sukanya Banerjee, for instance, conceptualizes imperial citizenship through Indian claims to free movement across imperial borders, to occupy public offices, and to vote.[57] Jared McDonald attends to imperial citizenship claims by Khoesan people in South Africa to fair wages and equality before the law.[58] Zaki Nahaboo uses imperial citizenship as a lens to study demands for Black political representation in Mauritius.[59] The right to a fair trial has not been included in such studies largely because the right to legal protection was understood by contemporaries as a right of subjecthood rather than of citizenship, and all settlers (as well as most Indigenous peoples) were automatically British subjects. In Western Australia, there was already a clear protocol for obtaining legal protection. From 1861 onwards, all British subjects had the right to bring cases before the Supreme Court. Supreme Court cases could be appealed to the governor. And where justice was still believed not to have been served, the British subjects could appeal to the Privy Council to overturn colonial case law. Theoretically, therefore, there was no need to claim imperial citizenship to obtain a fair trial.

However, the cases of Carley, Gribble, Angelo, and Cowan demonstrate that the existence of a theoretical right to a fair trial was subject to the transparency and accountability of local legal systems. Where corruption hindered the functionality of Western Australia's legal system, the promise of legal protection to British subjects was simply not enough. The right to a fair trial had to be actively demanded from the imperial government, elevating it from a passive right of subjecthood to a claims-based right of citizenship. This underscores the situational malleability of imperial citizenship as a means of leveraging imperial power in local colonial conflicts. Far from being limited to strict definitions of what constituted citizenship or what rights citizenship conferred, these cases reveal that colonist understandings of and demands upon imperial authority shifted and adapted in response to a wide variety of issues encountered in colonial life. Being an imperial citizen did not come with specific expectations of rights and responsibilities, but was for the most part an abstract belief that the imperial government could solve everyday problems colonial governments were either unable or unwilling to address.

Notes

1 For an overview of the responsible government campaign in Western Australia, see Ann Curthoys and Jessie Mitchell, *Taking Liberty: Indigenous Rights and Settler Self-Government in Colonial Australia, 1830–1890* (Cambridge: Cambridge University Press, 2018), 361–404.
2 Malcolm Allbrook, "'A Disguised and Unquestionable Form of Slavery': Aboriginal Labour on the Nineteenth-Century Pearling Fleet in North-West Australia," *Australian Journal of Biography and History* 6 (2022): 79–101 (87), DOI: 10.22459/AJBH.06.2022.04.
3 Curthoys and Mitchell, *Taking Liberty*, 364.
4 *Ibid.*, 372.
5 Allbrook, "A Disguised and Unquestionable Form of Slavery," 90–91.

6 See Henry Reynolds, *This Whispering in Our Hearts Revisited* (Sydney: University of New South Wales Press, 2018); John Harris, *One Blood: 200 Years of Aboriginal Encounter with Christianity: A Story of Hope* (Sutherland: Albatross Books, 1990); Su-Jane Hunt, "The Gribble Affair: A Study in Colonial Politics," in John Brown Gribble, *Dark Deeds in a Sunny Land; or, Blacks and Whites in North-West Australia* (Nedlands: University of Western Australia Press, 1987).
7 Malcolm Allbrook, *Henry Prinsep's Empire: Framing a Distant Colony* (Canberra: Australian National University Press, 2014), 209–214; Jane Lydon, *Imperial Emotions: The Politics of Empathy across the British Empire* (Cambridge: Cambridge University Press, 2020), 123–142.
8 David Carley to Secretary of State for the Colonies, 11 January 1886, Oxford, Bodleian Libraries (BodL), MS Brit. Emp. s. 18 C128/91.
9 *Ibid.*
10 *Ibid.*
11 David Carley to Frederick Chesson, 3 January 1884, BodL, MS Brit. Emp. s. 18 C128/79.
12 David Carley to Frederick Chesson, 8 October 1884, BodL, MS Brit. Emp. s. 18 C128/81.
13 Carley to Secretary of State for the Colonies, 11 January 1886.
14 Frederick Napier Broome to Lord Granville, 12 July 1886, BodL, MS Brit. Emp. s. 18 C163/105.
15 *Ibid.*
16 *Ibid.*
17 *Ibid.*
18 *Ibid.*
19 John Gribble to Lord Granville, 25 May 1886, quoted in Gribble, *Dark Deeds*, 27–31.
20 *Ibid.*
21 *Ibid.*
22 John Gribble, "The Revd J. B. Gribble and His Ecclesiastical Superiors," *Daily News* (Perth), 22 May 1886.
23 Gribble to Lord Granville, 25 May 1886.
24 *Ibid.*
25 *Ibid.*
26 *Ibid.*
27 *Ibid.*
28 *Ibid.*
29 Colonial Office minutes, "Case of Rev. J. B. Gribble," 9 June 1886, The National Archives, London (TNA), CO 18/206, no. 13241.
30 *Ibid.*
31 Edward Fox Angelo to the Secretary of State for the Colonies, 23 October 1886, TNA, CO 18/207, no. 22545.
32 Edward Fox Angelo to the Secretary of State for the Colonies, 30 October 1886, TNA, CO 18/207, no. 23207.
33 *Ibid.*; Edward Fox Angelo to the Secretary of State for the Colonies, 12 January 1887, TNA, CO 18/209, no. 5375.

34 Edward Fox Angelo to the Secretary of State for the Colonies, 11 November 1886, TNA, CO 18/207, no. 424.
35 Colonial Office minutes, "Treatment of Natives," 11 November 1886, TNA, CO 18/207, no. 424.
36 Colonial Office minutes, "Treatment of Natives," 6 December 1886, TNA, CO 18/207, no. 1467.
37 Colonial Office minutes, "Treatment of Natives," 9 April 1887, TNA, CO 18/209, no. 10434.
38 John Walkinshaw Cowan to the Secretary of State for the Colonies, 21 October 1886, TNA, CO 18/207, no. 445.
39 *Ibid.*
40 *Ibid.*
41 John Walkinshaw Cowan to the Government Resident at Roebourne, 15 October 1886, enclosed in Cowan to the Secretary of State for the Colonies, 21 October 1886.
42 *Ibid.*
43 *Ibid.*
44 *Ibid.*
45 Colonial Office minutes, "Alleged Ill-Treatment of Natives," 3 December 1886, TNA, CO 18/445, no. 445.
46 *Ibid.*
47 Reynolds, *This Whispering in Our Hearts Revisited*, 78, 82, 85; Allbrook, *Henry Prinsep's Empire*, 211.
48 Lydon, *Imperial Emotions*, 138–139.
49 Allan Greer, "1837–38: Rebellion Reconsidered," *The Canadian Historical Review* 76, no. 1 (1995): 1–18, www.muse.jhu.edu/article/574662 (accessed 11 March 2025); J. L. McCracken, *The Cape Parliament, 1854–1910* (Oxford: Clarendon Press, 1967); Lambert, "The Responsible Government Question in Natal."
50 John Brown Gribble to Frederick Chesson, 17 December 1886, BodL, MS Brit. Emp. s. 18 C137/21.
51 Allbrook, *Henry Prinsep's Empire*, 214.
52 Curthoys and Mitchell, *Taking Liberty*, 385.
53 Henry Reynolds, *This Whispering in Our Hearts Revisited*, 73.
54 Frederick Broome to Secretary of State for the Colonies, 3 December 1886, TNA, CO 18/207 no. 445.
55 Curthoys and Mitchell, *Taking Liberty*, 389.
56 *Ibid.*, 396–401.
57 Sukanya Banerjee, *Becoming Imperial Citizens: Indians in the Late-Victorian Empire* (Durham, NC: Duke University Press, 2010).
58 Jared McDonald, *Khoesan and Imperial Citizenship in Nineteenth Century South Africa* (New York: Routledge, 2023).
59 Zaki Nahaboo, "Rémy Ollier and Imperial Citizenship," *Interventions* 20, no. 5 (2018): 717–733, DOI: 10.1080/1369801X.2018.1487317.

Part II

Settler imperial citizenship within responsible governments

4

Securing settler futurity against indigenous resistance: New Zealand, 1860–1861

On 22 February 1860, Governor Thomas Gore Browne declared martial law in Taranaki, a region on the western coast of New Zealand's North Island, marking the beginning of the Taranaki Wars, which would rage on and off for the next ten years. The spark of the conflict was the New Zealand government's purchase of a 600-acre piece of land called the Pekapeka block from the Te Āti Awa iwi. Pekapeka was owned and occupied by a multitude of people with overlapping claims to the land, with a patchwork of non-contiguous plots and areas held in common so that no individual could justifiably claim ownership of the whole block. One of these coresidents, a chief named Te Teira, offered to sell his portion of Pekapeka to the government, while another coresident, Wiremu Kingi, challenged the sale, claiming that Te Teira did not have the right to sell land with overlapping titles. Governor Browne decided that it was more prudent for the future of the colony to recognize Te Teira's right to sell Pekapeka than to recognize Kingi's right to veto land sales, and he signed a deed of purchase with Te Teira's family for the entire block of land. He declared martial law and sent soldiers to occupy the land two days before the deed was signed, demonstrating his knowledge that transgressing Kingi's land rights would lead to armed resistance, and he purposefully escalated tensions by invading the dubiously purchased land with a force of 400 imperial soldiers and settler militia, who opened fire on Kingi's forces on 17 March. Fighting paused a year later on 18 March 1861, but would resume as the Waikato War in 1863–1866 and Tītokowaru's War in 1868–1869, so that the fighting from 1860 to 1861 later became known as the First Taranaki War.

According to the Waitangi Tribunal of 1996, this invasion was "an unlawful attack by the armed forces of the Crown on Māori not at that time in rebellion,"[1] and such questionable legality was not lost on contemporaries in New Zealand. Newspapers such as the *Māori Recorder* criticized Governor Browne to such an extent that Browne issued a public proclamation against "the publication of opinions ... impugning the justice and legality of the course pursued by Her Majesty's Government," which he believed was spreading disaffection in the Māori population.[2] For some critics of the government, however, debating the legality of the war in local papers was not enough, and they instead turned to publishing pamphlets in Britain. The most prodigious of these pamphleteers was Octavius Hadfield, the archdeacon of Kapiti, who wrote three pamphlets: *One of England's Little Wars*, *A Sequel to "One of England's Little Wars,"* and *The Second Year of One of England's Little Wars*. Sir William Martin, former Chief Justice of New Zealand, wrote only a single a pamphlet entitled *The Taranaki Question*, but at 152 pages it was larger than all three of Hadfield's combined. George Selwyn, the bishop of New Zealand, contributed his voice to a lesser extent by enclosing a pastoral letter within a collection of *Extracts of Letters from New Zealand on the War Question*.

This chapter approaches these pamphlets as performances of imperial citizenship. I show that all three pamphleteers sought to go over Governor Browne's head to bring an end to a war they believed endangered the survival of fellow settlers, the future growth of the colony, and the continuation of British sovereignty in New Zealand. Their invocations of imperial authority to protect settler society support recent scholarship on the notion of New Zealand as a "garrison colony" and highlight the connection between settler colonialism and imperial military power.[3] However, their conviction that settler society would be best protected by the *removal* of imperial troops rather than the continuation of an imperial military campaign provides a new perspective on settler understandings of the link between imperial and settler power. Moreover, their attempts to invoke imperial intervention via pamphlets rather than directly petitioning government departments or officials points towards the multitude of methods that settlers employed to invoke imperial authority. By focusing on why Hadfield, Martin, and Selwyn adopted pamphleteering as their chosen method of performing imperial citizenship, this chapter underscores the strengths and weaknesses of different forms of imperial connection and the agency that imperial citizens possessed to choose the methods of connection most suitable to their purposes.

A war for sovereignty?

Although New Zealand had received responsible government in 1853, Britain retained control over two important areas of state administration: Māori affairs and armed forces. The two were connected, inasmuch as Britain believed that settler management of Māori affairs would lead to constant warfare, and it refused to foot the bill of colonial wars started by settler mismanagement.[4] Imperial soldiers therefore continued to be stationed at New Zealand until 1870, and, as Charlotte Macdonald points out,

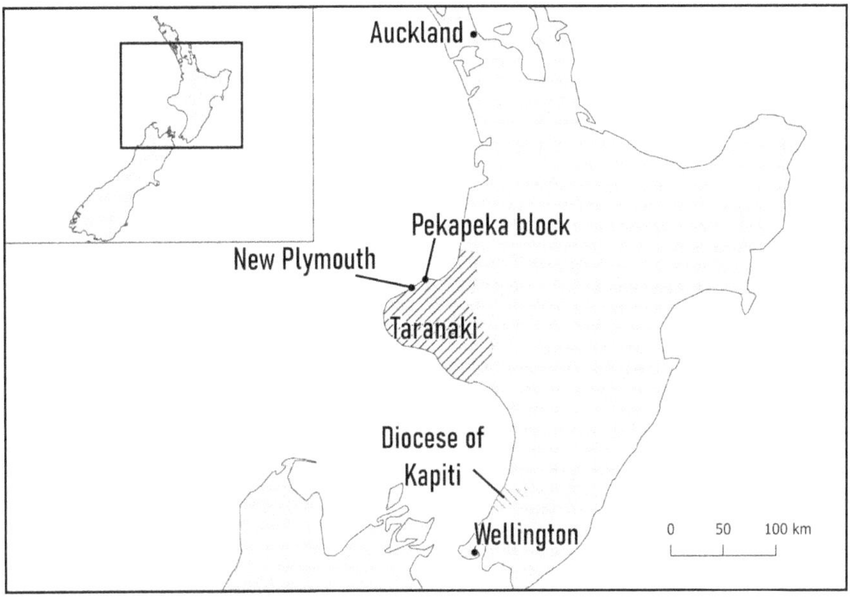

Map 4.1 New Zealand's North Island

this means that "the first three crucial decades of New Zealand as a British colony of settlement were predicated on the presence of a military garrison."[5] Britain's continuing control over New Zealand's defences is a crucial piece of context to understand why Octavius Hadfield, William Martin, and George Selwyn invoked imperial authority to intervene in the First Taranaki War. It was, after all, an imperial war fought by imperial soldiers, and it was the British rather than the New Zealand government that had the power to end it. According to James Belich, the fundamental cause of the war was not settler land hunger but Britain's interest in maintaining its sovereignty over New Zealand.[6]

On the ground, however, it was not always clear whether British sovereignty was truly believed to be in jeopardy, or whether the spectre of an imperilled British sovereignty was used rhetorically by settlers to maintain imperial military support. Influenced by a desire to reduce expenses incurred by colonial warfare, some voices in the British government and press advocated removing imperial troops and allowing New Zealand to fight the Taranaki War on its own. This possibility led the New Zealand press to assert their dependence on British support. Kenton Storey argues that by representing the war as a threat, not just to settler livelihoods but to the Queen's sovereignty, the New Zealand press hoped to justify Britain's continuing military support.[7]

In turn, a central element of Hadfield's, Martin's, and Selwyn's critiques of the war was that British sovereignty was not actually in danger at all. Hadfield, for instance, argued that the Māori were not fighting *against* British sovereignty, but for the *maintenance* of British law and order. In a reader letter to *The Times* dated 26 February 1861, he explained that

> there was no resistance of the law on the part of Wiremu Kingi and those acting with him ... It is a curious but an important feature of the present war, that the Natives regard themselves as fighting in support of law and order, in opposition to the illegal conduct of Governor Browne; and there can be no doubt that they are right in this view of the subject.[8]

According to Hadfield, it was Governor Browne's illegal land claim that challenged the Queen's sovereignty, and by resisting such an illegal move the Māori were fighting for the preservation of British law. Martin took a different tack, suggesting that Māori disaffection with Britain was not so widespread as was believed. In *The Taranaki Question*, he wrote:

> I know it has been asserted that a large portion of the Native population is hostile to the Queen's sovereignty. I am persuaded that such is not the case. My firm belief is that, if what is called disaffection were carefully sifted and examined, it would be found almost universally to be at bottom directed against particular persons or particular grievances, not really against the authority of the Crown.[9]

According to Martin, therefore, Māori resistance was not so much against Britain as against a select group of British people. Conversely, Selwyn argued that "William King has no ill-will whatever against any of our countrymen," and he demanded that "those who complain of his duplicity cease to force him into a position of hostility by the suspicions and threats."[10] From this view, the Māori military response did not come from a place of offence against Britain, but from defence of Māori rights. Based on these statements, Belich and others contend that Hadfield, Martin, and Selwyn simply did not consider British sovereignty to be at stake, believing instead that the sovereignty issue was being used to justify a war that was primarily designed by settlers to seize Māori land.[11]

If such was the case, then Hadfield's, Martin's, and Selwyn's invocation of imperial authority through their pamphlets would appear to be typical manifestations of a humanitarian desire to restrain settler violence through imperial oversight to protect Indigenous rights. However, Hadfield, Martin, and Selwyn made it clear that their motivations for invoking imperial authority were for settler rather than Māori benefit. Hadfield asserted that the Taranaki War posed an immediate danger to settler lives as well as to the future colonization of New Zealand, as he believed the Māori to be more than capable of wiping the settlement out. In a private letter to his brother,

Hadfield explained that "I did not write [my pamphlets] so much to defend the natives, who are perfectly able to take care of themselves, as ... to avert from the unfortunate settlers the ruin that must undoubtedly overtake them if the war is allowed to continue much longer."[12] Hadfield challenged the narrative that British military support could guarantee settler survival. He wrote in a letter to *The Times* that "no force that Great Britain could possibly maintain on this island would exterminate [the Māori] in fifty years," and that "nothing is more certain than that the whole white population of this island would be exterminated so soon as the war of Māori extermination began in good earnest."[13]

Martin similarly framed his pamphlet as a defence of settler futurity. He argued that the continuity of the settler presence in New Zealand was dependent on Māori confidence in settler justice, since the Māori would only consent to be governed by settlers if they were governed fairly. "Be just, and you may easily govern the Māori. Be just, and a moderate force will suffice. Be unjust, and a force far larger than England can spare will not suffice."[14] Martin's purpose in invoking imperial authority was thus not only to end the war, but to ensure that those responsible for starting the war were punished and any land unjustly seized be returned. "The restoration of peace will not suffice, unless peace be so made as to produce confidence, to create an assurance that injustice is not intended ... we must satisfy the people that our government yields to them direct and permanent benefit."[15] Martin placed less emphasis than Hadfield on the immediate threat of settlers being pushed into the sea, and instead emphasized the future threat of an ungovernable Māori population.

Conversely, Selwyn located his invocation of imperial authority in terms of future land acquisition. He echoed parts of Hadfield's concern about settler lives and Martin's concern about just governance, writing that "the lives and property of our fellow-settlers, scattered as they now are over at least 15,000 square miles of broken country, can only be preserved by the greatest forbearance, and the strictest justice in our dealings with the Native people."[16] But his primary focus was on the relative ease of taking land by force versus obtaining land through fair purchase. On the one hand, he argued that "no menaces of military interference are likely to have any effect upon men who, from their childhood, have been accustomed to regard it as a point of honour to shed their last drop of blood for the inheritance of their tribe."[17] On the other hand, he pointed out that "these very men, and others of their race, have already sold 30,000 acres in this settlement for tenpence an acre, a million of acres at Aburiri for a penny three farthings, the whole of the first Auckland Territory for about fourpence, and the whole of the middle Island south of Kaikoura for a mite per acre."[18] His point in making this comparison was to suggest that war with the Māori would only jeopardize their willingness to part with land in the future, whereas recognizing Māori land title and taking the time to settle all overlapping land claims, although it might be "a troublesome process,"[19] was "the only way in which the further acquisition of land can be brought about."[20]

Hadfield's, Martin's, and Selwyn's efforts to invoke imperial authority thus demonstrate an alternative interpretation of the impact of the First Taranaki War upon British sovereignty. Rather than seeking to protect Indigenous rights by restraining settler violence, they were instead seeking to protect settler lives and ensure the future of colonization in New Zealand by restraining imperial violence. Despite their attempts to disprove the contention that Wiremu Kingi's resistance constituted a challenge to British sovereignty, they nevertheless situated their demands to stop the war and recognize Kingi's land rights as necessary for the preservation of the British presence in New Zealand. As such, they effectively articulated a sovereignty-based argument, only one in which British sovereignty depended upon Māori consent rather than subjection. Their perspectives were not shared by the New Zealand press and government, who insisted upon an interpretation of British sovereignty that Hadfield, Martin, and Selwyn believed was jeopardizing their own lives and futures, and so they attempted to inject their dissenting viewpoints into political discussions in Britain to ensure that imperial policy was based upon, in their contention, a proper interpretation of sovereignty in New Zealand.

The pamphlet war

Hadfield, Martin, and Selwyn were not the only New Zealand settlers to publish pamphlets about the First Taranaki War in Britain. Their publications represent only one side of a "pamphlet war" between critics and supporters of Governor Browne and his invasion of Taranaki. Martin's pamphlet was countered by James Busby, a former British Resident turned newspaper editor and representative in the Auckland Provincial Council, who had played an important part in drafting the Treaty of Waitangi. Following the publication of Martin's *The Taranaki Question*, Busby responded with a pamphlet of his own entitled *Remarks upon a Pamphlet Entitled "The Taranaki Question,"* which set out to undermine Martin's criticisms of Governor Browne. Busby dismissed Martin's claim that Browne had violated Māori property rights, by asserting that "Sir W. Martin ascribes to the natives rights which they never possessed, and claims for them privileges to which they have not a shadow of a title."[21] Pointing to the Crown's right of pre-emption established through the Treaty of Waitangi as evidence that the Māori had relinquished the right to sell their lands to individuals and thereby relinquished their full title to the land, Busby argued that "the ascription to the natives of a right to have the title to their lands ... is as unreasonable and unfounded as would be the right of a lease holder to insist upon his title being dealt with as if it were a freehold."[22] Martin responded with a further pamphlet, *Remarks on "Notes Published for the New Zealand Government,"* agreeing that the Māori might have no *codified* land rights, but that they certainly had *customary* land rights which had "existed from time immemorial."[23]

Hadfield, too, found his pamphlet opposed by someone with a connection to the New Zealand government. Governor Browne's brother, Harold Browne, was a professor of divinity at Cambridge, and although he did not live in New Zealand, he came to his brother's defence in a pamphlet entitled *The Case of the War in New Zealand from Authentic Documents*. Harold Browne explained that the purpose was to defend his brother's "judgement, integrity, and humanity" against spurious attacks from "one, whom of all men living I have honoured most for his unparalleled missionary labours, I mean Archdeacon Hadfield."[24] Rather than following Busby's strategy of denying Māori property rights entirely, Harold Browne argued that their property rights were more complicated than Hadfield assumed them to be, and that those who knew better realised that Te Teira, rather than Kingi, held the property rights to Pekapeka. He challenged "the extreme simplicity of the case as stated by Archdeacon Hadfield" that the Pekapeka block was held in common by many landowners with overlapping titles and could not be sold without the consent of all claimants.[25] On the contrary, Harold Browne argued that some parcels of Māori land were held under such a communal tenure, but that "the natives have no fixed rules, the custom varies in different districts," and that in the Ngāti Awa iwi "a family of three or four people have been regarded as empowered to dispose of its [the iwi's] common property."[26] Pekapeka, according to Harold Browne, was owned by Te Teira and his family and did not require Wiremu Kingi's consent to be sold, thereby vindicating his brother's decision to purchase the land against Wiremu Kingi's objections.

This pamphlet war is revealing of the centrality of imperial citizenship to New Zealanders in the 1860s, who lived in a state of garrisoned sovereignty in which their safety and security were dictated by policy makers thousands of kilometres away. Each pamphleteer used their pamphlets to advocate pro- and anti-war policies in Britain, effectively participating in a political arena that had been deliberately closed to them when Britain withheld control over defence and Māori affairs from New Zealand's responsible government in 1853. At the same time, however, the pamphleteers' decision to use pamphlets as their method of performing imperial citizenship is also revealing of the difficulty of participating in imperial policy making from the distant colonies, for these pamphlets were not their first attempts made to invoke imperial authority.

Pamphleteering to resist governmental censorship

Prior to publishing their pamphlets, Hadfield, Martin, and Selwyn had each tried to petition the Colonial Office directly, and each found their petitions undermined by Governor Browne and the New Zealand government. Selwyn was the first to do so. On 28 April 1860, he wrote an angry letter to the colonial secretary protesting that a military engagement had been launched before sufficient efforts had been taken to settle matters peacefully, and he demanded that a civil tribunal be established to investigate the conflict before force continue to be used.[27] Browne forwarded the letter to the Colonial Office, but he did so alongside an extensive rebuttal from ministers of the New Zealand government. Totalling forty-five pages, the ministers's response challenged every line of Selwyn's three-page letter, but they particularly sought to undermine Selwyn's capacity to judge political matters objectively. Comparing him to "the abolitionists of North America" whom "few statesmen will hold that they take a sober and just view of the great question of humanity," the ministers argued that Selwyn's reputation as a "philanthropist" made him "liable, even beyond other men, to the disturbing influences of prejudice and passion."[28] The same thing happened to Hadfield, who had cowritten a letter to the Colonial Office on 1 June 1860 with the bishop of Wellington criticizing Browne for starting a war without notifying the settlers beforehand and endangering the future of the colony by angering one of the few Māori chiefs who did not support the Māori King Movement.[29] Once again, Browne forwarded the letter to the Colonial Office along with a rebuttal from ministers of the New Zealand government. The Colonial Office chose to believe the government ministers, and replied to Browne that "so far as his [the Secretary of State] information extends, he thinks that you [Browne] have shewn that the Bishop and Archdeacon have been inaccurately informed on some points, and that they have taken an incomplete view of others, and he finds no reason to withdraw the confidence of Her Majesty's Government in your administration."[30]

Martin's experience was not quite so antagonistic as that of Selwyn and Hadfield. On 7 May 1860, Martin codrafted a list of recommendations for the future administration of Māori affairs along with Selwyn and a politician named William Swainson. Martin *et al.* made various recommendations, ranging from dividing communally owned lands into separate individually owned plots to setting aside more money to pay Māori magistrates. But their tenth recommendation was specifically directed at the Taranaki

War: "that before the land be reserved or granted as before mentioned, the ownership be made the subject of careful investigation, by a competent tribunal, to be constituted for that purpose by the Governor in Council."[31] Such a recommendation implied that Browne had not properly investigated Wiremu Kingi's title claim and called for an independent investigation. No rebuttal was offered by Browne or the New Zealand government. Indeed, Browne sent the memorandum to the Secretary of State with the comment that "it is with extreme satisfaction that I call Your Grace's attention to the great similarity of the recommendations contained in these valuable memoranda and those submitted in my despatch No. 80 of 29th of September 1859."[32] Yet no independent tribunal was ever arranged, and this became a central critique within Martin's pamphlet, which reprimanded that "it is not lawful for the Executive Government to use force in a purely civil question, without the authority of a competent judicial tribunal. In this case no such authority has been obtained: no such tribunal has been resorted to."[33]

That Hadfield's, Martin's, and Selwyn's pamphleteering was, in each case, preceded by unsuccessful attempts to participate in imperial policy making via direct correspondance with the Colonial Office, and that in two of the three cases these attempts were rebuked with hostility by the New Zealand government, reveals that what historians have traditionally referred to as a pamphlet war was actually an extension of a pre-existing information war within government communication networks. Their pamphlets can be understood as extensions of their previous petitions to the Colonial Office, designed to undercut the ability of Governor Browne and ministers of the New Zealand government to counter their arguments. This use of pamphlets as a means of challenging government discourses connects to scholarship on the role of letters to newspaper editors as a method of political participation in nineteenth-century Britain. Allison Cavanagh argues that newspapers provided "empowered spaces" for ordinary people that "allowed them to access what they saw as a broader and more legitimate sphere of power than those encountered in daily life."[34] Cavanagh finds that everyday citizens wrote letters to the editor to address a wide array of personal grievances, and she argues that letter writers treated newspapers as empowered spaces because they perceived editors as "one who was empowered against vested interest, potentially one of 'us' rather than one of 'them.'"[35] This is precisely what Hadfield, Martin, and Selwyn did through their pamphlets. Encountering resistance within official government communication networks, they turned to public forms of communication to get their opinions in front of the British MPs who had the power to stop the war.

What is more, Hadfield had even attempted to use letters to the editor of British newspapers to consolidate his position in the information war against Harold Browne. On 15 November 1860, a month before publishing his pamphlet in rebuke of Hadfield, Harold Browne had written a letter to the editor of *The Times* complaining that Hadfield had "written a pamphlet ... impugning the justice of the present war."[36] While simultaneously defending his brother's actions, Harold pointed the finger of blame at Hadfield himself. He claimed that Hadfield had played a role in starting the war by withholding "important communications tending to peace."[37] This referred to a rumour in the New Zealand press that Hadfield had received a letter from Wiremu Kingi that would have prevented the outbreak of war, and that Hadfield had not passed it on to the government. Hadfield responded with his own letter to the editor of *The Times* written on 5 February 1861, two months prior to his second pamphlet published in April, calling Browne's accusation "an erroneous statement deliberately circulated on a mere superficial examination of information."[38] Browne retaliated with yet another letter in *The Times* on 19 April 1861, complaining that Hadfield "impugns the fidelity of my statements," but rather than challenging Hadfield directly, he simply referred readers to his pamphlet that had already been published.[39] Hadfield then attempted to issue his own rebuttal, but the editor of *The Times* refused to print it, forcing Hadfield to publish his rebuttal as his third pamphlet, *A Sequel to "One of England's Little Wars,"* which opens with a criticism of the editor of *The Times* for "want of fairness in this matter, when it is remembered that his columns are so frequently open to articles and letters defending the policy of the war."[40]

The intertwined nature of Hadfield's and Harold Browne's pamphlets and letters to the editor, in addition to the entanglement of Hadfield's, Martin's, and Selwyn's pamphlets and petitions to the Colonial Office, reveals the extended terrain of the information battle waged over the First Taranaki War. Unwilling to sit idly by when they believed the future of their colony was in jeopardy, Hadfield, Martin, and Selwyn moved between petitions, newspapers, and pamphlets in quick succession, seeking a medium through which they could influence imperial policy making without opposition from interested parties, such as New Zealand officials desirous of continuing their land war and Governor Browne's brother desirous of defending his family's honour. Their constant efforts demonstrate not only the significance they attached to their identity as imperial citizens, through which they invoked imperial authority in as many ways as they could think of to bring an end to the war, but also the difficulty of participating in imperial policy making. The ability to publish pamphlets and letters in the press may have offered Hadfield, Martin, and Selwyn the opportunity to circumvent opposition within government communication networks, but they offered such an opportunity to opponents as well. Invoking imperial authority therefore often came down to whose version of events the imperial government chose to believe, and it was always more likely that the imperial government would believe the institutionalized opinions of its own employees and powerful officials than a small group of outspoken activists.

Conclusion

As this chapter has shown, the information war over representations of the First Taranaki War was about much more than Māori land rights and British sovereignty. Motivating Octavius Hadfield's, William Martin's, and George Selwyn's criticisms of the injustice of the war was a fear that settler lives and property, and the very future of the colony, were jeopardized by provoking a war with the Māori. Such a fear was not limited to these three pamphleteers. As Mark Hickford and Kenton Storey recount, tensions were high across the whole North Island throughout the war: rents in New Plymouth soared as settlers living in the countryside flooded into the safety of the town, while people in Auckland constantly fretted that the war would spread there.[41]

What was unique about Hadfield, Martin, and Selwyn was their interpretation of the Empire's role in securing their safety. Storey shows that newspaper editors in New Zealand coped with the anxiety of war by trying to justify British military support, representing the war as a battle over British sovereignty.[42] By so doing, these editors conveyed an understanding that settler colonialism depended upon British imperial strength, reflecting Charlotte Macdonald's argument that New Zealand was a "garrisoned" colony rather than a settler colony. Hadfield, Martin, and Selwyn did the opposite: they coped with the anxiety of war by trying to end British military support, arguing that warfare was destroying Māori consent to be governed. As such, they conveyed an understanding that settler colonialism depended upon British imperial humanitarianism and justice. Such a viewpoint echoes scholarship on humanitarian governance, particularly Amanda Nettelbeck's argument that ideas of humanitarianism and justice were used by imperial officials to transform Indigenous peoples into governable subjects – the major difference being that Hadfield, Martin, and Selwyn were not imperial officials, or officials of any kind.[43] Rather than using humanitarianism for the purpose of increasing imperial power, they saw it as their duty as imperial citizens to remind imperial officials of their humanitarian duties in order to preserve settler society. In sum, they desired not a garrisoned colony, but a humanitarian one, empowered by just imperial governance to survive without resistance from Indigenous forces.

This chapter also explored the varied terrain of invoking imperial authority against the First Taranaki War, ranging through petitions to the Colonial Office, letters to British newspapers, and self-published pamphlets.

Hadfield's, Martin's, and Selwyn's ability to criticize government and participate in imperial policy making from New Zealand via letters to the editor and pamphleteering lends support to Allison Cavanagh's argument that the fourth estate (which is typically conceptualized as newspapers but can also be extended to pamphlet culture) can be understood as a "tool of citizenship" that enabled people who were not in positions of power to exert political influence.[44] Not only did the pamphleteers exert political influence, but they did so from thousands of kilometres away, showing that the imperial scale of the British media system as charted by Simon Potter enabled performances of imperial citizenship at the same time that it enabled distant imperial subjects to stay up to date on events around the world.[45]

Yet the very openness of this imperial fourth estate, which empowered Hadfield, Martin, and Selwyn to inject their opinions into the British public sphere via letters to the editor and pamphlets, also enabled their opponents to do the same. Such was by design: according to Jürgen Habermas, it was the job of the public sphere to encourage public debate and elevate the rational-critical debate of private people.[46] For Hadfield, Martin, and Selwyn, however, the openness of the fourth estate merely enabled government officials to extend their efforts to undermine and censor dissenting voices. In this sense, the imperial fourth estate worked to support the imperial government rather than hold it accountable. Instead of sidestepping the New Zealand government, writing letters to the editor and pamphlets merely dragged the pre-existing conflicts between Hadfield, Martin, Selwyn, and the New Zealand government into public view. In practice, therefore, invoking Empire through the fourth estate offered little improvement on doing so through official channels.

Notes

1 Waitangi Tribunal, *The Taranaki Report: Kaupapa Tuatahi* (Wellington, NZ: Legislation Direct, 1996), 80.
2 *New Zealand Gazette*, 25 January 1861, no. 4, p. 17.
3 Charlotte Macdonald, "Woolwich to Wellington: From Settler Colony to Garrisoned Sovereignty," *New Zealand Journal of History* 53, no. 1 (2019): 50–76, https://muse.jhu.edu/pub/426/article/883327 (accessed 11 March 2025).
4 Claudia Orange, *The Treaty of Waitangi* (Wellington: Allen & Unwin, 1987), 139–140.
5 Macdonald, "Woolwich to Wellington," 57.
6 James Belich, *The New Zealand Wars and the Victorian Interpretation of Racial Conflict* (Auckland: Auckland University Press, 1986), 77–79.
7 Kenton Storey, *Settler Anxiety at the Outposts of Empire: Colonial Relations, Humanitarian Discourses, and the Imperial Press* (Vancouver: University of British Columbia Press, 2016), 191.

8 Octavius Hadfield, *A Sequel to "One of England's Little Wars": Being an Account of the Real Origin of the War in New Zealand, Its Present Stage, and the Future Prospects of the Colony* (London: Williams and Norgate, 1861), 6–7.
9 William Martin, *The Taranaki Question* (Auckland: The Melanesian Press, 1860), 116.
10 George Selwyn, "Pastoral Letter of the Bishop of New Zealand, to the Members of the Church of England in the Settlement of New Plymouth," in New Zealand, *Extracts of Letters from New Zealand on the War Question, with an Article from the New Zealand Spectator of November 3rd 1860, and a Copy of the Native Offenders' Bill* (London: F. J. Wilson, 1861), 89–90.
11 Belich, *The New Zealand Wars*, 79–80; Karen Morin and Lawrence Berg, "Gendering Resistance: British Colonial Narratives of Wartime New Zealand," *Journal of Historical Geography* 27, no. 2 (2001): 196–222 (207), DOI: 10.1006/jhge.2000.0299; Kenton Storey, "Colonial Humanitarian? Thomas Gore Browne and the Taranaki War, 1860–61," *Journal of British Studies* 53, no. 1 (2014): 111–135 (127), DOI: 10.1017/jbr.2013.210.
12 Octavius Hadfield to Charles Hadfield, 8 January 1861, Wellington City Libraries, Octavius Hadfield Papers, 50008-26-1.
13 Hadfield, *A Sequel*, 11–12.
14 Martin, *The Taranaki Question*, 130.
15 *Ibid.*, 129.
16 Selwyn, "Pastoral letter," 98.
17 *Ibid.*, 92.
18 *Ibid.*
19 *Ibid.*, 87.
20 *Ibid.*, 92.
21 James Busby, *Remarks upon a Pamphlet Entitled "The Taranaki Question, by Sir William Martin, D.C.L., Late Chief Justice of New Zealand"* (Auckland: Philip Kunst, 1860), 6–7.
22 Busby, *Remarks*, 10.
23 William Martin, *Remarks on "Notes Published for the New Zealand Government" on Sir William Martin's Pamphlet Entitled The Taranaki Question* (London: W. H. Dalton, 1861), 6.
24 Harold Browne, *The Case of the War in New Zealand from Authentic Documents* (Cambridge: Deighton, Bell, 1860), 5–6.
25 *Ibid.*, *The Case of the War in New Zealand*, 5–6.
26 *Ibid.*, 37.
27 George Selwyn to Colonial Secretary, 28 April 1860, The National Archives, London (TNA), CO 209/154.
28 Memorandum by Ministers, 25 May 1860, TNA, CO 209/154.
29 Charles Abraham and Octavius Hadfield to the Colonial Office, 1 June 1860, TNA, CO 209/154.
30 Colonial Office to Thomas Gore Browne, 26 September 1860, TNA CO 209/154.
31 William Martin, George Selwyn, and William Swainson to Thomas Gore Browne, 7 May 1860, TNA, CO 209/154.

32 Thomas Gore Browne to the Colonial Office, 2 January 1861, TNA, CO 209/160.
33 Martin, *The Taranaki Question*, 67.
34 Allison Cavanagh, "Letters to the Editor as a Tool of Citizenship," in Allison Cavanagh and John Steel (eds), *Letters to the Editor: Comparative and Historical Perspectives* (Cham: Palgrave Macmillan, 2019), 95.
35 *Ibid.*, 94–95.
36 "The New Zealand War," *The Times*, 17 November 1860.
37 *Ibid.*
38 "New Zealand," *The Times*, 15 April 1861.
39 "War in New Zealand," *The Times*, 19 April 1861.
40 Octavius Hadfield, *A Sequel*, 2.
41 Mark Hickford, *Lords of the Land: Indigenous Property Rights and the Jurisprudence of Empire* (Oxford: Oxford University Press, 2011), 384; Storey, *Settler Anxiety*, 151.
42 Storey, *Settler Anxiety*, 151–153, 191–194.
43 Amanda Nettelbeck, *Indigenous Rights and Colonial Subjecthood: Protection and Reform in the Nineteenth-Century British Empire* (Cambridge: Cambridge University Press, 2019); see also Alan Lester and Fae Dussart, *Colonization and the Origins of Humanitarian Governance: Protecting Aborigines across the Nineteenth-Century British Empire* (Cambridge: Cambridge University Press, 2014).
44 Cavanagh, "Letters to the Editor as a Tool of Citizenship," 89–108.
45 Simon Potter, *News and the British World: The Emergence of an Imperial Press System, 1876–1922* (Oxford: Clarendon Press, 2003).
46 Jürgen Habermas, *The Structural Transformation of the Public Sphere: An Inquiry into a Category of Bourgeois Society* (Cambridge, MA: MIT Press, 1989).

5

Protestant freedom versus Catholic tyranny: Quebec, 1875–1877

The coexistence of significant anglophone and francophone populations in Quebec complicated democratic governance in the decades following responsible government in Canada, and indeed continues to spark tension into the present. Prior to Confederation in 1867, John Lambton, 1st earl of Durham, famously described Lower Canada (Quebec) as "two nations warring in the bosom of a single state,"[1] a state made worse by the 1840 Act of Union, which sandwiched English Upper Canada and French Lower Canada into the single Province of Canada. This had made the anglophone minority in Quebec significantly more powerful than the francophone majority by uniting them with the anglophone majority of Ontario. With Confederation in 1867, however, the province of Quebec had been given its own provincial government separate from that of anglophones in Ontario, so that the English in Quebec instantly became a minority voting block at both federal and provincial levels, and became significantly less powerful compared to the province's French majority.[2] In this context, the overarching sovereignty of the British Empire – within which Canada continued to remain despite its responsible government – took on a new meaning to anglophone Québécois. Experiencing for the first time what it was like to live as a minority, Anglo-Québécois looked to imperial authority to protect them from persecution. As will be seen, this persecution was most often expressed in terms of conservatism dominating liberalism, and particularly conservative Catholicism tyrannizing liberal Protestantism.

Quebec residents invoked imperial protection for the first time only two years after Confederation, and in that instance imperial authority proved singularly responsive and effective. In 1869, a Franco-Québécois man named Joseph Guibord had died under excommunication, and consequently was denied ecclesiastical burial by the bishop of Montreal. His widow sued the bishop for denying her husband burial rights, and after following the suit for five years through the Superior Court, the Court of Review, and the Court of Queen's Bench, the case was finally brought before the imperial authority of the Judicial Committee of the Privy Council. On 21 November

1874, the Privy Council ruled in favour of Guibord's widow, demonstrating that imperial authority could be invoked to protect Québécois rights against persecution by the Catholic hierarchy. Yet the imperial victory was only partial. A first burial attempt was made on 2 September 1875, but was stopped by an angry mob. A second attempt on 16 November 1875 succeeded thanks to an armed military escort, but the bishop immediately deconsecrated the plot of ground where Guibord was buried, rendering the entire process moot and calling the viability of imperial authority for protecting settler rights into question.

Less than a month after Guibord was buried on deconsecrated land, a second opportunity arose to test once and for all if the British Empire could protect Québécois rights. On 8 December 1875, the French Catholic Seminary of St Sulpice destroyed a Protestant church built by the Mohawk First Nation just outside Montreal. Although it did not directly affect them, Anglo-Protestants throughout the province interpreted the destruction of the church as an attack on Protestantism in general, and they immediately organized a Protestant Defence Alliance (PDA) to petition to the imperial government in defence of British liberties. This chapter examines the PDA's campaign through the lens of imperial citizenship, attending to the mobilization of Britishness as political leverage against the imperial government, the invocation of both direct and indirect forms of imperial authority via petitions and public opinion, and condemnation by opponents of the PDA for betraying the ideals of a national Canadian citizenship. I argue that imperial citizenship provided British settlers who found themselves in minority positions with a means of resisting perceived encroachments of their civil rights when local forms of citizenship failed. At the same time, however, I also argue that the realization of imperial citizenship rights was dependent on their recognition by British society, and that the particularity of the PDA's issues rendered their claims unrecognizable outside their local environment. The case thus demonstrates that the vagueness of the imperial citizenship concept, which at one level empowered it to be fitted to a variety of situations, could also detract from its ability to be recognized.

The Protestant Defence Alliance

On 22 December 1875, a group of around seventy Montreal Protestants met in a YMCA assembly hall to draft the constitution of the newly established PDA of Canada. These men (for they were all men) represented Montreal's Anglo-Protestant elite. Many were ordained Protestant clergy, and the rest including industrialists, academics, and financiers. Indeed, the meeting took place at the YMCA because the founder of Montreal's YMCA,

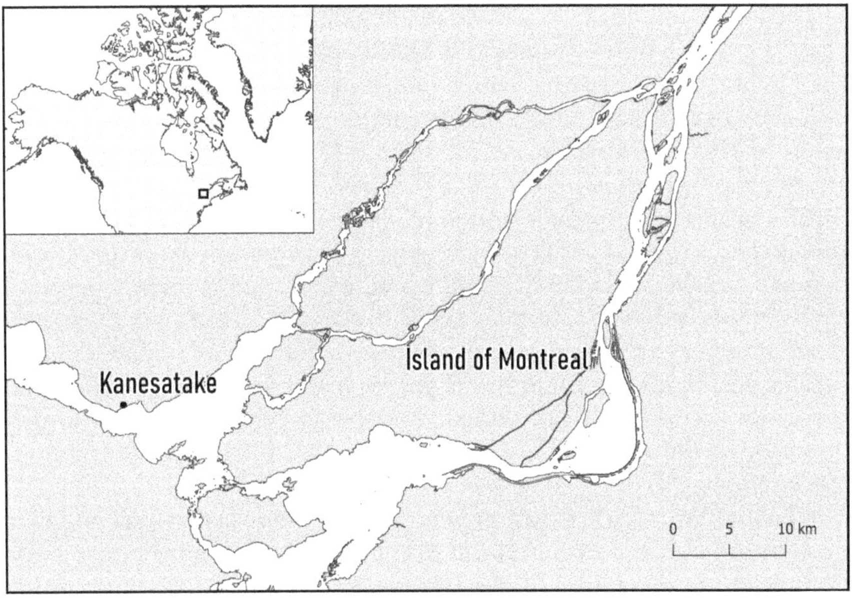

Map 5.1 Montreal region

Timothy James Claxton, was a major organizer of the Alliance and went on to become one of its vice-presidents. The purpose of the Alliance, as set out in the constitution, was "the resistance of all efforts on the part of the Roman Catholic hierarchy to violate the principles of civil and religious rights and liberties, and the guidance and protection of Protestants and others who may be exposed to the persecution of the Romish priesthood for conscience' sake."[3] The founders of the Alliance were careful to explain that they were anti-hierarchy, not anti-Catholic. They asserted that Catholic French-Canadians were enslaved by their hierarchy, and that the Alliance should therefore "help the French-Canadians to free themselves."[4] In fact, the Alliance deliberately chose not to call themselves the British Defence Alliance because they wanted to encourage people of non-British origin to join their ranks, and they would later change their name to the Civil Rights Defence Alliance in 1877 to encourage further Catholic participation. Nevertheless, Britishness remained a fundamental element of the society, and the founders explained that they fought "not only for Protestant liberty, but for the liberty of all British subjects."[5] The Government of Quebec, they claimed, was falling under the control of Ultramontane principles that were "in direct antagonism to the principles of British liberty," and that "as British subjects, we must contend for those liberties for which our forefathers shed their blood."[6]

The PDA's anti-Catholic sentiment and its juxtaposition of Catholic tyranny and British liberty locates the Alliance within the extensive history of anti-Catholicism across the British Empire. Anti-Catholicism experienced a resurgence in Britain following the union of the British and Irish parliaments in 1800, Catholic emancipation in 1829, and the restoration of the English Catholic hierarchy in 1850. This last was interpreted by many in Britain as an act of "papal aggression" and an attack on the Queen's sovereignty, and sparked virulent "anti-popery" movements built upon fears that the Catholic hierarchy was attempting to interfere in British politics.[7] Anti-Catholicism then spread to all of the settler colonies via mass emigration throughout the nineteenth century. In the Australasian and South African colonies, it manifested as a paranoia about papal aggression, and anti-Catholic rhetoric was common amongst Protestant settlers who perceived small and relatively insignificant Catholic communities as conspirators attempting to bring about a new Catholic empire.[8]

However, Anti-Catholicism took a different shape in Canada, and particularly in Quebec because of its high French Catholic population. Quebec Catholicism closely adhered to the Ultramontane ideology articulated by the First Vatican Council in 1870 and in Pope Pius IX's 1864 *Syllabus of Errors*, which codified papal infallibility and denounced rationalism and liberalism.[9] The Catholic bishop of Montreal, Ignace Bourget, was very closely involved in provincial governance and exerted his influence to maintain the primacy of French Catholic culture in the face of an increasingly Anglicized Canada. In response, English Québécois frequently interpreted the Catholic hierarchy as tyrannical and freedom-hating in opposition to narratives of modern, industrial, progressive, and Protestant Britishness.[10] The grievances most commonly cited by Protestants against the Quebec hierarchy were nepotism, the overrepresentation of Catholic clergy in public offices, the funnelling of public money into Catholic schools and churches, and executive interference in legal proceedings against Catholic priests.[11] The formation of the PDA in 1875 was a direct manifestation of these grievances, reflecting Protestant feelings of marginalization by the Quebec government, which was itself only a reaction to marginalization by English dominance across Canada as a whole. However, these feelings of Protestant marginalization were nothing new in 1875, and were merely the context for the creation of the PDA. The spark that pushed Quebec Protestants to organize was the destruction of a Protestant Mohawk church at Kanesatake by the Seminary of St Sulpice in December 1875, which served as evidence that the Catholic Church was willing and able to attack Protestants and their property.

The Mohawk had lived at Kanesatake village west of Montreal since 1721, when the French government had granted land to missionaries of the Roman Catholic Seminary of St Sulpice in return for removing the Mohawk from their previous village in central Montreal.[12] The land at Kanesatake was disputed from the very beginning: the Mohawk had been told that they were to possess a deed to the new village in return for abandoning Montreal, but the deed was instead registered to the seminary. This discrepancy went unnoticed until the 1780s, when settlers in the area began enclosing Mohawk land. The Mohawk tried to assert their ownership of the land and discovered that it legally did not belong to them. They sent many petitions to colonial and imperial authorities in the late eighteenth and early nineteenth centuries to regain ownership of the land to no avail, but relations with the seminary remained cordial.[13] This changed in the mid-nineteenth century with the decline of the fur trade and the rise of the timber industry: whereas hunting rights were guaranteed without possession of land, logging rights were contingent upon possession. When the Mohawk began logging on what they believed to be their own land in the 1830s, the seminary charged any Mohawk found cutting down trees with trespass, sparking significant resentment. In 1851, Methodist missionaries began visiting Kanesatake, and many Mohawk converted out of dissatisfaction with the seminary. The bishop of Montreal responded in 1852 by excommunicating four Methodist Mohawk chiefs, and from that point onwards Kanesatake was riven by conflict between Catholics and Mohawk converts. This conflict escalated via arrests and lawsuits until 8 December 1875, when the seminary tore down the Mohawk's Methodist church.[14]

The destruction of the Mohawk church became a rallying point for Quebec Protestants to organize the PDA, and was the cornerstone of the PDA's activities throughout its short existence. At the PDA's annual meeting on 13 March 1877, the "Case of the Oka Indians" took up more than three-quarters of the proceedings, and was the only substantial topic of discussion besides a brief note that someone in Lachine had been "outraged" at a Catholic *Fête-Dieu* (Feast of Corpus Christi) celebration and a short deliberation over a change of name. The Alliance used "the outrages inflicted by the Seminary of St Sulpice on the defenceless Indians of Oka" as an excuse for criticizing Catholic maladministration more generally.[15] Publishing 5,000 copies of a pamphlet on *The Indians of the Lake of Two Mountains*, the PDA asserted that the destruction of the church was only the most recent example of structural "aggressions of the new creed of Vaticanism … which threaten, if not soon arrested, to invade the civil rights of our people to such an extent that the most serious consequences to the peace and prosperity of Canada may be dreaded."[16]

The PDA organized a lawsuit against the seminary, but were frustrated that "dishonourable tricks and technical objections have caused much delay."[17] Failing to vindicate the Mohawk in local courts, the PDA turned to the federal government. They sent a deputation to Ottawa on 31 March

1876, but were merely told that the seminary were in full possession of the reserve at Kanasetake, and that their ownership "did not impose any duty on the Seminary towards the Indians."[18] With no help coming from the federal government, the PDA next looked to Britain, invoking imperial authority with the assertion that "the Queen has power to call these Stewards to account for their stewardship; and if unfaithful, she can deprive them, and give it to others."[19]

"Strong expulsions" of British opinion

To enact their vision of imperial citizenship against the Seminary of St Sulpice's oppression of Protestant Mohawk civil liberties, the PDA sent, or caused to be sent, three separate petitions to the British government. The first was a personal appeal from James Mathewson, committee member of the PDA and an Irish immigrant who had opened a grocery importation business in Montreal in 1834. Mathewson addressed his petition directly to Queen Victoria, informing her that the Seminary of St Sulpice held the Mohawk of Kanesatake under an "absolute and despotic ... bondage not unlike that of Egypt of old."[20] He contended that the seminary was purposefully persecuting the Mohawk in the hopes that the Mohawk would move elsewhere, leaving all the land to the seminary. In response, Mathewson requested Queen Victoria to "so appeal to their harsh oppressors as that a way may be opened for them remaining where they are," with the particular hope that land titles could be provided for each Mohawk family.[21] The Colonial Office responded by sending Mathewson a report from the Privy Council of Canada as well as a memorandum from the Canadian Minister of the Interior explaining that the Mohawk's claim to rights within the seminary's lands was a matter of law rather than of politics, and that a court case was currently underway to determine the "legality or otherwise of these supposed rights of the Indians."[22] In other words, the Colonial Office determined that it was a matter for the Canadian court system and did not involve the imperial government.

The PDA was not deterred, and their second and third petitions took a contrary perspective. The second was sent by the Congregational Union of Ontario and Quebec on 9 June 1876, while the third was sent by the Aborigines' Protection Society (APS) on 11 July 1877, but both were influenced and endorsed by the PDA. Following the court's decision that the Mohawk had no rights within the seminary's lands, the petitioners reiterated Mathewson's claim that the seminary was purposefully oppressing the Mohawk "with the intention of obliging them to leave ... that it may remain the exclusive property of the Seminary."[23] More than that, the petitioners challenged the legitimacy of the court's ruling against the Mohawk. They alleged that "owing to the wealth and influence of the Seminary, to the poverty and ignorance of the Indians, and to the technical points of law raised in the Courts, the sufferers have been unable to obtain any adequate redress from Your Majesty's Courts of Law in the Province of Quebec."[24] The PDA elaborated on this claim at a public meeting, explaining that "it is well known to us and should have been to any who proffered information to Lord Carnarvon, that the case has never been decided or even touched on its real merits."[25] Consequently, the petitioners asked Queen Victoria to appoint a commission to investigate the seminary's titles and, if found that the seminary had acted unjustly, to transfer administration of the Mohawk to another body. The petition from the APS made it clear that such was not the APS's official stance, but was that of "the Society's correspondents in Canada" from within the PDA.[26] The Colonial Office responded curtly to both petitions, stating that "as therefore the right of the Seminary has been affirmed by the Courts of Law ... Lord Carnarvon sees no ground for supposing that everything which could be urged on behalf of the Indians has not been put forward and duly considered," concluding that "Her Majesty's Government cannot interfere in any more active manner in the matter."[27]

The Colonial Office's rejection of these petitions would seem to indicate that the PDA's invocation of imperial authority failed. The PDA, however, had a back-up plan. In early 1876, the committee asked one of its members, a lecturer at McGill College named Philip Carpenter, to reach out to the editors of British newspapers to bring their case before the British public. Carpenter wrote to the APS that the PDA fully expected the imperial government to reject any petition.[28] The purpose of the petitions, he explained, was to generate outrage in Britian that could pressure the Canadian government to challenge the seminary's land claims. He asserted that "they <u>do</u> care here, from Govt downwards, for strong expulsions of opinion from Brit. papers; they care nothing for what is said <u>here</u>. That is why I address you."[29] He hoped that "a strong expression of opinion <u>for</u> the Indians through the English press" would remind Canadian politicians of British liberties and responsibilities.[30] "If British Connection means anything, let our Govt understand that they are <u>bound to maintain</u> civil and religious liberty in general, and that in particular they are bound to take the part of the Indians."[31] The PDA therefore approached invoking imperial authority through two separate avenues: by directly petitioning for imperial intervention, and by indirectly channelling British public opinion into political leverage in Canada, hoping to "shame our own men" with British disappointment.[32]

Sadly, the PDA discovered that even leveraging the indirect power of imperial public opinion was beyond their reach, primarily because the British public was uninterested in their plight. To be sure, the Alliance did succeed in making the British papers three times. A letter to the editor of the *Daily News* from Philip Carpenter was published on 4 January 1876, and the editor then wrote an editorial on the subject the following day.[33] A month later, a pamphlet sent to the *Belfast News-Letter* was published on 8 February 1876.[34] But these letters were drowned out by British obsession with the many riots that plagued Montreal at the time. In the first week of January, just when the *Daily News* published Carpenter's letter, news of bread riots in Montreal generated more than nine different articles in papers including *The Times*; the *Manchester Courier*; and, indeed, the *Belfast News-Letter*. This followed a trend that had continued throughout 1875, when British newspapers actively discussed Montreal riots against mandatory smallpox vaccination in August and riots between Catholics and Protestants in September.

This extended cacophony of articles on rioting compared to the short trickle of articles on the PDA reflected the relative relevance of each story to the British public. The conflict between the Seminary of St Sulpice and the Mohawk impacted practically no one in Britain, whereas riots in Montreal had the potential to endanger loved ones and interrupt businesses. Carpenter's hope that a strong expression of opinion from the British press would shame Canadian politicians into action very well may have been correct, but the British press simply was not interested enough in the issue to make such an expression of opinion. Failing to invoke imperial authority either directly or indirectly, the PDA was forced to rely on local authorities, which largely failed to achieve a satisfactory settlement to the conflict. The Seminary of St Sulpice continued to assert its property rights over Kanesatake and reject any obligations towards the Mohawk, despite multiple armed conflicts and legal disputes culminating in a Privy Council decision in 1912 that the seminary possessed the duties of a charitable trust.[35] The dispute between the seminary and the Mohawk was not resolved until 1945, when the Canadian government purchased the land from the seminary, but the land was never given to the Mohawk and title remains disputed to this day.[36]

Canadian backlash against imperial citizenship

Not only did the Alliance's efforts to invoke imperial authority fail, they also provoked significant backlash from Canadians invested in responsible government. The months after the Alliance was formed witnessed a heated debate in Ontario and Quebec newspapers. On 8 February 1876, the *Toronto Globe* proclaimed that the PDA's demand for federal and imperial intervention would be a violation of the British North America Act, which guaranteed provincial rights, specifically to avoid majorities in one part of the country strong-arming minorities in other provinces, as anglophones had strong-armed francophones in Quebec prior to Confederation.[37] Asserting that "the Province of Quebec has a perfect right to take such measures as it deems proper ... so long as there is no departure from what is laid down in the Confederation Act," the *Globe* remonstrated that the PDA and Quebec Catholics "must learn to live together in peace and harmony without at every turn invoking Federal interference and Imperial vetoes."[38] The following week, Sir Henri-Gustave Joly, Liberal member of the Legistlative Assembly and future premier of Quebec, wrote a letter in the *Morning Chronicle* denouncing the PDA for trying to challenge Catholic political dominance through federal and imperial petitions rather than through provincial elections.[39] Pointing to the fact that anglophone Protestants historically voted in favour of the Conservative Party (who were aligned with the Catholic hierarchy), Joly called on the PDA to "begin by doing their duty as *citizens* ... If they think that the Liberal Party deserves their support, let them, in the constituencies where they are in a majority, return Liberal members, and, without endangering the peace of the Province, they will obtain a Government which will secure to every Church and every religious belief equal rights and equal liberties."[40]

In response, the PDA wrote its own letter to the *Montreal Daily Witness* on 13 March 1876, arguing that their critics' focus on politics and provincial rights was missing the point.[41] The PDA, they asserted, was completely apolitical and did not care about squabbles between Liberals and Conservatives, nor about provincial rights. On the contrary, the PDA was fighting something much larger and more sinister than Canadian politics: the Catholic Church's global conspiracy against freedom. "A fierce struggle is going on, not in Canada merely, but all over the world, between a party determined to destroy all freedom of human thought and action, and those who hold to liberty, progress and equal civil rights."[42] Imagining itself involved in a global Manichean battle between Protestantism and Catholicism, the PDA looked at imperial authority not as an interference in provincial politics, but as the only power capable of connecting the Protestants of the world in a union strong enough to resist Catholic despotism. As such, the PDA sidestepped Joly's call for them to act as citizens by reformulating the definition of citizen. Rather than acting as Canadian citizens to participate in local politics, the PDA positioned themselves as imperial citizens participating in a global battle for civil liberties.

Moreover, the admonition to act as Canadian citizens through democratic participation rather than invoking imperial intervention clashed with PDA members' experiences of abandonment within Canadian politics. Since 1867, Quebec Protestants had been electing an anti-Catholic politician named Lucius Seth Huntington as MP for Shefford, just outside Montreal, but his fears of Catholic conspiracies were openly mocked. Huntington gave a speech calling for Protestants to unite against Catholic despotism in early 1876, and his fellow MPs united against him. Prime Minister Alexander Mackenzie sent letters of apology to the bishops of Quebec and Toronto. Fellow Liberal MP for Quebec Luther Holton accused Huntington of fomenting religious strife. And Conservative MP Louis François Roderigue Masson warned Protestants not to interfere in Catholic politics.[43] This backlash against a politician willing to speak against Catholic interests convinced PDA members that there was no hope in working through Canadian politics. As one of its members explained to the APS, "the whole body of Canadian politicians are dumb dogs in the matter. Both the party in, and the party who hope to be in, counsel peace with the Hierarchy."[44]

Not only was their anti-Catholicism dismissed by Canadian politicians, it was also censored within Quebec newspapers. There were three competing English-language newspapers in 1870s Montreal. The *Montreal Gazette* was the mouthpiece of the Conservative Party of Quebec, which was aligned with Ultramontane Catholicism and dominated Quebec politics throughout the mid-to-late nineteenth century.[45] The *Montreal Herald* was an organ of the Liberal Party of Quebec, which, although hostile to the powerful Ultramontane Quebec Church hierarchy and known as the "party of Protestant Dissent" for much of the nineteenth century, had begun in the 1870s to downplay sectarianism in order to promote non-denominational unity.[46] And the *Montreal Witness* was an independent paper dedicated to virulent Protestantism, temperance, and social morality issues.[47] The *Witness* was the only one of these papers that would express support for the PDA, and was also the only paper that would report on the PDA's annual meetings. Uncoincidentally, the *Witness* was actively suppressed by the powerful bishop of Montreal, who in 1875 banned the newspaper because of its anti-Catholic rhetoric.[48]

Indeed, whereas the *Witness* vigorously criticized the Seminary of St Sulpice for its destruction of the Mohawk church, the *Gazette* and *Herald* united in support of the seminary. The *Gazette* insisted that the seminary had a legal right to do so as the owner of the land and that their actions had been sanctioned by the courts.[49] The *Gazette* further denounced all who attempted "to make political capital out of the unfortunate events," and argued that it was not the seminary but the Mohawk's lawyers who were to blame – for failing to establish a legal right to the land.[50] The *Herald* concurred that "in the dispute between the Oka Indians and the Seminary, the law was with the Seminary," and that the Mohawk had no grounds for disputing the destruction of their church since "the Indians have no property in the soil of the seigniory which can be enforced in a Court of Law."[51] Thus, openly ridiculed in the House of Commons and banned from responding to public debates in a press environment that actively challenged its interests, the PDA had little faith in the promise of Canadian democracy. Feeling that their Canadian citizenship was worthless against the global reach of Catholic tyranny, the PDA put their faith in imperial citizenship instead.

Conclusion

As this chapter demonstrates, imperial authority could retain a special significance for settler minorities within self-governing colonies. Confederation granted each Canadian province its own quasi-sovereign government in order to prevent the different ethnic populations of each province from dominating other provinces. In Quebec, however, provincial autonomy enabled the large French majority to politically dominate the small English minority. The federal structure of the Canadian government could theoretically intervene in provincial maladministration, but the federal government's dependence on Quebec's support translated into an unwillingness to compromise Quebec's provincial autonomy, rendering Anglo-Québécois feeling forsaken by their new nation. Consequently, Anglo-Québécois came to see imperial sovereignty as a means of making the Canadian government listen to their concerns, and to see imperial citizenship as a stand-in for the national citizenship that did not seem to count for much. Replacing national with imperial citizenship was not without its critics, with some denigrating Anglo-Québécois for neglecting their voting rights and failing to respect voting outcomes that were adverse to their interests. Yet for the PDA, who felt that a Catholic conspiracy was silencing dissent and controlling election outcomes, voting as Canadian citizens seemed useless. Neither did directly petitioning the imperial government come with much promise given Canada's self-governing status. Instead, the PDA hoped to indirectly apply imperial authority by shaming Canadian politicians through expressions of abhorrence in the British press. The British press, however, proved uninterested overall in the destruction of an Indigenous church in Quebec, and no strong expression of abhorrence appeared.

The PDA's experience invoking imperial authority against the Catholic hierarchy in Quebec contributes to ongoing efforts to place anti-Catholicism in Canada within its wider imperial context. The popular narrative within Canadian history, as established by eminent Canadian historian J. R. Miller, is that Canadian anti-Catholicism was "less an echo of theological and social controversies in Britain and the United States" but rather "very much a Canadian problem" concerning the formation of a nationalist Canadian identity.[52] Conversely, imperial historians John Wolffe and Géraldine Vaughan argue that Canadian anti-Catholicism was intimately connected with imperial rhetoric of Britishness and British values.[53] They demonstrate that the PDA's articulation of Catholicism as the enemy of British liberty was common across all settler colonies and contributed to the formation of a common British identity.

However, Wolffe's and Vaughan's emphasis on anti-Catholicism as a mechanism of preserving Britishness as a cultural identifier overlooks the functionality of anti-Catholic Britishness as leverage against the British government. Vaughan develops the category of "theologico-political anti-Catholicism" to describe the way in which ultra-Protestant societies around the Empire used Catholicism as a scapegoat for corruption in their societies and a foil for British identification with liberty, and the PDA certainly fits this description. Yet the PDA went one step further. It used Catholicism as a scapegoat for its members' feelings of political marginalization, and then it used British identification with liberty as justification for the British government to interfere in Canadian politics and for the British public to decry the Canadian government's lack of action. The PDA's articulation of anti-Catholicism was therefore not only a manifestation of an imperial discourse of British identity, but also a method of invoking imperial authority as imperial citizens.

Importantly, however, the specificity of the PDA's demands upon imperial authority illustrates the limitations of the imperial citizenship concept. Most of the case studies in this book connected imperial belonging with relatively common political demands, whether that be the right to a fair trial in Western Australia, the desire for physical safety in New Zealand, or the ability to participate in policy making in Natal. Despite their local particularities, these are all traits that most people in the Empire could relate to. Freedom from papal tyranny, on the other hand, was not truly relevant to anyone who was not a Protestant in Quebec. Indeed, despite the existence of anti-Catholic societies throughout the Empire, Wolffe shows that these were fringe organizations, and that their concerns were irrational anxieties about Catholic influence that simply did not exist.[54] This disconnection between the PDA's experiences and those of other British subjects detracted from the British public's capacity to recognize their right to imperial interference, rendering their appeals to British popular opinion dead on arrival.

Notes

1 John Lambton, earl of Durham, *The Report and Despatches of the Earl of Durham, Her Majesty's High Commissioner and Governor-General of British North America* (London: Ridgways, 1839), 8.

2 Garth Stevenson, *Community Besieged: The Anglophone Minority and the Politics of Quebec* (Montreal: McGill-Queen's University Press, 1999), 26–30.

3 "The Protestant Defence Alliance of Canada," *Montreal Daily Witness*, 25 December 1875.
4 *Ibid.*
5 *Ibid.*
6 *Ibid.*
7 Saho Matsumoto-Best, *Britain and the Papacy in the Age of Revolution* (London: The Boydell Press, 2003), 143–154.
8 John Wolffe, "Anti-Catholicism and the British Empire, 1815–1914," in Hilary Carey (ed.), *Empires of Religion* (London: Palgrave Macmillan, 2008), 46–49.
9 J. R. Miller, "Anti-Catholic Thought in Victorian Canada," *Canadian Historical Review* 66, no. 4 (December 1985): 474–494 (476), DOI: 10.3138/CHR-066-04-03.
10 Géraldine Vaughan, "'Britishers and Protestants': Protestantism and Imperial British Identities in Britain, Canada and Australia from the 1880s to the 1920s," *Studies in Church History* 54 (2018): 359–373, DOI: 10.1017/stc.2017.20.
11 For examples, see "Protestant Defence Alliance," *Montreal Star*, 5 February 1876; and "The Archambault Case," *Montreal Star*, 1 October 1874.
12 John Thompson, *A Brief History of the Land Dispute at Kanesatake [Oka] from Contact to 1961* (Ottawa: Treaties and Historical Research Centre, 1991), 9.
13 *Ibid.*, 13–25.
14 *Ibid.*, 25–13; Harry Swain, *Oka: A Political Crisis and Its Legacy* (Vancouver: Douglas & McIntyre, 2010), 21–22.
15 "Protestant Defence Alliance Meeting," *Montreal Daily Witness*, 14 March 1877.
16 Protestant Defence Alliance, *The Indians of the Lake of Two Mountains and the Seminary of St Sulpice* (Montreal: Witness Printing House, 1876), 6.
17 "Protestant Defence Alliance Meeting."
18 *Ibid.*
19 Philip Carpenter to Frederick Chesson, 1 January 1876, Oxford, Bodleian Libraries (BodL), MS Brit. Emp. s. 22 G83b/1–9.
20 J. A. Mathewson to Queen Victoria, 19 November 1875, The National Archives, London (TNA), CO 42/740, no. 13368.
21 *Ibid.*
22 David Laird to Colonial Office, 13 September 1875, enclosed in Colonial Office minutes, "Persecution of Protestant Indians at Oka by Roman Catholic Clergy," TNA, CO 42/740, no. 13368.
23 Congregational Union of Ontario and Quebec to Queen Victoria, 9 June 1876, Library and Archives of Canada, Department of Indian Affairs files, RG10, Vol. 1991, file 68221.
24 *Ibid.*
25 "Protestant Defence Alliance Meeting."
26 APS to the Secretary of State for the Colonies, 11 July 1877, TNA, CO 42/751, no. 8416.
27 Colonial Office to APS, 23 July 1877, TNA, CO 42/752, no. 8416.

28 Philip Carpenter to Frederick Chesson, 17 March 1875, BodL, MS Brit. Emp. s. 22 G83b/1–6.
29 Philip Carpenter to Frederick Chesson, 17 December 1875, BodL, MS Brit. Emp. s. 22 G83b/1–8.
30 Philip Carpenter to Frederick Chesson, 1 January 1876, BodL, MS Brit. Emp. s. 22 G83b/1–9.
31 Philip Carpenter to Frederick Chesson, 28 July 1875, BodL, MS Brit. Emp. s. 22 G83b/1–7.
32 Carpenter to Chesson, 17 March 1875.
33 "Priestly Outrage on the Protestant Indians of Lower Canada," *Daily News*, 4 January 1876; leader, *Daily News*, 5 January 1876.
34 Leader, *Belfast News-Letter*, 8 February 1876.
35 Thompson, *A Brief History of the Land Dispute at Kanesatake*, 31–39.
36 Tom Fennario, "Mohawk Land Dispute Unresolved 3 Decades after Siege of Kanehsatake," *APTN News*, 11 July 2020, www.aptnnews.ca/national-news/siegekanehsatake30th/ (accessed 18 March 2025); Thompson, *A Brief History of the Land Dispute at Kanesatake*, 43–47.
37 "Intolerance Catching," *Toronto Globe*, 8 February 1876.
38 *Ibid.*
39 "Opinions of the People," *Morning Chronicle*, 19 February 1876.
40 *Ibid.*
41 "The Protestant Defence Alliance and the Leaders of Political Parties," *Daily Daily Witness*, 13 March 1876.
42 *Ibid.*
43 Robert Hill, *Voice of the Vanishing Minority: Robert Sellar and the Huntingdon Gleaner, 1863–1919* (Montreal: McGill-Queen's University Press, 1998), 92.
44 Carpenter to Chesson, 1 January 1876.
45 P. B. Waite, "White, Thomas," in *Dictionary of Canadian Biography* (Toronto: University of Toronto Press, 1982).
46 Lorne Ste Croix, "Penny, Edward Goff," in *Dictionary of Canadian Biography*; James Forbes, "'A Deplorable Speech': The Liberal Party vs Anti-Catholicism during the Alexander Mackenzie Administration, 1873–1878," *Journal of the Canadian Historical Association* 28, no. 1 (2017): 193–216, DOI: 10.7202/1050899ar.
47 Roderick MacLeod, "Dougall, John Redpath," in *Dictionary of Canadian Biography*.
48 *Ibid.*
49 Leader, *Montreal Gazette*, 10 December 1875.
50 "The Oka Indians," *Montreal Gazette*, 20 December 1875.
51 "The Oka Indians," *Montreal Herald*, 16 December 1875.
52 J. R. Miller, "Anti-Catholicism in Canada: From the British Conquest to the Great War," in Terrence Murphy and Gerald Stortz (eds), *Creed and Culture: The Place of English-Speaking Catholics in Canadian Society, 1750–1930* (Montreal: McGill-Queen's University Press, 1993), 38. See also Miller, "Anti-Catholic Thought in Victorian Canada"; and J. R. Miller, *Equal Rights: The*

Jesuits' Estates Act Controversy (Montreal: McGill-Queen's University Press, 1979).

53 Wolffe, "Anti-Catholicism and the British Empire," 43–63; Vaughan, "Britishers and Protestants"; Géraldine Vaughan, *Anti-Catholicism and British Identities in Britain, Canada and Australia, 1880s–1920s*, Histories of the Sacred and Secular, 1700–2000 (Cham: Palgrave Macmillan, 2022).

54 Wolffe, "Anti-Catholicism and the British Empire," 48.

6

Mass petitioning as participatory imperial politics: Cape Colony, 1884–1885

Between September 1884 and June 1885, a deluge of seventy-two petitions from all corners of the Cape Colony were sent to the Colonial Office. The size of these petitions ranged from Clanwilliam's modest forty-six signatures on 5 November 1884 to Cape Town's sprawling 4,054 signatures on 15 October 1884. Forty-seven towns in total sent petitions, shown on Map 6.1. Not only have these petitions gone unmentioned in the historiography of South Africa, but the idea of settlers living under a responsible government publicly petitioning the imperial government at such a scale is completely anomalous within the broader historiography of the British Empire. Using a database of over 1 million petitions presented to the British House of Commons between 1780 and 1918, Richard Huzzey and Henry Miller find that nearly all petitions from settler colonies revolved around demands for self-government, so that "the number of petitions and signatures relating to Canada, Australia, New Zealand, and southern Africa waned once responsible or representative government was granted."[1] Similarly, A. J. Christopher's study of petitions to the House of Commons from the Cape Colony specifically finds that, out of seventy-eight petitions written by settlers between 1833 and 1914, the vast majority (sixty-three) were written prior to receiving responsible government in 1872, and he records only one petition from the 1880s.[2] The seventy-two Cape Colony petitions of 1884–1885 do not appear in such studies because they were sent through the High Commissioner of South Africa directly to the Secretary of State for the Colonies, bypassing the House of Commons entirely. These seventy-two petitions therefore offer a rare and valuable window into the entanglement of imperial and settler sovereignties in self-governing colonies.

All seventy-two petitions related to a series of conflicts in Bechuanaland (modern-day Botswana) commonly referred to as the Bechuanaland Wars. In 1882, two separate wars broke out between a number of rival African nations. In the north, fighting erupted between a Ratshidi chief named Montshiwa and two Rapulana chiefs named Matlaba and Moshete. Meanwhile, in the south, a separate conflict arose between a Batlhaping

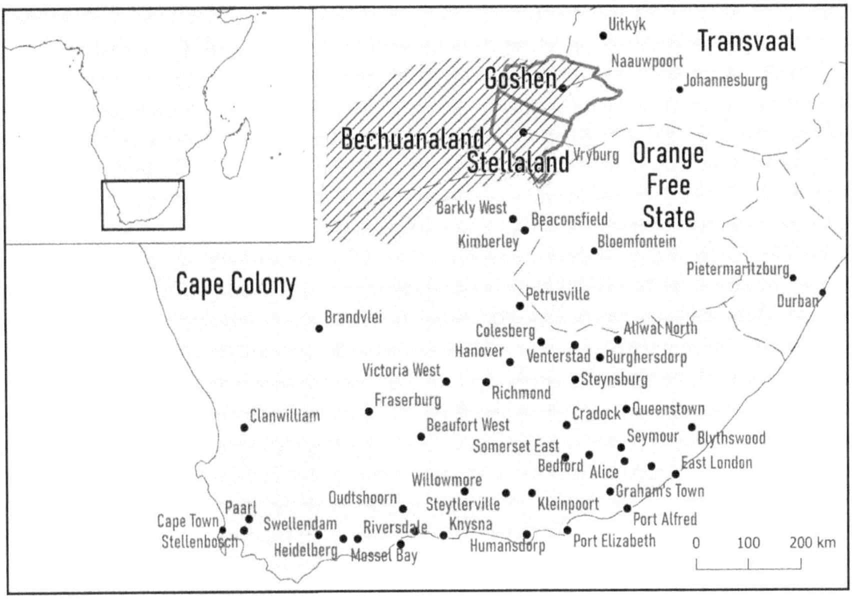

Map 6.1 Bechuanaland petitions

chief named Mankurwane and a Korana chief named David Massouw. All of these chiefs employed settler mercenaries known as freebooters, mostly Afrikaners from the Transvaal but also a few British colonists from the Cape. Montshiwa and Mankurwane achieved victories with the help of their white freebooters, but those freebooters ultimately betrayed their African employers and proclaimed their own republics: Goshen in the north and Stellaland in the south, which later merged into the United States of Stellaland in 1883. Stellaland was ostensibly an independent republic, but it was heavily supported by the Transvaal government. The 1881 Pretoria Convention, which established peace following the First Anglo-Boer War, had fixed the Transvaal's borders and forbidden it to expand without British approval. Establishing Stellaland was therefore a surreptitious means for the Transvaal government to extend its borders to the west.

Stellaland posed a major problem for the Cape and British governments alike, albeit for different reasons. For the Cape government, and the mining magnate and MP Cecil Rhodes in particular, Stellaland threatened the trade routes into the interior of Africa that fuelled the mining industry with firewood and cheap labour. For the British government, the Transvaal's westward expansion came with the possibility of linking up with Germany's new colony in South West Africa established in 1884, which threatened to undermine British supremacy in the region. Britain and the Cape therefore had a shared interest in annexing Bechuanaland, but they held competing visions for how annexation would unfold. Britain wanted the freebooters to be expelled by military force, the land to be restored to its African owners, and the Cape to ultimately assume responsibility for administering the region.[3] The Cape, on the other hand, wanted to settle the matter peacefully by recognizing freebooter land claims, and only wanted to assume responsibility for administering Bechuanaland if it could dispose of the land as it desired.[4] The seventy-two settler petitions were written precisely at this moment of impasse between Britain and the Cape over how to respond to the Bechuanaland issue. Recognizing that South Africa was on the precipice of either a major military offensive or a major land settlement, settlers throughout the colony took to petitioning the Colonial Office to sway its decision one way or the other.

On first glance, the fact that settlers were petitioning about events beyond the borders of the colony and therefore outside the jurisdiction of their responsible government appears to suggest that invoking imperial authority was unrelated to their own sovereignty. Lorenzo Veracini theorizes this very phenomenon in his conceptualization of settler colonialism. Recognizing that settler and imperial claims to sovereignty were contradictory, he argues that both sovereignties could coexist because they were directed over different territories, with settler sovereignty directed over domestic territory and imperial sovereignty directed over foreign territory.[5] On the ground, however, it was not so easy to demarcate between domestic and foreign territory, nor between settler and imperial sovereignty. The Bechuanaland Wars were waged outside the Cape's borders, but settlers from across the political spectrum feared that, if mishandled, conflict would spread into the colony. Petitioners thus invoked imperial authority to influence domestic and foreign affairs simultaneously, and attending to how and why they did this offers valuable insight into the entanglement of imperial and colonial authority in self-governing spaces.

Determining the extent of colonial–imperial cooperation in Bechuanaland

On 21 September 1884, Colonial Secretary Edward Stanley informed Hercules Robinson, governor of the Cape Colony, that before deciding upon a course of action in Bechuanaland, he desired "to understand the extent of co-operation to be given by the Colony on account of trade routes and otherwise if active measures taken."[6] In response, a public meeting was held in Cape Town on 24 September to survey public opinion on whether or not the colony should contribute to an imperial intervention in Bechuanaland, should one occur, and telegrams were sent to the other major towns suggesting they do the same.[7] Over the course of September and October 1884, more than twenty-two public meetings took place in towns throughout the Cape Colony to discuss whether or not they desired imperial intervention in Bechuanaland and to what extent they would be willing to assist an imperial force if it was sent.

Six towns were in support of both imperial intervention and colonial cooperation.[8] They unanimously asserted that the Empire had a duty to enforce the Convention of London, otherwise trade routes to the north would be closed and British supremacy in the region would be undermined "with disastrous results to all loyal subjects of Her Majesty in this country."[9] More than that, however, these towns asserted that the Cape Colony, as an independent nation, had to take a leading position in Bechuanaland if it was to retain its dominant position in relation to the other colonies in the region. At the Cape Town meeting, for example, it was declared that "If they wished the Cape Colony to have a history, they must come to the front, and assert themselves now ... People spoke of the trade route; but there was a still more important thing, and that was the history of this country ... Only by this means could they secure a voice in the South Africa of the future ... to keep the Cape Colony to the front."[10]

Conversely, fourteen towns rejected any notion of colonial cooperation, preferring either an entirely imperial intervention or no intervention at all.[11] The public meetings in Paarl and Steynsburg indicated that their reticence to condone colonial involvement was rooted in a fear that doing so "can only serve to disturb the harmony existing between colonists," and "will create nothing else than race-hatred and cause a disastrous separation between colonists."[12] The *Graham's Town Journal* further explained that the problem with a joint imperial–colonial endeavour was that, if Cape colonists were to intervene in Transvaal matters, it would sow conflict between British and Afrikaner settlers. Imperial interference, on the other hand, would direct Afrikaner anger outside the colony. "If a man is misconducting himself in the streets, a policeman who wishes to apprehend him will hardly expect much aid from the offender's brothers and cousins, and might by insisting on such aid raise up a much larger difficulty than at first existed."[13] As such, the *Journal* insisted that "if force has to be used, it must be by the Imperial power,"[14] and that "the Colony should be kept out of all complications in Bechuanaland."[15]

Resolutions from all town meetings were dutifully transmitted to the Colonial Office so that the Secretary of State for the Colonies could base his Bechuanaland policy on local colonial opinion. This outpouring of democratic deliberation over imperial policy showcases the strong desire that many colonists had to participate in imperial policy making. Moreover, the

15–6 majority support for imperial intervention with no colonial involvement seems to have successfully influenced the Colonial Office's policy. On 10 November 1884, the Colonial Office commissioned Sir Charles Warren to initiate military operations in Bechuanaland with only nominal colonial assistance.[16] As part of their deal with the imperial government, the Cape government had demanded an opportunity to attempt a peaceful settlement before any military operations began. High Commissioner Robinson had little faith in the idea, writing to the Colonial Office that "without force I do not believe that Ministers can effect any settlement ... which will be satisfactory to Her Majesty's Government."[17] However, given that "military preparations would occupy at least two months," he suggested that the Cape government be allowed to try such a settlement while an armed force was being mustered, and Warren was instructed to wait at least six weeks before starting military operations in Bechuanaland.

The Upington/Sprigg settlement

While Warren was waiting, the Cape government sent two Cape politicians friendly to Afrikaners' interests, Thomas Upington and Gordon Sprigg, to Bechuanaland to cut a deal. On 22 November Upington and Sprigg arrived at a peaceful settlement that essentially granted the freebooters everything they wanted, recognizing their land claims and granting them independent self-government. Robinson informed the Colonial Office on 29 November that such an agreement could not be accepted by the imperial government, and he authorized Warren to occupy Bechuanaland as planned.[18] After months of preparations and negotiations with the Transvaal, Warren entered Bechuanaland on 28 February 1885.[19] The Colonial Office's dismissal of the Cape government's settlement, especially given that Robinson never intended to agree to any settlement and ordered Warren to prepare for military involvement from the start, aligned with colonists' desires to keep the colony out of Bechuanaland affairs, and would seem to suggest that their voices were listened to. However, the public resolutions took up to a month to reach England via the post, so that Sir Charles Warren's commission on 10 November was declared *before* the Secretary of State for the Colonies had received most of the town resolutions. The only resolutions to reach the Colonial Office prior to 10 November were those from Aliwal North, Kimberley, Cape Town, Cradock, Knysna, Barkly West, Kaffraria, and Venterstand. Five of these eight towns had supported colonial cooperation with an imperial intervention, so that the Colonial Office's decision to retake Bechuanaland without colonial assistance was actually against the wishes of the majority of town resolutions that it had received at the time.

It therefore seems doubtful that town resolutions actually informed the Colonial Office's policy making.

Nevertheless, to colonists from the fourteen towns that opposed colonial cooperation, their ability to influence Bechuanaland policy seemed validated by Warren's commission on November 10. As residents of Graham's Town put it, "there was an agitation throughout the Colony to get the Imperial Government to do its duty … The voice of the Colony was heard by the people of England."[20] When Upington and Sprigg later made their deal with the freebooters against imperial interests, those opposed to colonial cooperation took it as a direct rejection of their democratic voices, while those in support of a colonial invasion celebrated the efficacy of their imperial lobbying. A new round of petitions was signed between 27 November and 13 December from seventeen different towns, nine criticizing the Upington/Sprigg settlement and eight defending it.

Those in opposition to the Upington/Sprigg settlement unanimously agreed that no settlement should be made without a representative of the imperial government present, namely Sir Charles Warren. Moreover, they repeatedly justified their opposition to the Upington/Sprigg settlement by citing the racial divisions in South Africa, referring to the hostility between English and Afrikaner settlers. The Aliwal North petition, for example, argued that the settlement's plan for annexing Bechuanaland to the Cape was not feasible "on account of the divisions existing among the leading races, which would assuredly lead to complications."[21] The meeting at Graham's Town elaborated: "We would warn the British Government that if they accept the action of the Ministers it will end in misery and war in South Africa."[22] According to those at the meeting, the invaders in Bechuanaland would not respect the settlement and would rebel against the Cape, but the Cape, "in the present divided feeling of the country," would be unable to put down the rebellion and would lose the seemingly inevitable civil war.[23]

On the other hand, those in support of the Upington/Sprigg settlement took the complete opposite perspective. Rather than believing a show of imperial force would act as a deterrent against warfare, supporters of the settlement believed that a heavy-handed military response would push the Transvaal into a military response of its own. The petition from Riversdale, for example, argued that "the sending of an armed force to Land Goshen may appear to be the first step towards the breaking out of a war which will involve our country in great disaster."[24] The Beaufort West petition elaborated that those opposed to the Upington/Sprigg settlement were consigning South Africa to a future of intercolonial conflict and hostility, whereas they asserted that "the Imperial Government should enter upon amicable co-operation with the Colony and the Transvaal Republic in the regulation of the matters in connexion with Bechuanaland, whereby, according to the conviction of this meeting, threatening and serious troubles, even bloodshed, will be averted."[25]

As outlined above, the imperial government ultimately decided to ignore the Upington/Sprigg settlement and send Sir Charles Warren with an armed host into Bechuanaland. And once again, the impact of settler petitions on that outcome is dubious. Governor Robinson proclaimed the settlement unsatisfactory and authorized Warren's expedition on 29 November, but only two of the seventeen petitions for or against the settlement had even been drafted by that date, and none of them had arrived on the desk of the Secretary of State for the Colonies. There can therefore be little to no connection drawn between these petitions and imperial decision making.

Imperial policy beyond Bechuanaland

However, to those petitioners who opposed the Upington/Sprigg settlement, Warren's expedition signalled the efficacy of their extended efforts to influence imperial policy, prompting a third and final round of petitions. Six of the towns that had previously challenged the Upington/Sprigg settlement (Kimberley, King William's Town, East London, Port Elizabeth, Aliwal North, and Graham's Town) wrote further petitions in April and May 1885 to express their approval of Warren's success in Bechuanaland and to offer suggestions for imperial policy going forwards. Three of the petitions recommended that Warren remain in South Africa after settling affairs in Bechuanaland and conduct similar expeditions into "all the native territories beyond the Cape Colony," thereby expanding imperial administration along "the entire coast line between East London and Delagoa Bay."[26] This primarily referred to Zululand, which in 1884 had been engulfed in a civil war that ended with the Transvaal confiscating nearly 3 million acres of land.[27] With the Transvaal inching closer to obtaining an outlet to the ocean, the petitioners suggested that Warren head them off "to restore that distracted country to order and prosperity" and "secure the Colonies and South Africa from the danger of foreign interference."[28]

The other three petitions looked even farther afield, commenting on the rapidly deteriorating situation in Sudan. Observing the "loyal action of other Colonies in offering assistance to the Mother Country," the petitioners recommended that the Cape should offer "a fully-equipped contingent for service in the Soudan ... at the expense of the Colony."[29] At the time these petitions were signed between mid-April and early May 1885, Britain was reeling from the death of Charles Gordon during the fall of Khartoum in January, Britain's loss in the Battle of Kirbekan in February, and the failure of the Suakin Expedition in March. The petitioners felt that the Cape Colony owed it to the Empire to provide troops in recompense for Warren's assistance in Bechuanaland. Moreover, in light of Canada's contribution of 386 voyageurs on the Nile Expedition and Australia's contribution of 770 soldiers on the Suakin Expedition, the petitioners felt that it was their government's duty to copy "the patriotic conduct of those sister Colonies."[30] Aliwal North liked the idea of making such a patriotic contribution, yet believed that "the unfortunate circumstances of this country prevents it from following in the footsteps of its sister Colonies."[31] Although this statement is not elaborated upon, it most probably referenced the fact that, unlike Canada and Australia, the Cape Colony had multiple vulnerable fronts bordering hostile African, German, and Afrikaner populations that required military forces to remain in the region.

The impact of this third round of petitions is just as dubious as the first two. Britain pulled out of the war in Sudan on 17 May, only a couple weeks after these petitions were written, so there was never a chance for the Cape to offer troops. Conversely, Britian did annex Zululand, but not until 1887, and not until Germany began showing interest in the area.[32] Such outcomes would seem to indicate that the petitions failed. However, the extensive scholarship on the history of petitioning contends that obtaining a specified outcome is only one small element of why people petition in the first place. Historians of Indigenous petitions to the imperial government stress that, although such petitions nearly always failed to achieve their desired outcome, they nonetheless remained important tools for articulating claims to sovereignty and protecting community identities.[33] Such an approach to petitions as tools of identity formation is particularly applicable to the Bechuanaland petitions given the racialized divisions between British and Afrikaner settlers. To assess the impact of all three rounds of petitions, we must therefore consider how the petitions were being used to demarcate racial boundaries.

British humanity versus Afrikaner democracy

Interestingly, public meetings from majority Afrikaner regions as well as majority British regions were equally defensive regarding their loyalty towards Britain. It is standard fare to begin petitions with a declaration of loyalty to the petitioned authority, and each of the seventy-two Bechuanaland petitions opened with a typical statement such as "This meeting of loyal subjects of Her Majesty the Queen of England is of opinion ..."[34] Beyond these formal statements, however, were currents of defensiveness in response to perceptions of loyalty under question. British-majority communities were concerned about allegations of disloyalty from politicians back in England. For example, a public meeting in Cape Town attended primarily by British settlers lamented "recent expressions of opinion in the House of Commons imputing to Your Majesty's subjects in this Colony an indifference to the maintenance of the tie which now binds them to the Empire," while a public meeting in East London regretted that the loyalty of the Cape had "been somewhat questioned of late in England."[35] Afrikaner-majority communities, on the other hand, were concerned about allegations of disloyalty from neighbouring British settlers. An Afrikaner-dominated meeting at Beaufort West, for instance, resolved that "Whereas certain persons ... have accused the members of the Afrikander Bond and the Farmers Protection Association of disloyalty ... this meeting wishes to assure Her Majesty the honoured Queen of England emphatically of their loyalty as British subjects."[36]

Such efforts on the part of both British and Afrikaner settlers to establish their loyalty to the Empire required them to locate their demands for either imperial intervention or imperial neutrality within a framework of service to the Empire, and each group did so using a particular discourse of Britishness. British-majority communities adopted a humanitarian discourse to align their desire for imperial military invention with the British Empire's identity as a humane and civilizing force. Nearly all petitions from British-majority communities included a statement along the lines of this excerpt from a Graham's Town petition: "Your Petitioners, therefore, earnestly desire that Your Majesty's Government will take prompt and sufficient measures to restore order in Bechuanaland and to preserve the rights of the natives, to whom imperial protection has been graciously promised ... for the efforts of Christianity and civilization."[37] A Kimberley petition went as far as to proclaim that, beyond any economic or political benefits, imperial intervention was to preserve "above all the lives and properties of friendly natives."[38] By articulating their invocations of imperial authority as necessitated by Britain's duty to protect and civilize its Indigenous subjects, and not a boon primarily benefiting petitioners themselves, the petitions from British-majority communities sought to frame their demands as acts of loyalty to the Empire's honour and moral standing.

Afrikaner-majority communities, on the other hand, adopted a democratic discourse to align their desire for imperial neutrality with the British Empire's identity as the harbinger of liberty and freedom. Unlike those from British-majority communities, Afrikaner petitions made virtually no mention of African welfare or the Empire's civilizing duty. Instead, nearly every Afrikaner petition made reference to the fact that Afrikaners represented a majority of the Cape's settler population and therefore had a democratic right to determine local policy. The Kleinpoort petition, for example, stated that demands for imperial intervention "do not represent the views of the majority of Colonists, but only those of a small section of the community."[39] Such petitions directly linked their democratic rights to a discursive connection between Britishness and liberty, as when the Beaufort West petition emphasized how much they valued "the freedom and privileges they enjoy under the English flag."[40] Afrikaner petitions also invoked the rights and freedoms Britain had guaranteed to the Cape via "their interests and privileges under Responsible Government," arguing that the Upington/Sprigg settlement should stand since it was made by "the true representatives of the people."[41]

The use of their petitions to establish British settlers as humanitarian and Afrikaners as democratic indicates that petitioning the imperial government was not solely about influencing policy towards Bechuanaland. Indeed, Bechuanaland was only one arena within the vast South African landscape that required colonial and imperial cooperation, with conflicts in Zululand and Basutoland also calling for Britain and the Cape to come to an agreement for sharing responsibilities. Bechuanaland therefore represented only one battle in a wider war over who in the Cape could influence imperial policy. Failing to achieve imperial intervention or neutrality in Bechuanaland may have represented a loss in that battle, but the overall war effort could nevertheless be salvaged if British or Afrikaner settlers were at least able to strengthen their overall legitimacy in the eyes of British policy makers. This war over settler political identities would continue at an even larger scale throughout the South African War of 1899–1902, when thousands of pamphlets were circulated around South Africa and England to sway people's perceptions of the patriotism or humanity of British and Afrikaner settlers.[42] The Bechuanaland petitions thus represent one isolated instance of a broader pattern of using technologies of political participation to establish settler identities within an imperial framework.

Conclusion

These petitions demonstrate the convergence of notions around participatory democracy and imperial subjecthood. Settlers throughout the Cape Colony applied their expectations, grounded in responsible government, that their government be responsible to their voices and opinions, and applied it to the overarching authority of the imperial government. This blurs the boundaries between imperial and responsible governance, revealing that settlers did not shift their perception of political subjectivity from the Empire to their colony on a one-for-one basis. On the contrary, they combined their attachment to responsible colonial governance with their attachment to imperial authority, hoping to gain the benefits of both.

Moreover, the way that petitioners connected events in Bechuanaland to their own self-interest demonstrates the arbitrary nature of concrete delineation between domestic and foreign affairs that is typically understood as the dividing line between settler and imperial jurisdiction within a responsible government structure. The Transvaal's invasion of Bechuanaland was most assuredly a matter of imperial jurisdiction, given that Bechuanaland was independent and the Transvaal was a foreign state. Yet colonists in the Cape asserted in their petitions that multiple domestic issues within their own jurisdiction were intimately contingent upon events in foreign territory. Most obviously, conflict in Bechuanaland interfered with the Cape's access to trade routes into the northern interior of Africa, with nearly all petitions including a statement that "the future expansion and development of the trade of this colony … greatly depend upon the action taken by the Imperial Government."[43] Thanks to the imperial customs and Shipping Acts of 1857 and 1869, responsible governments had complete jurisdiction over their own trade, customs, and navigation, the only proviso being that they could not directly injure British commerce.[44] The Cape's trade with the interior of Africa was thus its own internal business. However, since the efficacy of the trade route was dependent upon Britain's ability to maintain stability in Bechuanaland and enforce its conventions with the Transvaal, the Cape's jurisdiction over its trade was intimately interwoven with Britain's jurisdiction over foreign policy. Petitioning imperial authority was therefore just as much about pursuing domestic trade policies as it was about influencing foreign affairs.

Additionally, the emphasis across all of the petitions on race tensions between English and Afrikaner populations within the Cape Colony shows that questions of domestic law and order were directly entangled with those concerning foreign warfare. By the 1880s, the Cape Colony was largely in control of defending its own borders, but the authority to negotiate with foreign entities or send troops onto foreign soil still rested entirely with the British government. The Transvaal's invasion of Bechuanaland was therefore undoubtedly an imperial concern. Yet the interconnectedness of the populations of the Transvaal, the Cape, and Bechuanaland meant that political boundaries between the three entities were blurry. Large populations of Afrikaners, British colonists, and Tswana peoples straddled borders in all three regions, with the relationship between Afrikaners in the Cape and the Transvaal remaining a particularly troubling unknown element. Those petitioners who supported the Upington/Sprigg settlement believed that if Transvaal Afrikaners were offended, Cape Afrikaners would rise up in rebellion to avenge them. Conversely, petitioners who challenged the Upington/Sprigg settlement believed that if Transvaal Afrikaners were placated, Cape Afrikaners would rise up in rebellion to take advantage of the

Cape's weakness. In both scenarios, the alleged interconnection between Afrikaner populations inside and outside the Cape was believed to render domestic defence directly dependent upon foreign policy. Thus, in terms of defence as well as trade, the petitions from the Cape Colony invoked imperial authority in foreign territory for the maintenance of settler sovereignty in the domestic sphere.

Notes

1 Richard Huzzey and Henry Miller, "Colonial Petitions, Colonial Petitioners, and the Imperial Parliament, ca. 1780–1918," *Journal of British Studies* 61, no. 2 (2022): 261–289 (268), DOI: 10.1017/jbr.2021.185.
2 A. J. Christopher, "South African Petitions to the House of Commons, 1833–1914: Grievances, Protests, Advice and Information," *Historia* 63, no. 1 (2018): 1–23, DOI: 10.17159/2309-8392/2018/v63n1a1.
3 Anthony Sillery, *The Bechuanaland Protectorate* (Oxford: Oxford University Press, 1952), 53; Deryck Schreuder, *Gladstone and Kruger: Liberal Government & Colonial "Home Rule" 1880–85* (London: Routledge, 1969), 459–460.
4 Sillery, *The Bechuanaland Protectorate*, 58; Schreuder, *Gladstone and Kruger*, 461–462.
5 Lorenzo Veracini, *Settler Colonialism: A Theoretical Overview* (Cham: Palgrave Macmillan, 2010), 53–74.
6 Edward Stanley, 15th earl of Derby, to Hercules Robinson, 21 September 1884, in British House of Commons, *Further Correspondence Respecting the Affairs of the Transvaal and Adjacent Territories, October 1884* (London: Eyre and Spottiswoode, 1884), 76.
7 "Affairs of Bechuanaland," *Graham's Town Journal*, 25 September 1884.
8 Cape Town, Knysa, Aliwal North, Kimberley, Beaconsfield, and Barkly West.
9 "Resolutions Passed at the Cape Town Meeting Held on 24 September 1884," in British House of Commons, *Further Correspondence Respecting the Affairs of the Transvaal and Adjacent Territories, February 1885* (London: Eyre and Spottiswoode, 1885), 141.
10 "The Crisis in Bechuanaland," *Cape Argus*, 27 September 1884.
11 Georgetown, Mossel Bay, Graham's Town, Queenstown, Cradock, the Free Presbytery of Kaffraria, Port Elizabeth, Venterstad, Colesburg, Burghersdorf, Steynsburg, Kleinport, Oudtshoorn, and Paarl.
12 "Resolutions Passed at the Paarl Meeting Held on Monday the 27th October 1884," in British House of Commons, *Further Correspondence Respecting the Affairs of the Transvaal ... February 1885*, 44; "Resolutions Passed at Steynsburg by a Bond Meeting on 25 October 1884," in British House of Commons, *Further Correspondence Respecting the Affairs of the Transvaal ... February 1885*, 29.
13 Leader, *Graham's Town Journal*, 29 September 1884.
14 *Ibid.*

15 Leader, *Graham's Town Journal*, 27 September 1884.
16 Colonial Office to Sir Charles Warren, 10 November 1884, in British House of Commons, *Commission and Instructions to Major-General Sir Charles Warren, K.C.M.G., as Special Commissioner to Bechuanaland, November 1884* (London: Eyre and Spottiswoode, 1884), 4.
17 Hercules Robinson to earl of Derby, 17 October 1884, in British House of Commons, *Further Correspondence Respecting the Affairs of the Transvaal ... October 1884*, 139.
18 Hercules Robinson to earl of Derby, 29 November 1884, in British House of Commons, *Further Correspondence Respecting the Affairs of the Transvaal ... February 1885*, 39.
19 Charles Warren to earl of Derby, 28 February 1885, in British House of Commons, *Further Correspondence Respecting the Affairs of the Transvaal and Adjacent Territories, May 1885* (London: Eyre and Spottiswoode, 1885), 21.
20 "Meeting on Bechuanaland Affairs," *Graham's Town Journal*, 1 December 1884.
21 "Resolutions Passed at a Public Meeting Held Saturday Evening," in British House of Commons, *Further Correspondence Respecting the Affairs of the Transvaal ... February 1885*, 75.
22 "Meeting on Bechuanaland Affairs."
23 *Ibid.*
24 "Resolutions Passed at Public Meeting Held at Riversdale, December 13th, 1884," in British House of Commons, *Further Correspondence Respecting the Affairs of the Transvaal ... February 1885*, 7.
25 "Resolutions Adopted at Beaufort West, 2 December 1884," in British House of Commons, *Further Correspondence Respecting the Affairs of the Transvaal ... February 1885*, 34.
26 "Resolutions Passed in King William's Town, 14 April 1885," in British House of Commons, *Further Correspondence Respecting the Affairs of the Transvaal and Adjacent Territories, August 1885* (London: Eyre and Spottiswoode, 1885), 3; "Resolutions Passed in East London, 29 April 1885," in British House of Commons, *Further Correspondence Respecting the Affairs of the Transvaal ... August 1885*, 13.
27 John Laband, "British Boundary Adjustments and the uSuthu-Mandlakazi Conflict in Zululand, 1879–1904," *South African Historical Journal* 30 (1994): 33–60, DOI: 10.1080/02582479408671781.
28 "Resolutions Passed in Grahamstown, 21 May 1885," in British House of Commons, *Further Correspondence Respecting the Affairs of the Transvaal ... August 1885*, 21.
29 "Resolutions Passed in Port Elizabeth, 16 April 1885," in British House of Commons, *Further Correspondence Respecting the Affairs of the Transvaal ... May 1885*, 187.
30 "Resolutions Passed in Kimberley, 8 April 1885," in British House of Commons, *Further Correspondence Respecting the Affairs of the Transvaal ... May 1885*, 142.

31 "Resolutions Passed in Aliwal North, 4 April 1885," in British House of Commons, *Further Correspondence Respecting the Affairs of the Transvaal … August 1885*, 15.
32 John Laband, *Rope of Sand: The Rise and Fall of the Zulu Kingdom in the Nineteenth Century* (Johannesburg: Jonathan Ball, 1995), 376.
33 Robert Travers, "Indian Petitioning and Colonial State-Formation in Eighteenth-Century Bengal," *Modern Asian Studies* 53, no. 1 (2019): 89–122, DOI: 10.1017/S0026749X17000841; Prashant Kidambi, "The Petition as Event: Colonial Bombay, circa 1889–1914," *Modern Asian Studies* 53, no. 1 (2019): 203–239, DOI: 10.1017/S0026749X17000555; Chima Korieh, "'May It Please Your Honor': Letters of Petition as Historical Evidence in an African Colonial Context," *History in Africa* 37 (2010): 83–106, DOI: 10.1353/hia.2010.0034; Ann Curthoys and Jessie Mitchell, "Bring This Paper to the Good Governor: Aboriginal Petitioning in Britain's Australia Colonies," in Saliha Belmessous (ed.), *Native Claims: Indigenous Law against Empire, 1500–1920* (Oxford: Oxford University Press, 2011), 182–198; Ravi de Costa, "Identity, Authority, and the Moral Worlds of Indigenous Petitions," *Comparative Studies in Society and History* 48, no. 3 (2006): 669–698, DOI: 10.1017/S0010417506000260.
34 "Resolutions Adopted at the Meeting of the Colesberg Branch of the Africander Bond, 4 October 1884," in British House of Commons, *Further Correspondence Respecting the Affairs of the Transvaal … February 1885*, 6.
35 "Petition from Cape Town, 15 October 1884," in British House of Commons, *Further Correspondence Respecting the Affairs of the Transvaal … February 1885*, 1; "Public Meeting in East London, 4 December 1884," in British House of Commons, *Further Correspondence Respecting the Affairs of the Transvaal … February 1885*, 74.
36 "Resolutions adopted at Beaufort West," 34.
37 "Petition from Grahamstown, October 1884," in British House of Commons, *Further Correspondence Respecting the Affairs of the Transvaal … February 1885*, 7.
38 "Petition from Kimberley, October 1884," in British House of Commons, *Further Correspondence Respecting the Affairs of the Transvaal … February 1885*, 45.
39 "Resolutions Adopted at Kleinpoort, 27 October 1884," in British House of Commons, *Further Correspondence Respecting the Affairs of the Transvaal … February 1885*, 19.
40 "Resolutions Adopted at Beaufort West."
41 "Resolutions Adopted at Murraysburg, 13 December 1884," in British House of Commons, *Further Correspondence Respecting the Affairs of the Transvaal … February 1885*, 48.
42 John Galbraith, "The Pamphlet Campaign on the Boer War," *The Journal of Modern History* 24, no. 2 (1952): 111–126.
43 "Petition from the Loyal Subjects of Mossel Bay to Her Majesty the Queen," in British House of Commons, *Further Correspondence Respecting the Affairs*

of the Transvaal and Adjacent Territories, December 1884 (London: Eyre and Spottiswoode, 1885), 9.

44 Alpheus Todd, *Parliamentary Government in the British Colonies*, 2nd edn (London: Longmans, Green, 1894), 179.

Part III

Indigenous imperial citizenship

7

Petitioning for African voting rights: Cape Colony, 1887

In 1887, the Cape Colony underwent a major test of its self-governing capabilities under responsible government by attempting to disenfranchise Black voters through the Parliamentary Registration Act (PRA). This Act reformed the system of voter registration in various ways, with the most controversial reform buried in Clause 17: "No person shall be entitled to be registered as a voter by reason of his sharing in any communal or tribal occupation of lands."[1] When the Cape had first obtained representative government institutions in 1853, the Constitution Ordinance had made no distinction between land held under communal and individual tenure. All that had been required was that eligible voters had "occupied ... any house, warehouse, shop, or other building, being either separately or jointly, with any land ... occupied therewith, of the value of twenty-five pounds sterling."[2] This language was vague, and the £25 threshold was low in order to prevent voters of British descent, who tended to have higher incomes, from dominating voters of Afrikaner descent, as well as Coloured voters, who tended to have lower incomes.[3] Many British settlers were, predictably, concerned that such a franchise would lead to Afrikaners and Coloured people teaming up to control the government, but British dominance in the Cape legislature continued for three decades after the 1853 Constitution was signed.

However, this balance began to shift in the 1880s for two reasons. First, a series of annexations throughout the 1870s and 1880s drastically increased the Black population by incorporating several densely populated African kingdoms into the Cape, and a century of missionary activity and trade relations meant that a significant number of this new population were educated and held enough property to qualify for the franchise. It was estimated by contemporary politicians that between 1882 and 1886 the proportion of Black voters had increased from 12 per cent of the electorate to 42 per cent, sparking considerable panic that white voters would soon be "swamped" out of politics.[4] Second, a new political party called the Afrikaner Bond was formed in 1881 to champion Afrikaner nationalism in reaction to British political and cultural supremacy.[5] The Bond became a powerful voting bloc in the Cape parliament, and it was hostile to Black voters because they typically voted for settlers of British descent. The Bond therefore sought to exclude as many Black Africans from the franchise as possible to maintain its political influence.

Explicitly disenfranchising Black Africans based on race alone was largely out of the question. The tradition of "Cape liberalism," stretching back to the criminalization of racial discrimination in Ordinance 50 of 1828, made such a notion a political non-starter.[6] Moreover, the imperial government was likely to disallow any legislation that explicitly subjugated a racial group, as it did when Canadian and Australian governments attempted to legislate against Asian immigrants in the 1870s.[7] Various methods of indirectly restricting the Black franchise were proposed, such as raising the property qualification to £100 or instituting a literacy test, but such measures would have affected Afrikaners as well as Black Africans. Conversely, stipulating that land held under communal tenure (as opposed to individual freehold) could not be used to meet the property qualification effectively targeted Black Africans alone, as most of the Black population in the Cape lived on communal locations or reserves, whereas most white-owned property was held under individual tenure. Historians disagree on just how many Black Africans were disenfranchised by the PRA, with numbers ranging from 3,000 to 30,000.[8] But even the most conservative estimates hold that more than 40 per cent of the Black voting population were struck off the registration lists because of Clause 17's exclusion of communally held land.

Many Black voters looked to the imperial government to disallow the Act despite its lack of explicit racial language. Five separate petitions were sent to the imperial government from different Black communities to request that the Act be disallowed.[9] The first, signed by A. Hatha on behalf of a public meeting at Seymour, was enclosed in a congratulatory Golden Jubilee address to Queen Victoria. The second and third, signed by Frank Makwena and prominent Black journalist John Tengo Jabavu on behalf of the Port Elizabeth and King William's Town Native Committees, informed the Colonial Office that signatures were being collected and a delegation to England being arranged. The fourth, signed by 126 inhabitants of the Oxkraal location in Queenstown, asked whether it was true that Britain had promised Cape delegates at the 1887 Colonial Conference that "no further Imperial interference so far as we Natives are concerned shall take place in the future. If this be true Your Majesty's loyal subjects feel that they are doomed."[10] The fifth, written by Jabavu, was directed to the Aborigines' Protection Society (APS), asking that a question in the House of Commons be raised to pressure the Colonial Office into listening to the other petitions.

Most settlers in the Cape Colony dismissed these petitions, believing that responsible government had removed the colony from imperial oversight.

The *Cape Times*, for example, despite calling for the dismissal of the PRA in order to protect Black voting rights, held that petitioning the imperial government was pointless. It wrote that "the appeal to the Queen has its fascination for the helpless, and for those who suffer wrong; but there is no place for it in our institutions. The beautiful traditions of the Throne have long vanished from the region of practical politics."[11] Historians largely agree with this belief. John Miller calls Indigenous petitions to British authorities "futile and quixotic" for the same reason that Sarah Carter and Maria Nugent call them "invariably (and perhaps inevitably) ... failures" and Michael Belgrave refers to them as "undertaken in ignorance of the constitutional conventions": because self-government supposedly precluded imperial intervention.[12] Ann Curthoys similarly maintains that "after the granting of responsible government, any thought of the British government retaining the power to intervene on behalf of Indigenous people was quite illusory."[13] Consequently, those who examine the PRA give at most a passing reference to the imperial petitions. Recognizing that the petitions existed and failed without offering any analysis of *why* they failed, South African historians have constructed a narrative in which petitioning the imperial government was merely something that Black communities needed to get out of their system before getting on with the more important work of organizing against the Cape and then the South African governments.[14]

As this chapter demonstrates, however, the petitions for imperial disallowance of the PRA were not dismissed out of hand as outside imperial jurisdiction. On the contrary, the Colonial Office investigated the petitioners' claims and deliberated with the Law Officers of the Crown as to whether intervention was warranted. Attending to details of this investigation and the reasoning provided by the Law Officers for not disallowing the PRA reveals that the question of imperial intervention was not decided by Britain's lack of jurisdiction in a self-governing colony. Instead, Britain's decision not to disallow the PRA was based on the Colonial Office's subpar investigative efforts as well as Black petitioners' inability to get accurate information onto the desks of the right people in the British governmental machine. Both of these factors point to the role of government control over official communication networks in determining the outcome of imperial citizenship claims. By attending to *how* the imperial government rejected petitions for imperial protection of Black voting rights, I show that the retreat of imperial sovereignty was not as cut and dried as historians assume, and that concerted effort had to be made by key government officials (particularly the governor and the Secretary of State for the Colonies) to prevent imperial intervention.

Equally important to understanding *why* petitions against the PRA failed is understanding *how* the petitioners attempted to convince the imperial government of their right to vote as imperial citizens. Historians of Indigenous performances of imperial citizenship tend to place overwhelming emphasis on rhetorical claims to Britishness. They argue that since imperial citizenship was an abstract concept with no grounding in codified law, claims to imperial citizenship had to be situated within other discourses of reciprocity such as recompense for loyalty to the Empire or assimilation to British culture. The petitioners examined in this chapter, however, combined rhetorics of loyalty and assimilation with legal arguments grounded in constitutional law. This forced the imperial government, in turn, to respond to imperial citizenship claims on a legal basis. Consequently, although imperial citizenship was never codified as an official status, attending to how both petitioners and the imperial government used constitutional law to invoke and deny imperial intervention reveals that imperial citizenship was more than a rhetorical performance. The betrayal of imperial citizenship by the Colonial Office is thus even more brutal and tragic. Rather than dismissing imperial citizenship claims as non-legal make-belief, the Colonial Office and the Cape government deliberately worked together to undermine Black African voting rights in the face of Britain's responsibility to enforce the Constitutional Ordinance of 1853.

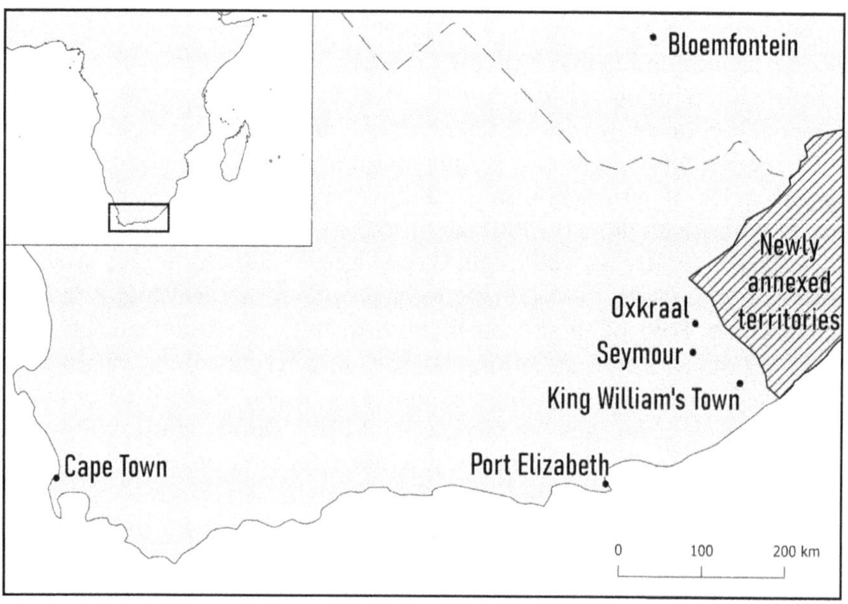

Map 7.1 Parliamentary Registration Act petitions

Debating communal tenure as qualification to vote

On 3 August 1887, the Colonial Office received a long letter from John Tengo Jabavu enclosed in a note from Sir Robert Fowler, MP for the City of London and treasurer of the APS. Jabavu's letter explained that the PRA was "in reality aimed at Disfranchising the natives in the colony," and called for the British government to exercise its imperial authority to disallow the Act.[15] Jabavu held that "the franchise we enjoy was given the natives specially by Her Majesty's Government after the Colonists had denied it to us."[16] As it was Queen rather than the Cape that provided Black Africans with their "sacred rights of citizenship," Jabavu reasoned that it was "the Queen that should take them away."[17] The Colonial Office agreed that the Act was "intended to effect a good deal of practical disfranchisement," and instructed Governor Sir Hercules Robinson "to report fully on the exact effect of this measure as regards Native claimants of the franchise."[18]

Governor Robinson's reply freely admitted that the Act was designed to disenfranchise Black voters, writing that "the effect of this legislation will doubtless be to remove from the lists of voters the names of very many natives."[19] Robinson also freely admitted that doing so was in disagreement with the Constitution Ordinance of 1853, which he acknowledged granted the franchise to every adult male British subject who occupied "any house or other building, either separately, or jointly with any land occupied therewith, of the value of £25."[20] This language, particularly the phrases "any house" and "any land," clearly included property held under tribal or communal tenure. However, Robinson argued that the Act was not *altering* the Constitution Ordinance, but merely *clarifying* the spirit of the Ordinance, which had previously been unwritten. He explained that voting lists had been filled with African voters who used their portion of communally owned land to make up the £25 qualification requirement, and he claimed that "this practice is not in accordance with the intention of the Constitution Ordinance, inasmuch as no definite value can be affixed to the precarious use of land held under such conditions."[21] To defend this claim, he enclosed a report from the Cape Attorney General stating that "where grants of land have been made to communities without naming the individual members thereof or giving any holding or occupation other than in common, it is impossible to affix a definite value ... It was never intended by any legislation in this Colony to encourage so rude and barbarous a system."[22] Robinson thereby argued that the Act was fixing a loophole in the Constitution Ordinance rather than altering the franchise requirements, and disenfranchising only those Africans who had never been intended to have the franchise in the first place.

Problematically, however, Robinson's representations of African land tenure were hotly contested in the Cape Colony. When the Act was debated in the Cape parliament in June 1887, MPs went back and forth on the issue. Critics of the Act argued that communal tenure as existed in the Cape Colony was virtually equivalent to European individual tenure in nearly every respect. Individuals occupied sections of communally owned land for their own exclusive use, their occupied land was inalienable and inheritable, and occupants were entitled to all proceeds of cultivation from their land.[23] They further pointed to interpretations of the Constitution by William Porter, who had been the Attorney General at the time the Constitution was written, which demonstrated that the Constitution had purposefully allowed occupation rather than ownership of land in order to enfranchise Black Africans.[24] Porter had written that:

> If they [Black Africans] have in general little fixed property to protect, they have another sort of property which they should be enabled to protect. They have their labour to protect; they have to protect the right to carry their labour to their own market, and to sell it at their own price; they have to protect right of making the most of whatever powers of mind and body God has given them. They have to protect themselves from oppressive vagrant laws calculated to compel them to do forced work; and, having all this to protect, they have sense enough to know the men who would oppose them if not checked, and the men who would stand up for them and take their part.[25]

Porter had clearly demonstrated that having no fixed property was not meant to be a barrier to voting rights, and that Black Africans had been intended to benefit from the vague language in the Constitution since its inception. As such, opponents in parliament argued that the Act was "a violation of the Constitution Ordinance," which made it liable to disallowance by the imperial government.[26]

Interestingly, proponents of the Act did not directly dispute these claims. Instead, their arguments centred on whether or not Black Africans *deserved* the franchise. Rhodes, for instance, asked parliament if they truly believed "it was right that men in a state of pure barbarism should have the franchise and vote?"[27] He insisted that "the natives did not want it," and that white people ought to stop treating Black people as political equals, but rather "be the lords over them, and let them be a subject race."[28] Some MPs agreed, while others focused on the value of Black property. They argued that "a Kafir hut" was worth next to nothing, being "simply a big eagle's nest, built of grass," and that even if all the land held under communal tenure was divided among all occupants, the plots would be small and of poor quality.[29] According to such logic, "very few native voters would possess the right in these divisions to be registered even on the communal qualification."[30] That such arguments focused on whether Black Africans *should* have the franchise, rather than whether they already had a constitutional right to vote, vividly demonstrates that African land tenure was not really the issue at all, and that the PRA was not about clarifying the original intention of the Constitution. Indeed, even Rhodes, who heartily supported the Act, remarked that "it was a perfect farce to call this Bill an interpretation of the Constitution Ordinance. He preferred to call a spade a spade. This was not an interpretation of the Constitution Ordinance, but the basis upon which the country is to be governed."[31]

Challenging specious arguments

John Tengo Jabavu actively followed these parliamentary debates. He recognized that supporters of the Act were attempting to alter the Constitution to disenfranchise Black voters, and that they were using the language of "clarifying the spirit of the Constitution" and "fixing loopholes" to avoid the imperial veto. He concluded that the best means of protecting the Black franchise was to demonstrate the fallacies behind the Act's pretensions and thereby invoke the imperial government's guarantee of Black voting rights via the Constitution. That is why Jabavu initially wrote the letter to the APS that pushed the Colonial Office into demanding a report from Governor Robinson. However, when Jabavu learned that the Colonial Office had asked Robinson to report on the effects of the Act, he warned the APS that "Sir Hercules Robinson's report will, I have no doubt, be that of his ministers, and they are past masters in duplicity."[32] He therefore took it as his "bounded duty to briefly recapitulate the cardinal points of our case for your benefit so that you may be the better enabled to cope with the specious arguments that will be advanced."[33]

Chief among these cardinal points was the nature of communal tenure. Anticipating Hercules Robinson's claim that communal occupancy did not have a fixed value, Jabavu explained that "it is argued that the white man's land is of money value; the black man's under the tribal or communal tenure, which is secure as any white man's holding, counts for nothing."[34] On the contrary, he asserted that "it ought to be clearly understood that in these reserves each male adult has individual rights to the land on which his house stands, and also to the land he cultivates for his exclusive benefit, and the title, according to native practice, is as strong as the title of any citizen within the London Corporation."[35] Jabavu further wrote that the rights of communal occupancy were "even recognized in Colonial Law Courts either by the right of prescription or under the native law," by which he was referring to an 1883 Government Commission on Native Laws and Customs.[36]

In 1883 the Cape government had conducted an investigation into the nature of land tenure in the newly annexed African districts, and the published report of this investigation determined that under communal tenure "the occupier of any kraal, garden, or plot of land may lawfully sell his right of occupation."[37] The report also recognized that "the rights of occupation to any kraal, garden, or plot of land shall be heritable," demonstrating the government's awareness that occupation under communal tenure was not merely usufructuary but came with rights to perpetual use and occupation akin to ownership under individual tenure.[38] Jabavu was thus pointing out that the Cape government *knew* that communal tenure was just as secure, heritable, and capable of having a fixed value as individual tenure, and that its claims to be fixing a loophole in the Constitution were blatantly false. The APS accepted Jabavu's arguments and on 6 September 1887 forwarded to the Colonial Office further evidence of the suitability of communal tenure to make up the franchise qualification.[39]

A betrayal of imperial citizenship

According to imperial regulations, the Colonial Office was responsible for scrutinizing colonial legislation, but if any legislation potentially required imperial intervention it had to be referred to the Law Officers of the Crown for a final verdict.[40] The Colonial Office accordingly sent the PRA to the law officers on 4 October 1887, and on 17 October the law officers determined that "in our opinion the 17th section of the Act of 1887 is not at variance with the Constitution Ordinance."[41] Armed with the Law Officers' report, the Colonial Office informed Jabavu that the Act would not be disallowed and that stripping voting rights from people who were never meant to have them according to the Constitution "can hardly be called disfranchisement."[42] Jabavu's belief that the imperial government would protect Black voting rights thus turned out to be illusory, yet it is important to understand *why* the imperial government did not intervene. The decisions by the Law Officers and the Colonial Office would seem to indicate that Jabavu's claims regarding the equivalency of communal and individual tenure had been investigated and found unsatisfactory, or that research into the 1853 Constitution had found that communal tenure was not originally intended to count towards qualification. But such was not the case.

On the contrary, the Law Officers were entirely unaware of debates over the nature of communal tenure. The Colonial Office only provided the Law Officers with four documents: the text of the 1853 Constitution, the text of the 1887 PRA, and the two reports from Robinson and Upington making the false claims that communal land could not count towards qualification because it could not be precisely valued. The Law Officers were not provided with Jabavu's letter or accounts of Cape parliamentary debates, and their report mentions nothing about whether or not communal land could be assigned a fixed price or communal title was sufficiently secure to be used in qualification calculations. The only question they considered was whether or not former Attorney General William Porter's opinion – that the Constitution should enable Black people with no property to vote – was enough to justify disallowing the Act. They determined that Porter's opinion was only meant as guidance and was "not put forth or to be received as an authoritative exposition of the law,"[43] essentially deciding that simply because the former Attorney General interpreted the Constitution liberally did not mean that the spirit of the Constitution was liberal.

Jabavu's invocation of imperial protection of Black voting rights in the Cape therefore failed not because the Law Officers refused to recognize his claim upon imperial citizenship, but because they approached his claim without adequate information. The Law Officers held some responsibility for their oversight, but like judges in the courtroom it was their job to evaluate the information presented to them, not to do independent research. The Law Officers could only use the evidence provided by the Colonial Office and the Cape government. Both bodies possessed Jabavu's claims, as well as records of Cape parliamentary debates over communal tenure and official documents such as the 1883 Commission on Native Laws and Customs that contained pertinent information, and yet both provided only those details that supported their own opinions. Consequently, the failure of Jabavu's claim to imperial citizenship lay largely in the structure of imperial government communication, which enabled a select few individuals – particularly governors and Secretaries of State for the Colonies – to control the flow of information within the imperial government.

The manner in which Jabavu's petition was rejected provides valuable insight into the operation of imperial citizenship that previous historical accounts have failed to observe. There is certainly no shortage of historical scholarship on the PA or Jabavu himself, yet none of this scholarship makes more than a passing reference to Jabavu's petition to the Colonial Office. D. R. Edgecombe and Julie Evans *et al.* both mention that Jabavu as well as several other Black organizations and communities petitioned Britain to disallow the Act, but they discuss these petitioners as if they were supplicants who "begged the Queen to withhold her assent" in return for "their loyalty and their long record as allies of the British Government," rather than recognizing their actions and performances of citizenship based upon constitutionally guaranteed rights.[44] Edgecombe and Evans *et al.* also fail to give any indication of what Britain's response was to the petitions. Farai Nyika and Johan Fourie's investigation into the number of Africans disfranchised by the PRA similarly moves from the statement that "Jabavu led a small delegation that entreated the British Crown to veto the Act" to the conclusion that "the Registration Bill was passed" with no consideration whatsoever of the content, impact, or significance of these petitions, not to mention their inaccuracy in that Jabavu never actually brought a delegation to London.[45] Beaurel Visser's examination of Black African resistance efforts provides the most detail on the nature of the debate over the capacity of communal tenure to meet the franchise qualifications, and acknowledges that Jabavu's petitions failed because the Law Officers of the Crown ruled that communal tenure should not qualify towards the franchise.[46] But Visser, too, fails to attend to *why* the Law Officers made this decision, and indeed does not cite any Colonial Office records at all. The chronic inattention to imperial aspects of the history of the PRA reveals the historiographical assumption that petitioning the imperial government was futile when, in reality, Jabavu's petitions were actively investigated and sabotaged by government officials.

Khwezi Mkhize is the only scholar to perceive Jabavu's petition as a performance of imperial citizenship, yet his analysis goes no further than to recognize that Jabavu perceived the 1853 Constitution as "a social contract between the imperial government and the Cape's citizens."[47] Mkhize does not explore how Jabavu went about attempting to convince the imperial government to fulfil its part of the social contract or how the imperial government responded. By focusing on Jabavu's perception of himself as an imperial citizen and not delving into the mechanics of how and why his citizenship claims failed, Mkhize only contributes to scholarly assumptions that imperial citizenship was a fanciful concept based solely upon rhetorical claims based in loyalism, respectability, and Britishness.

On the contrary, a closer examination of Jabavu's petitions disproves the teleological assumption that performances of imperial citizenship were futile. To be fair, many contemporaries of Jabavu were themselves unsure whether Britain retained the authority to interfere in the Cape Colony. For instance, when the *Cape Times* learned that the Secretary of State for the Colonies had not dismissed Jabavu's petition and was investigating the issue, it wrote with a panic and dismay that is worth quoting in full.

> Sir Henry Holland might have said boldly that in matters of internal legislation he would not advise any interference with the discretion of the Cape Parliament. He might have explained to the advocates of native rights that by an understanding with the representatives of the Cape Colony at the recent Conference the Imperial Government virtually abandoned its power of revising the decisions of the Colonial Parliament in strictly domestic questions ... And under this theory the Royal veto would be as obsolete with reference to Colonial as it has long been with reference to Imperial legislation.

> It appears, however, that we have overestimated the extent and value of the new departure. Sir Henry Holland professes to adhere to the strict letter of the Constitution Ordinance; and upon that letter he will shape his course in the somewhat difficult strait now before him.[48]

This excerpt captures the moment that contemporaries in the Cape Colony realized that their self-government was not free from imperial interference, and underscores the importance of appreciating the real possibility that Britain could have acted on Jabavu's petition.

The Colonial Office's investigation into the PRA was a tangible consequence of Jabavu's petition that carried a serious potential for intervention. The influence of the Colonial Office's omission of pivotal information on the Law Officer's judgement that the 1853 Constitution had not protected communal tenure reflects the significance of imperial networks and information flows for the period of transition from imperial to settler administration. The imperial government no longer possessed an untrammelled authority to dictate colonial policies, but neither was it "inconceivable," as Philip Buckner argues, that the British government would act against the decisions of a colonial parliament.[49] Instead, the exercise of imperial sovereignty was contingent upon imperial interpretations of colonial events. And those interpretations were themselves contingent upon governmental communication. Petitions were one method of communicating with the Colonial Office, but the Colonial Office was then free to omit any parts of those petitions as they passed between different government departments. The impotency of petitions suggests that the consolidation of the sovereign settler state in the late nineteenth century was contingent upon the failure of alternative trajectories of continued imperial intervention. The Cape's disfranchisement of Black voters was not a direct result of responsible government, nor did responsible government ensure the passage of the PRA. Instead, the passing of the PRA was determined as much by the bestowal of self-government as by the inability of petitioners to challenge false representations of communal tenure and the 1853 Constitution within government communication networks.

Conclusion

In their now classic book *Drawing the Global Colour Line*, Marilyn Lake and Henry Reynolds contend that the development of exclusionary immigration policies in the settler colonies was a "British betrayal of the idea of imperial citizenship."[50] They describe a series of conflicts in the late nineteenth century between self-governing colonies demanding the right to decide the legal status of their minority populations and a Colonial Office fighting to affirm the principle of non-discriminatory law throughout the Empire. The Colonial Office, they argue, responded to these conflicts "with a mixture of diplomacy, delay and duplicity," sometimes disallowing offensive bills "but usually [giving] way if the colonists were sufficiently determined."[51] Betrayal and duplicity are the perfect descriptors of the Colonial Office's response to petitions against the PRA when it received Jabavu's petition and then withheld it from the Law Officers. Yet the decision to withhold Jabavu's petition goes beyond a simple willingness to allow self-governing colonies to institute racially exclusionary policies. The Colonial Office actively participated in the Cape government's efforts to deny the reality of communal tenure and to violate the Constitution Ordinance of 1853. This betrayal indicates that the failure of imperial citizenship was rooted not only in its lack of codification, but also in its inconvenience to imperial administrators.

While it is easy to explain the Cape government's desire to misrepresent communal tenure and thereby avoid imperial disallowance of the PRA, it is difficult to say why Governor Robinson and the Colonial Office participated in the ruse by withholding crucial information. Lake and Reynolds suggest that the Colonial Office was willing to betray the idea of imperial citizenship because they feared what settlers would do if their claims to sovereignty were denied, and particularly because they feared another American-style revolution.[52] While all-out war between the Cape and Britain was unlikely, the Cape still held economic and demographic leverage that Britain was only too aware of. Duncan Bell and John Darwin demonstrate that, by the mid-nineteenth century, the settler colonies had become "a critical element in British world power," so that during the intense interimperial competitions between 1870 and 1945 the settler colonies "assumed an unprecedented role in British political discourse."[53] It is likely that the Colonial Office's willingness to sabotage Jabavu's petition was a consequence of the larger context of British dependence on settler economic and military contributions during this period.

Regardless of the Colonial Office's motives, its sabotage of Black Africans' constitutional right to vote underscores the reality that invoking imperial intervention was more than a simple matter of sovereignty. Britain had the clear political jurisdiction and, indeed, a constitutional duty to disallow the PRA. The efforts made by the Secretary of State for the Colonies and the governor to manipulate the Law Officers' decision making process to avoid disallowing the Act show that individual perspectives and decisions played an important role in establishing what self-governing colonies could and could not do. Indeed, the findings of this chapter suggest that we can invert the link between the failure of Indigenous petitions to the Empire and colonial self-government: it was not self-government that made petitions fail, it was the failure of petitions that confirmed and entrenched self-government. By forcing the British government to make hard choices about how it was going to govern the settler colonies after self-government, Indigenous petitions instigated the solidification of policies that were previously vague and undetermined.

Notes

1 Cape of Good Hope, *Statutes of the Cape of Good Hope Passed by the Seventh Parliament during Sessions 1884–1888* (W. A. Richards and Sons, 1889), 394.
2 Cape of Good Hope, *Statutes of the Cape of Good Hope, 1652–1886* (Cape Town: W. A. Richards and Sons, 1887), 297.
3 Stanley Trapido, "The Origins of the Cape Franchise Qualifications of 1853," *The Journal of African History* 5, no. 1 (1964): 37–54, DOI: 10.1017/S0021853700004497.
4 Sir Gordon Sprigg in the Cape House of Assembly, 15 June 1887, quoted in D. R. Edgecombe, "The Non-Racial Franchise in Cape Politics, 1853–1910," *African Historical Review* 10, nos 1–2 (1978): 23, DOI: 10.1080/00232087885310031.
5 T. R. H. Davenport and Christopher Saunders, *South Africa: A Modern History* (London: Palgrave Macmillan, 2000), 107–111. See also T. R. H. Davenport, *The Afrikaner Bond: The History of a South African Political Party, 1880–1911* (Oxford: Oxford University Press, 1966).
6 Edgecombe, "The Non-Racial Franchise," 24–25; Stanley Trapido, "'The Friends of the Natives': Merchants, Peasants and the Political and Ideological Structure of Liberalism in the Cape, 1854–1910," in Shula Marks and Anthony Atmore (eds), *Economy and Society in Pre-Industrial South Africa* (London: Longman, 1980), 247–274 (248).
7 Alpheus Todd, *Parliamentary Government in the British Colonies*, 2nd edn (London: Longmans, Green, 1894), 154–159.
8 Farai Nyika and Johan Fourie, "Black Disenfranchisement in the Cape Colony, c. 1887–1909: Challenging the Numbers," *Journal of Southern African Studies* 46, no. 3 (2020): 455–469, DOI: 10.1080/03057070.2020.1741177.
9 Colonial Office minutes, "Jubilee Address," 3 August 1887, The National Archives, London (TNA), CO 48/514, no. 17107; Colonial Office minutes, "Franchise for Natives," 3 August 1887, TNA, CO 48/514, no. 17102; Colonial Office minutes, "Registration Act," 24 August 1887, TNA, CO 48/514, no. 18553; Colonial Office minutes, "Registration Bill," 28 September 1887, TNA, CO 48/514, no. 21190; Colonial Office minutes, "Parl. Voters Registration Bill," 3 August 1887, TNA, CO 48/515, no. 15420.
10 Colonial Office minutes, "Registration Bill," 28 September 1887.
11 "The Native Protest," *Cape Times*, 30 July 1887.
12 J. R. Miller, "Petitioning the Great White Mother: First Nations' Organizations and Lobbying in London," in *Reflections on Native–Newcomer Relations:*

Selected Essays (Toronto: University of Toronto Press, 2004), 217–241 (223); Sarah Carter and Maria Nugent (eds), *Mistress of Everything: Queen Victoria in Indigenous Worlds* (Manchester: Manchester University Press, 2017), 10; Michael Belgrave, *Dancing with the King: The Rise and Fall of the King Country, 1864–1885* (Auckland: Auckland University Press, 2017), 306.

13 Ann Curthoys, "The Dog that Didn't Bark: The Durham Report, Indigenous Dispossession, and Self-Government for Britain's Settler Colonies," in Karen Dubinsky, Adele Perry, and Henry Yu (eds), *Within and without the Nation: Canadian History as Transnational History* (Toronto: University of Toronto Press, 2015), 25–48 (39–40).

14 For examples of such superficial coverage, see Nyika and Fourie, "Black Disenfranchisement"; Edgecombe, "The Non-Racial Franchise"; Beaurel Visser, "African Resistance to the Parliamentary Voters' Registration Act," *Journal of Southern African Studies* 48, no. 6 (2022): 975–991, DOI: 10.1080/03057070.2023.2167392; and Julie Evans, Patricia Grimshaw, and David Phillips, *Equal Subjects, Unequal Rights: Indigenous People in British Settler Colonies, 1830–1910* (Manchester: Manchester University Press, 2003).

15 John Tengo Jabavu to Robert Fowler, 2 July 1887, Oxford, Bodleian Libraries (BodL), MS Brit. Emp. s. 18 C153/154.

16 *Ibid.*

17 John Tengo Jabavu to Frederick Chesson, 15 August 1887, BodL, MS Brit. Emp. s. 18 C139/15.

18 Colonial Office minutes, "Parliamentary Voters Registration Bill," 3 August 1887, TNA, CO 48/515, no. 15420.

19 Colonial Office minutes, "Parly Voters Registration Act," 31 August 1887, TNA, CO 48/515 no. 19036.

20 *Ibid.*

21 *Ibid.*

22 *Ibid.*

23 "Parliamentary Registration Bill," *Cape Argus*, 16 June 1887.

24 "Parliamentary Registration Bill," *Cape Argus*, 24 June 1887.

25 "The Native Vote," *Cape Times*, 16 May 1887.

26 "Parliamentary Registration Bill," *Cape Argus*, 23 June 1887.

27 "Parliamentary Registration Bill," 24 June 1887.

28 *Ibid.*

29 "Parliamentary Registration Bill," *Cape Argus*, 28 June 1887.

30 "Parliamentary Registration Bill," 23 June 1887.

31 "Parliamentary Registration Bill," 24 June 1887.

32 John Tengo Jabavu to Frederick Chesson, 29 August 1887, BodL, MS Brit. Emp. s. 18 C139/16.

33 *Ibid.*

34 *Ibid.*

35 *Ibid.*

36 *Ibid.*

37 Cape of Good Hope Commission on Native Laws and Customs, *Report and Proceedings: With Appendices of the Government Commission on Native Laws and Customs. Presented to Both Houses of Parliament by His Excellency the Governor, January, 1883* (Cape Town: W. A. Richards and Sons, 1883), 41.

38 Cape of Good Hope, *Report and Proceedings*, 41. Recent studies of African communal tenure also demonstrate that occupation conferred ownership rights on families that could only be broken by severance of family ties to the community. See Willemien du Plessis and Juanita Pienaar, "The More Things Change, the More They Stay the Same: The Story of Communal Land Tenure in South Africa," *Fundamina* 16, no. 1 (2010): 73–89, https://journals.co.za/doi/pdf/10.10520/EJC34404 (accessed 11 March 2025).

39 Colonial Office minutes, "Parly Voters Registration Act," 6 September 1887, TNA, CO 48/515 no. 18184.

40 Todd, *Parliamentary Government in the British Colonies*, 137–138.

41 Colonial Office minutes, "Parly Voters Registration Act," 17 October 1887, TNA, CO 48/515, no. 21004.

42 *Ibid.*

43 *Ibid.*

44 Edgecombe, "The Non-Racial Franchise," 29–31; Evans *et al.*, *Equal Subjects, Unequal Rights*, 162–163.

45 Nyika and Fourie, "Black Disenfranchisement," 461.

46 Visser, "African Resistance," 975–991.

47 Khwezi Mkhize, " 'To See Us as We See Ourselves': John Tengo Jabavu and the Politics of the Black Periodical," *Journal of Southern African Studies* 44, no. 3 (2018): 413–430 (428–429), DOI: 10.1080/03057070.2018.1462993.

48 "The Registration Bill," *Cape Times*, 29 August 1887.

49 Phillip Buckner, "The Creation of the Dominion of Canada, 1860–1901," in Phillip Buckner (ed.), *Canada and the British Empire* (Oxford: Oxford University Press, 2010), 66–86 (70).

50 Marilyn Lake and Henry Reynolds, *Drawing the Global Colour Line: White Men's Countries and the International Challenge of Racial Equality* (Cambridge: Cambridge University Press, 2008), 5.

51 *Ibid.*, 124.

52 *Ibid.*, 128.

53 Duncan Bell, *Reordering the World: Essays on Liberalism and Empire* (Princeton: Princeton University Press, 2016), 33–37; John Darwin, *The Empire Project: The Rise and Fall of the British World-System, 1830–1970* (Cambridge: Cambridge University Press, 2009), 11.

8

Indigenous credibility in the imperial metropole: New Zealand, 1882

The 1880s witnessed a revolution in Māori tactics of resistance against settler colonialism in New Zealand. The previous four decades were marked by the New Zealand Land Wars of 1843–1872, in which various Māori iwis conducted a series of interconnected campaigns against settler and imperial forces that resulted in the loss of thousands of Māori lives and millions of acres of territory. With military strength and morale shattered, many Māori communities turned to legal and constitutional avenues of resistance. Over 1,000 petitions were presented to the New Zealand General Assembly in the 1880s alone, and by 1892, a separate Māori parliament called Te Kotahitanga was established to rival the authority of the New Zealand parliament.[1] A crucial element of this constitutional and legal revolution in resistance politics was its imperial scale. Calling upon the Treaty of Waitangi of 1840, signed with the British Crown, many Māori looked to the imperial government as a treaty partner to recognize and respect Māori sovereignty against encroachment by the New Zealand settler government. Three separate petitions were presented to Queen Victoria in 1882, 1883, and 1884 to uphold Britain's obligations towards the Māori according to the Treaty of Waitaingi: one from the Ngāpuhi iwi, one from the four Māori members of the House of Representatives, and one from the Waikato iwi. The petitions of 1882 and 1884 were brought to Britain in person by delegations from each iwi at great expense, demonstrating the investment made in invoking imperial authority as a form of resistance against settler colonialism.

Bringing the petitions to Britain in person enabled Māori petitioners to take control of their own narrative and sidestep the power that settler and imperial government officials exerted over imperial communication explored in previous chapters. However, while personal delegations could overcome some of the limitations of petitioning by post, they also came with unique vulnerabilities of their own, particularly that of personal credibility. Delegates are politically powerful figures because they are able to represent the collective views and opinions of a much larger group of people, but only to the extent that they are perceived as representative of that group. It was therefore crucial for Māori delegates to be able to convince British audiences that they

Map 8.1 Māori petitions in 1882, 1883, and 1884

possessed the backing and support of their iwis back home, and it was equally crucial for the New Zealand government to undermine the delegates' credibility in order to prevent the imperial government interfering in its affairs. This chapter explores how Māori delegates and the New Zealand government went about establishing and sabotaging credibility, focusing on the 1882 delegation. As will be seen, Māori delegates used various tactics to establish their credibility, ranging from giving ceremonial gifts and presenting evidence of collective support to piggy-backing off the social capital of the Aborigines' Protection Society (APS). The New Zealand government, too, used a variety of sabotage tactics, from attacking the validity of the Treaty of Waitangi to spreading false rumours about the delegates themselves. Attending to this battle over Māori delegate credibility highlights the extralegal element behind invoking imperial authority, wherein legality and constitutionality could, in practice, be less important than personality and perception in determining if and how imperial citizenship would be recognized.

The 1882 Ngāpuhi petition

In 1882, seven rangatira (hereditary political leaders) of the Ngāpuhi iwi of northern New Zealand deputed a man named Hirini "Sydney" Taiwhanga to present a petition on the behalf of the Ngāpuhi to Queen Victoria. Son of an important chief and missionary, Taiwhanga studied in mission and theological schools and worked for the first forty years of his life variously as a carpenter, sailor, surveyor, and teacher around the Bay of Islands, New Zealand.[2] Throughout these years, Taiwhanga gained experience in petitioning for redress of personal grievances against the New Zealand government, and this experience (in addition to his fluency in English) led him to become a frequent amanuensis and lobbyist for the Ngāpuhi in the 1870s and 1880s.[3] This history strengthened Taiwhanga's standing among the Ngāpuhi as a passionate and articulate advocate, while simultaneously solidifying his reputation among the settler population as a troublemaker. The duality of his personal reputation became critical to the success or failure of his delegation to Britain, with the British public having to choose which narrative to believe.

Taiwhanga's petition to Queen Victoria contained three requests, each corresponding to longstanding Māori grievances against the New Zealand government, and each rooted in the Treaty of Waitangi. Signed in 1840 between the British government and over 500 rangatira from across New Zealand, the Treaty of Waitangi has been interpreted variously over the past two centuries as the founding document of both pakeha (White New Zealander) sovereignty and also Britain's guarantee of Māori independence. It has been assumed since Ruth Ross's seminal work in the 1970s that these contradictory interpretations are the result of manipulative discrepancies between English and Māori translations of the Treaty,[4] although it is also important to recognize that the Colonial Office's understanding of sovereignty in 1840 was not mutually exclusive with sovereign pluralism, and both translations of the Treaty could have been equally valid at the time of its signing.[5] Regardless, the Māori version of the Treaty guaranteed the continuation of "te tino rangatiratanga," variously translated as sovereignty, self-determination, or chiefly autonomy, as well as the unqualified possession of their lands.[6] The Ngāpuhi in the 1870s and 1880s determined that the New Zealand government had violated these guarantees.

A Ngāpuhi mass meeting in 1881 outlined three specific grievances: land rights, fishing rights, and dog taxes.[7] Land was the foremost issue: the Native Land Courts established in 1865 had facilitated a massive alienation of Māori land amounting to over 3 million acres, and Public Work Acts of 1864 and 1876 had empowered the New Zealand government to take land for public development without Māori consent. Fishing rights were the second issue, with the 1877 Fisheries Act downgrading Māori rights to foreshores from possession to usage. The third issue was the imposition of a dog tax in 1880, against the protests of Māori political leaders. Dogs are *tapu* (of sacred significance) within Māori societies. Economically they were central to hunting practices and their meat was also a key source of protein, while culturally dogs play an important role in Māori cosmology. For settlers, on the other hand, Māori dogs were pests that preyed upon sheep. Imposing a tax to reduce the dog population thus signified the prioritization of settler capitalism over Māori subsistence and culture, and would eventually lead to the Dog Tax Rebellion of 1898.[8] Observing that the confiscation of land, the rejection of fishing rights, and the attack on Māori culture constituted violations of the Treaty of Waitangi's guarantee of Māori self-determination, the Ngāpuhi drafted three demands that became the three requests of their petition. First, they asked that a separate Māori parliament be established for the Māori to govern themselves. Second, they asked for the repeal of all laws contrary to the spirit of the Treaty of Waitangi. And third, they asked for the return of all land confiscated against the spirit of the Treaty of Waitangi.[9]

Taiwhanga was elected at a public meeting to present this petition to Queen Victoria on the behalf of the Ngāpuhi and, with funds provided by senior Ngāpuhi chief Parore Te Āwha, travelled to England along with two fellow delegates in June 1882.[10] However, the New Zealand government had mobilized to sabotage his mission before he even arrived in London. On 4 May an officer from the New Zealand native department reported to the Minister of Native Affairs that Taiwhanga had been chosen to bring a petition to England, and suggested that a report should be sent to the New Zealand Agent-General in London, Sir Francis Dillon Bell, detailing how Taiwhanga was a "thoroughly imprincipled [*sic*] man."[11] Consequently, the government solicited reports from two witnesses who were certain to denigrate Taiwhanga's character: James Clendon and Edward Williams, a magistrate and a judge of the Native Land Court who had confiscated Taiwhanga's land in 1876 (in contradiction of the Treaty of Waitangi) and forcibly evicted him and his family.[12]

Williams refused to write such a report because he "could not give an unbiased one,"[13] but Clendon happily wrote at length that Taiwhanga was the son of a "fourth-rate" chief who conducted "nefarious transactions" as a surveyor, was "the principal cause of all the disturbances at Kaikohe," and was "a perfect exemplification of education wasted."[14] Such personal attacks on Taiwhanga's character were bigoted, to be sure, but they were nonetheless honest from Clendon's perspective. Clendon had encountered Taiwhanga several times previously as a magistrate, often in contexts in which Taiwhanga was resisting settler encroachment on Māori land. For example, in 1881 Clendon had arrested Taiwhanga because the latter had refused to be illegally evicted from his house.[15] It is therefore unsurprising that Clendon, an important cog in the wheel of the settler colonial project, should think so little of an Indigenous person devoted to resisting settler colonialism.

However, Clendon went beyond personal defamation to spread unsubstantiated allegations about the validity of Taiwhanga's petition that he certainly knew were false. In particular, Clendon claimed that the petition brought to England was a forgery compiled by Taiwhanga alone and did not represent wider Māori opinion, which was demonstrably untrue.[16] Māori mass meetings at Orakei, Waitangi, and Waimate in 1881 and 1882 discussed in detail the very same grievances outlined in the petition, and passed resolutions mirroring its demands, disproving the claim that the petition was a forgery or was in any way not supported by the Ngāpuhi.[17] Some concern about the sending of a representative to England did surface at these meetings, but only because of the cost associated with such a mission, not because of disagreement over Taiwhanga's character or the validity of his grievances. Moreover, minutes from the 1882 meeting at Waimate explicitly state that

> after a lengthy korero [discussion] a resolution was brought before the runauga nui [great council] to raise subscriptions with a view to send home a delegate to Her Imperial Majesty Queen Victoria, with a petition showing the grievances under which the natives are labouring, and to urge Her Majesty to hear and grant its prayer. A ballot for delegates was then taken, and it resulted in the choice of the irrepressible Sydney [Hirini] Taiwhanga.[18]

By showing that there was a consensus vote to send Taiwhanga to England, this excerpt disproves Clendon's claim that Taiwhanga was acting on his own behalf and did not represent wider Māori grievances. Moreover, Clendon was certainly aware of these facts. These mass meetings were well attended by government officials who took careful notes of proceedings, and they were also widely reported on in New Zealand newspapers. Images of these mass meetings were so popular as to reach British newspapers as well.[19] It is inconceivable that a magistrate and judge on the Native Lands Court would have been ignorant of the meetings, and the blatantly false claims made in his report are more convincingly construed as deliberate attempts to thwart the Colonial Office's investigation through libel.

In London, Sir Francis Dillon Bell used Clendon's report "to belittle the appeal and discredit the petitioners," but without effect.[20] The Secretary of State for the Colonies, Lord Kimberley, agreed to hear the petition on 17 July, and he made no reference to Taiwhanga's character or representativeness of Ngāpuhi opinion. Indeed, when Taiwhanga told Lord Kimberley that he "came on behalf of the natives generally, and not on account of a special grievance," Kimberley accepted the claim without comment.[21] Claudia Orange argues that Taiwhanga's petition "failed completely" at the 17 July meeting, since Lord Kimberley "firmly denied any responsibility on the part of the British Crown or government," but that is not entirely accurate.[22] What Lord Kimberley actually said was that "without communication with the New Zealand Government he could say nothing in the matter," and that "full information will be obtained here of the state of affairs in New Zealand."[23] Far from signalling a failure or a repudiation of responsibility, this interview marked the beginning of an imperial investigation into the validity of Taiwhanga's petition and a protracted battle over the representation of his character and trustworthiness. There is some indication that Bell's propaganda against Taiwhanga had already convinced a number of the Colonial Office staff to ignore the petition. Evelyn Ashley, Undersecretary of State for the Colonies, opined in a private memo that "these Māories should not be treated as representative men but as private individuals. I think it is clear that they have come 'on their own work' to use a vulgar but expressive sentence. And they are not men of importance."[24] This statement was clearly influenced by the propaganda emanating from Bell. Nevertheless, Lord Kimberley wrote to the New Zealand government a week later asking for full reports on the matter,[25] showing the Colonial Office's willingness to investigate Taiwhanga's grievances and contemplate further action.

Cross-cultural diplomatic gifts

The New Zealand government's attacks on Taiwhanga's character did not cause Kimberley to reject the petition immediately, but he did refuse to allow Taiwhanga to meet Queen Victoria. Internal memos reveal that the Colonial Office itself was at first amenable to setting up a royal interview, and proposed to send the delegation to Osbourne House via the public ferry at Southampton.[26] But Sir Francis Dillon Bell's lobbying led the Colonial Office to change its mind, with Undersecretary the Hon. Evelyn Ashley relaying to Lord Kimberley that "in conversation with me here he [[Bell] was very decidedly against the Queen receiving the Māories," and Lord Kimberley concluded that it would be too impolitic to ignore Bell's protests for a second time.[27] This decision greatly distressed the Māori delegates, who had come in person to Britain not just to present a petition but to exchange gifts with Queen Victoria, their treaty partner. When the APS had first forwarded the Māori petition to the Colonial Office they had not fully grasped the significance of these gifts, mentioning only in passing that "we may add besides the memorial to which we have referred, they have brought native presents for Her Majesty."[28] But when the delegates learned that there would be no opportunity to present their gifts, they became "greatly exercised on this subject," and the APS relayed to the Colonial Office that the delegates "will not go until this question is settled."[29]

Taiwhanga's distress stemmed from the significance of gift exchange within Māori culture, a significance that the Colonial Office did not seem to understand. Gift exchange has, of course, been an integral element of global diplomatic cultures for centuries, and many historians point to the importance of gifts in forging and maintaining relationships in imperial and colonial spaces.[30] An overarching theme within the historiography of gift diplomacy is the danger of divergent cultural understandings of gift exchange leading to misinterpretations of the meaning of cross-cultural gifts, and this was a particular problem for Māori–British diplomacy. British imperial officials engaged extensively in gift exchange with many Indigenous groups around the world primarily as a means of securing loyalty and goodwill,[31] but Māori cultures imbue gifting with additional spiritual and intimate sacredness that most British observers did not appreciate. Within Māori cosmology, all objects possess an energy or life force known as *hau*, which is inherently reciprocal, and to gift an object is to establish a covenant to nurture its *hau* and reciprocate in the future. Ngāruahine scholar Amber Nicholson describes *hau* as "a spiritual force impelling behaviour – an ethic of reciprocity," and this notion is a central element of Māori politics and diplomacy.[32] Gifting between Māori iwis was the standard way of forging alliances and settling disputes, and the Treaty of Waitangi itself was conceptualized as a gift exchange by which Māori signatories gifted certain governance rights to the British Crown in return for the gift of recognizing Māori land and political rights as British subjects.[33] The Colonial Office did not share the same perspective on the sacred political implications of gifts, and largely saw Taiwhanga's offerings as trivial affirmations of loyalty that did not require the Queen's presence. Consequently, Lord Kimberley's refusal to allow the delegation an opportunity to present their gifts was probably not intended to give offence, but nevertheless represented a refusal to continue the reciprocal diplomatic relationship between Crown and Māori.

Moreover, the particular gifts brought to London represented specific political concepts within Māori culture. It is very difficult to determine the exact significance of the gifts, which is typically expressed through unique patterns or signatures on the objects themselves. I have been unable to find provenance connecting any Māori artefacts held in British or New Zealand collections to Taiwhanga's visit,[34] so I have no information on the unique patterns or signatures on the objects. But Taiwhanga did provide a brief description of the gifts to the APS that offers some hints towards their basic significance. The gifts included two whalebone clubs (*patu parāroa*), two greenstone clubs (*mere pounamu*), four baskets of woven flax (*kete*), and three mats of woven flax and kiwi feathers (*whariki*). The delegates had also intended to give the Queen a tie and a pair of stockings that they had previously worn. Each of these objects carried cultural symbolism and political connotations that contextualize the significance of gifting them to the Crown. Whalebone clubs (*patu parāroa*) and greenstone clubs (*mere pounamu*) are both associated with chiefly power and authority.[35] Flax (*harakeke*) is often used as a metaphor for relationships and interconnection, and flax baskets (*kete*) are associated with wisdom.[36] Flax and kiwi feather mats (*whariki*) are associated with diplomacy, communication, and politics.[37] And gifting personal clothing is a longstanding demonstration of respect in Māori culture, often performed for important visitors or chiefs on formal occasions.[38] Taiwhanga referenced this practice by calling his gift of clothes a love token for the Queen, but one of Taiwhanga's British philanthropist friends named Charlotte Weale (who is the focus of the next chapter) secretly destroyed his pieces of clothing before handing the gifts over to the Colonial Office, believing them unfit royal presents.[39] Thus, although it is impossible to identify the exact meaning of these particular gifts, their general context and connotations are quite clear. Gifting the items to the Crown was a recognition of Queen Victoria's chiefly authority, wisdom, and ongoing diplomatic relations with the Māori, and an attempt to establish a *hau* obligation of reciprocity to recognize Māori self-determination.

Overturning Lord Kimberley's decision to refuse these gifts was one of the few successes of Taiwhanga's alliance with the APS. Taiwhanga explained to the APS that presenting the gifts to Queen Victoria was a critical element of his diplomatic strategy, and the APS relayed to Lord Kimberley that "if they take back the presents to New Zealand the natives will suppose that the Queen has rejected them, and much bad blood will ensue."[40] There was some pushback from within the Colonial Office, with Undersecretary Ashley suggesting that the gifts should be refused "if the Queen's acceptance of these presents could imply a recognition of their having been sent by any large body of Māoris."[41] But Lord Kimberley ultimately agreed to pass them on to Queen Victoria, who sent confirmation that she had received the gifts and was "much pleased."[42] This miniature episode over Māori presents to the Crown demonstrates on a small scale the indeterminate outcomes of Indigenous petitions in this period. New Zealand's Agent-General at first succeeded in blocking the exchange of gifts, but rather than accepting this outcome Taiwhanga continued to lobby through the APS and utilized their social capital to change Lord Kimberley's mind. This framework of contestation between New Zealand government officials and Taiwhanga via the APS continued throughout the Colonial Office's investigation of the petition.

Lord Kimberley's investigation

The investigation was problematically biased from the outset, because the Colonial Office relied on the same government sources that had been responsible for the initial disinformation about Taiwhanga's petition and credibility. When Lord Kimberley demanded a full report from the New Zealand government, Governor Sir William Jervois delegated the task to Prime Minister Fred Whitaker, and Whitaker commissioned reports from none other than James Clendon and Edward Williams, the same people who had been approached to defame Taiwhanga prior to his arrival in England. Williams once again declined to comment citing lack of objectivity,[43] but Clendon was happy to reiterate all he had already said. He recapitulated Taiwhanga's poor moral character and the false claim that "the petition Hirini represented as conveying the complaints of his countrymen was his own ... and was totally different from the draft petition he had exhibited."[44] This time Clendon went even further than his earlier defamation, and alleged that he had evidence proving Taiwhanga had not actually been elected by the Ngāpuhi.

> I made some enquiries and was informed by "Te Hatene," "Maihi Rawiti" and several other chiefs that "Hirini"'s visit to England was entirely on his own account. That he had not been chosen by the natives as their "delegate," neither had any subscription, whatever, been raised to defray his expenses, beyond a few pounds from his near relatives and friends, in fact they all stated that a person, or persons of more ability and position than "Hirini Taiwhanga" would have been elected, had the native people desired to send "representatives" to England.[45]

All of this was simply hearsay, as Clendon never provided any supporting evidence, but similar statements were made by Frederick Manning, the judge of the Native Lands Court responsible for stripping Taiwhanga of his surveying licence. Manning said of Taiwhanga that "I have only known him as a scheming unprincipled native and notorious mischief maker."[46] Manning also claimed that "I do not think at present that the 'mission' can be said to represent seriously any well defined party having serious or determinately defined views," and "as to the Petition itself, the principle remark I have to make is that I am perfectly certain that Taiwhanga himself does not believe one word of the allegations made in it from beginning to end."[47] Just as with Clendon's earlier defamations, however, these claims that Taiwhanga's petition did not represent Ngāpuhi opinion and that he was not deputed to England with the consent of the Ngāpuhi community were demonstrably false. Widespread reporting of Ngāpuhi support for the petition and for Taiwhanga as delegate during mass meetings at Orakei, Waitangi, and Waimate in 1881 and 1882 rendered these claims groundless.

In addition to the reports submitted as part of Kimberley's official investigation, various New Zealand government officials and public personalities tried to publicly discredit Taiwhanga's delegation. Sir William Fox, member of the New Zealand parliament between 1855 and 1881, attacked the delegation in a paper read in his absence at the Royal Colonial Institute. Fox despaired that Britain was too ignorant of Māori history to properly respond to the delegation, and was particularly concerned that Britons would uncritically believe the delegation's protests against infractions of the Treaty of Waitangi. Fox alleged that the Māori delegation could not be trusted to know "anything at all about the treaty," while the British press "was not much better informed."[48] He set out to educate Britain on what he believed was the true nature of the Treaty, namely, that it was worthless. "The right of the Crown to the islands of New Zealand," he proclaimed, "does not rest on the Treaty of Waitangi; it rests on the discovery by Captain Cook in 1769."[49] Consequently, the Treaty could not be understood as creating any obligation to the Māori on Britain's part in return for sovereignty of the soil, since Britain was already the sovereign by right of discovery when the Treaty was written. Moreover, even if the Treaty was to be taken seriously when it was first signed, it had long been nullified, because "it was flagrantly broken through by Honi Heke and a portion of the Ngāpuhi tribe, who took up arms against the Queen in 1844."[50] Fox therefore argued that Taiwhanga's protests against infringements of the Treaty of Waitangi could not be taken seriously.

Nearly the entire audience at the Royal Colonial Institute agreed with Fox. Sir Charles Clifford, a retired member of the New Zealand parliament, argued that the Treaty was "a sham, a delusion, and a snare."[51] The bishop of Nelson said that the Treaty was "practically almost as far off as the Magna Carta or Doomsday Book,"[52] implying that it was no longer relevant to contemporary politics. Charles Pharazyn, an elderly member of the New Zealand Legislative Council, opined that "we hear treaties spoken of as if treaties could be made with a lot of savages. The treaty read this evening shows what it was written on to be mere waste paper."[53] But the audience also went further than Fox, disparaging the Māori delegates themselves as well as the treaty they based their demands upon. The bishop of Nelson argued that the delegates had no authority to speak on the behalf of the Māori, as they "represented only the minority; that at a large meeting of chiefs the majority had determined not to send a mission here."[54] Pharazyn, on the other hand, directly attacked Taiwhanga with a list of his immoral antecedents, prompting laughter from the audience with a quip that "it is hardly to be wondered at that he was not introduced to the Queen."[55] These attacks from Fox, Clifford, Pharazyn, and the bishop of Nelson substantiated those included in Kimberley's official investigation, creating the illusion that everyone in New Zealand disparaged Taiwhanga's delegation. Of course, in reality, these attacks only represented settler points of view, as neither Kimberley's investigation nor the discussion at the Royal Colonial Institute included any Māori voices. It therefore came down to the delegates themselves to defend their credibility.

Taiwhanga's anti-disinformation campaign

There was little the delegates could do in defence of their credibility while in Britain awaiting a response to their petition. It took many months for reports to work their way through the postal system from New Zealand to the Colonial Office. Taiwhanga and his fellow delegates ran out of funds after supporting themselves in London for three whole months and had to return home in September 1882, but it was not until February 1883 that Lord Kimberley came to a final decision in response to the petition. Thus, rather than directly countering the allegations against his credibility, Taiwhanga's strategy was to rebuild his reputation in Britain before going on a second delegation. Locally, he worked to solidify his reputation among the settler community by writing letters to newspapers in defence of his character. He responded to Pharazyn's attack at the Royal Colonial Institute by countering that Pharazyn was one of the "land sharks, the land rings, and land robbers" who would say anything to obtain more land.[56] He also responded to allegations against his personal character by stating that such allegations were made "without proved [*sic*] or foundation contrary to the provisions of both Acts Libel and Defamation of character."[57] At the same time as he was defending his character locally, Taiwhanga was also trying to establish his reputation in Britain. He did this by working to capitalize on the APS's social capital, hoping that if he could get the society to vouch for him as a legitimate Māori representative, he would be able to nullify any allegations the New Zealand government might mobilize against him.

On two different occasions he explained his intention by working through the APS to "give Sir D. Bell and others here no chance of passing any more remarks as they did to me last time,"[58] and specifically "to prevent Sir D. Bell and Lady Martin stating I am no rank at all and I am also an antecedents character [*sic*]."[59] To do this, Taiwhanga repeatedly emphasized to the APS how much support he had from Māori people across the colony. Sometimes this involved providing corroborating evidence from local newspapers, as when Taiwhanga wrote that "I enclose you five Whanganui newspapers you will see all the Māoris greatly supporting me to revisit England with the Petition."[60] At other times, Taiwhanga pointed to the amount of money raised as evidence of widespread Māori support, highlighting that "all the chiefs and tribes up now as one man, greatly supporting the second visit to England ... willing to sacrifice any money to send me."[61] More often, Taiwhanga attempted to establish his representativeness of Māori opinion by detailing the democratic processes behind his petitions. Just after arriving back in New Zealand, Taiwhanga informed the APS that

> the whole of Ngāpuhi tribe[']s collecting (£100) pounds to defray my expenses for travelling to each tribe of New Zealand to consult with them to sign a petition which our committee intends to present to the Queen ... If I succeed with the signing of the petition, then we going to have a great meeting of all the head chiefs of each tribe, into one place to appoint one or more of our numbers for bearers of the petition to England.[62]

In so doing, Taiwhanga illustrated that any petition he might bring in the future would be based upon widespread consultation and consensus. Following this consultation process, Taiwhanga informed the APS that he had obtained 8,500 signatures on his new petition,[63] and that at a great meeting between rival iwis the Ngāpuhi had secured a union in support of his petition, for which "the whole meeting and the whole assembly all agreeable as one man, and there was a loud applause and clasping of hands."[64] Set within the context of the New Zealand government's disinformation against Taiwhanga's representativeness and his own intention to prevent such remarks being made again, these assertions of widespread Māori support can be understood as
efforts to counter future disinformation through the APS's information network.

Unfortunately, Taiwhanga never did make it back to England and the APS never had another opportunity to mobilize the counterarguments that Taiwhanga provided them with. Two further Māori petitions were sent to the British government at the same time as Taiwhanga was preparing his second trip, one in 1883 from the four Māori members of the House of Representatives and one in 1884 from Tāwhiao, king of the Waikato iwi. The New Zealand government played the exact same disinformation game in response to these petitions as well, claiming that the 1883 petition "bears ample internal evidence that it does not contain [Māori] sentiments and cannot really have emanated from them."[65] It again argued that Tāwhiao, the petitioner in 1884, should "only [be] received [by the] Imperial Government [as a] New Zealand subject [of the] Queen. [He] does not represent more than one thousand natives."[66] Neither of these claims was true, and the APS used some of the information provided by Taiwhanga to refute them. For instance, the APS pointed out that Tāwhiao did have broad-based support, since "the expenses of his mission have been defrayed by contribution from tribes living in all parts of the colony,"[67] a detail previously emphasized by Taiwhanga. But the majority of Taiwhanga's counterarguments were specific to himself and could not be leveraged against the disinformation targeting the 1883 and 1884 petitions, and both eventually fell victim to misrepresentation.

Conclusion

It is difficult to say definitively why the 1882 Ngāpuhi petition to Queen Victoria did not receive the Colonial Office's support. Claudia Orange emphasizes the role of New Zealand's status as a responsible government, arguing that "Britain had no right to intrude in the affairs of a self-governing colony and was unable to do so."[68] Michael Belgrave, on the other hand, counters that Britain did have the authority to intervene in Māori affairs via Section 71 of the New Zealand Constitution Act, which empowered the British government to install separate Māori self-government and to pass legislation for that purpose without the consent of the responsible government.[69] Belgrave therefore suggests that "it did appear that there was a middle ground, a constitutional place where Māori demands for self-government could possibly be met."[70] To explain why this middle ground did not come to fruition, Belgrave points to arguments made by the New Zealand government (primarily the Attorney General and Prime Minister, Robert Stout) that Section 71 was created in the 1850s to be temporary and was no longer practicable. However, these arguments were made in 1884 in response to a later delegation, and no discussion of Section 71 took place during Taiwhanga's 1882 delegation. Instead, as this chapter has explored, the bulk of discussion about the 1882 delegation concerned how far it represented Māori opinion back in New Zealand. Thus, although there are no documents in which Lord Kimberley explicitly credits credibility as a deciding factor, it nevertheless appears likely that the extensive efforts of the New Zealand government to undermine the delegation's credibility as representatives of the Ngāpuhi had a material effect on the Colonial Office's response.

The centrality of credibility in the imperial government's response to the 1882 delegations reflects the very similar programme of signature veracity in the history of mass petitioning. Mass petitions, similar in concept to delegations, enable people to concentrate the collective authority of a large group into one smaller unit, in this case, a piece of paper. Susan Zaeske argues that women in the United States transformed their political identities "from that of subjects to that of citizens" by moving away from "individual prayers regarding personal grievances" to large-scale collective petitions with millions of signatures to substantiate their political authority.[71] Yet collective petitioning also invited scepticism about the veracity of signatures, and as Richard Huzzey and Henry Miller detail, signatures were often disputed as being forged, written by young children, or written under pressure or duress.[72] Such disputes plagued the mass petitions signed by Cape Colonists discussed in Chapter 6, such as when an angry father wrote to the Cape Government that "a certain petition, about to be presented to you from some of the inhabitants of this place, has been signed by about 50 pupils attending a school known as the Paarl Gymnasium. Among the number is my own son, 11 years of age. The master of his class recommended him to sign ... I would further beg to be allowed to withdraw the signature."[73] Indeed, when the four Māori members of the New Zealand House of Representatives sent a petition with each of their signatures to the imperial government in 1883, the New Zealand government responded that the signatures appeared fake and "cannot really have emanated from them."[74]

Delegations offered an alternative means of channelling collective authority, enabling petitioners to avoid scepticism of signature veracity by drawing authority from an important community leader chosen to represent the collective. Yet as this chapter demonstrates, the authority of a community leader was difficult to transmit across cultures and vast differences. Indigenous delegates needed not only to possess authority from their constituents, but also to be recognized as possessing that authority. And just as Indigenous scholars in other contexts have aptly demonstrated, relying on recognition by imperial or colonial authorities ultimately places the balance of power in imperial and colonial hands.[75] By sending a relatively unknown delegate with no status symbols recognizable to British audiences, the Ngāpuhi forced Britons to rely on the New Zealand government to provide context as to who Taiwhanga was and whom he represented.

Seemingly learning from this experience, another Māori delegation would be sent to Britain in 1884 headed by King Tāwhiao, a powerful political figure with monarchical credentials immediately recognizable by British audiences. However, as Charles Reed demonstrates, King Tāwhiao failed to be recognized in Britain as a serious political agent because he lacked the markers of European respectability that Taiwhanga had possessed. The London press ridiculed Tāwhiao for calling himself a king when his shabby clothes, tattooed face, and rude behaviour seemed so clearly to demonstrate his "savageness." "Despite the decidedly modern nature and method of Tāwhiao's claims, he could only be understood as an exotic exhibition or relic of the past rather than a vehicle for modern politics."[76] Zoë Laidlaw points out that Indigenous peoples in Britain were caught in a double bind when it came to being perceived as either too civilized to be authentically Indigenous or too uncivilized to be taken seriously, a bind that Tāwhiao certainly got caught up in.[77] However, as this chapter demonstrates, there was also a double bind when it came to being perceived as a credible representative of Indigenous communities. Tāwhiao appeared "savage" enough to be recognized as a representative of "savages," but he was too "savage" to be recognized as a political agent. Taiwhanga, on the other hand, was recognized as modern enough to be a political agent, but his modernity made his motives suspicious and undermined his ability to be perceived as a representative of popular Māori opinion. Whether in terms of unrecognized respectability on Tawhaio's part or unrecognized credibility on Taiwhanga's, the dependence of Indigenous delegations on British recognition was yet another limiting factor that seemingly doomed their invocations of imperial authority.

Notes

1 Claudia Orange, *The Treaty of Waitangi* (Wellington: Allen & Unwin, 1987), 186–190.

2 Claudia Orange, "Taiwhanga, Hirini Rāwiri," In *Dictionary of New Zealand Biography*, 1993, https://teara.govt.nz/en/biographies/2t4/taiwhanga-hirini-rawiri (accessed 11 March 2025).

3 For examples of Taiwhanga's early petitions, see Hirini Taiwhanga to Donald McLean, 28 May 1873, Wellington, Archives New Zealand (ANZ), Taiwhanga's papers, N.O. 83/102; "Petition Regarding Native Schools Act, 1867," 29 June 1876, in New Zealand, *Appendix to the Journals of the House of Representatives*, 1876, Session 1, J-04; "Petition of Hirini Taiwhanga," 17 September 1878, in New Zealand, *Appendix to the Journals of the House of Representatives*, 1878, I-3; and Hirini Taiwhanga to William Rolleston, 23 March 1881, ANZ, Taiwhanga's papers, N.O. 81/934.

4 See Rachael Bell, "'Texts and Translations': Ruth Ross and the Treaty of Waitangi," *New Zealand Journal of History* 43, no. 1 (2009): 39–58, www.nzjh.auckland.ac.nz/docs/2009/NZJH_43_1_03.pdf (accessed 11 March 2025).

5 Andrew McIndoe, "A Pluralistic Imperialism? Britain's Understanding of Sovereignty at the Signing of Treaty of Waitangi," *Auckland University Law Review* 21 (2015): 60–85, www.nzlii.org/nz/journals/AukULawRw/2015/5.pdf (accessed 11 March 2025).

6 Orange, *The Treaty of Waitangi*, 40–42.

7 *Ibid.*, 185–200.

8 Catherine Cumming, "The Hokianga Dog Tax Uprising," *Counterfutures* 11 (2021): 19–23, DOI: 10.26686/cf.v11.7351.

9 Māori petition to Queen Victoria, in John Wodehouse, earl of Kimberley, to Arthur Gordon, 8 August 1882, in British House of Commons, *Correspondence Respecting Native Affairs in New Zealand, and the Imprisonment of Certain Māories, Presented to Both Houses of Parliament by Command of Her Majesty August 1882* (London: Eyre and Spottiswoode, 1882), 287–289.

10 "Bay of Islands," *Thames Advertiser*, 29 March 1882.
11 Thomas William Lewis to John Bryce, 4 May 1882, ANZ, Taiwhanga's papers, N.O. 82/1586.
12 Hirini Taiwhanga to James Clendon, 10 August 1880, ANZ, Taiwhanga's papers, N.O. 81/502; Taiwhanga to Rolleston, 23 March 1881.
13 Edward Williams to W. Morpeth, 31 May 1882, ANZ, Taiwhanga's papers, N.O. 82/1654.
14 James Clendon to W. Morpeth, 31 May 1882, ANZ, Taiwhanga's papers, N.O. 82/1586.
15 Taiwhanga to Rolleston, 23 March 1881.
16 Clendon to Morpeth, 31 May 1882.
17 "The Native Meeting at Waitangi," *New Zealand Herald*, 25 March 1881; "The Opening of the Great Native Meeting at Waitangi," *New Zealand Herald*, 24 March 1881; "The Orakei Parliament," *New Zealand Herald*, 23 March 1881; "The Orakei Parliament," *New Zealand Herald*, 22 March 1881; "The Orakei Parliament," *New Zealand Herald*, 21 March 1881; "The Orakei Parliament," *New Zealand Herald*, 14 March 1881; "The Māori Parliament," *New Zealand Herald*, 12 March 1881.
18 "Bay of Islands."
19 "New Zealand Sketches: The Maori Parliament at Orakei," *Illustrated London News*, 4 December 1880.
20 Orange, *The Treaty of Waitangi*, 207.
21 "The Māori Land Question," *The Standard*, 18 July 1882.
22 Orange, *The Treaty of Waitangi*, 207.
23 "The Māori Land Question," *The Standard*, 18 July 1882.
24 Colonial Office minutes, "The Māori Presents to the Queen," 1 August 1882, The National Archives, London (TNA), CO 209/241, no. 13567.
25 Lord Kimberley to Arthur Gordon, 8 August 1882, in British House of Commons, *Correspondence respecting Native Affairs in New Zealand*, 287.
26 Colonial Office minutes, "The Māori Mission," 14 August 1882, TNA, CO 209/241, no. 14376.
27 *Ibid.*
28 Colonial Office minutes, "An Interview for a Deputation of Māories," 6 July 1882, TNA, CO 209/241, no. 12002.
29 Colonial Office minutes, "Presents Brought by the Māori Chiefs for the Queen," 23 July 1882, TNA, CO 209/241, no. 13061.
30 For example, see Zoltán Biedermann, Anne Gerritsen, and Giorgio Riello (eds), *Global Gifts: The Material Culture of Diplomacy in Early Modern Eurasia* (Cambridge: Cambridge University Press, 2017); Nicholas Thomas, *Entangled Objects: Exchange, Material Culture, and Colonialism in the Pacific* (Cambridge, MA: Harvard University Press, 1991); Alison Bennett, "Diplomatic Gifts: Rethinking Colonial Politics in Uganda through Objects," *History in Africa* 45 (2018): 193–220, DOI: 10.1017/hia.2018.5.
31 Amanda Nettelbeck, "Bracelets, Blankets and Badges of Distinction: Aboriginal Subjects and Queen Victoria's Gifts in Canada and Australia," in Sarah Carter

and Maria Nugent (eds), *Mistress of Everything: Queen Victoria in Indigenous Worlds* (Manchester: Manchester University Press, 2017), 212–217.

32 Amber Nicholson, "Hau: Giving Voices to the Ancestors," *The Journal of the Polynesian Society* 128, no. 2 (2019): 137–162 (138), DOI: 10.15286/jps.128.2.137–162.

33 Amiria Henare, "Taonga Māori: Encompassing Rights and Property in New Zealand," in Amiria Henare, Martin Holbraad, and Sari Wastell (eds), *Thinking through Things: Theorising Artefacts Ethnographically* (London: Routledge, 2006), 57–60.

34 The Queen certainly possessed the gifts at some point, since her secretary sent a thank-you note to the Colonial Office to confirm receipt, and there are many Māori objects in the Royal Collections without provenance that are potential candidates. However, in private correspondence with the Royal Collection's assistant curator of non-European art, I was informed that it would be very difficult to say conclusively which objects are Taiwhanga's gifts.

35 Emily Cunliffe, "Whales and Whale Bone Technology in New Zealand Prehistory" (MA thesis, University of Otago, 2014), 40; Basil Keane, "Pounamu – Jade or Greenstone – Symbols of Chieftainship," *Te Ara – the Encyclopedia of New Zealand* (Ministry for Culture and Heritage Te Manatu Taonga, 12 June 2006), https://teara.govt.nz/en/pounamu-jade-or-greenstone/page-5 (accessed 11 March 2025).

36 Erenora Puketapu-Hetet, *Māori Weaving* (Auckland: Pitman, 1989), 4; Lauren Fuka, "Object Monday: Māori Kete Baskets," Maxwell Museum of Anthropology, 10 May 2021, https://maxwellmuseum.unm.edu/maxwell-at-home/objects/object-monday-m%C4%81ori-kete-baskets (accessed 19 March 2025).

37 Puketapu-Hetet, *Māori Weaving*, 55.

38 Serge Tcherkézoff, "On Cloth, Gifts and Nudity: Regarding Some European Misunderstandings during Early Encounters in Polynesia," in Chloë Colchester (ed.), *Clothing the Pacific* (Oxford: Berg, 2003), 62–67.

39 Charlotte Weale to Frederick Chesson, 31 July 1882, Oxford, Bodleian Libraries (BodL), MS Brit. Emp. s. 22 G98/2–9.

40 Colonial Office minutes, "Presents Brought by the Māori Chiefs for the Queen."

41 Colonial Office minutes, "The Māori Presents to the Queen."

42 Colonial Office minutes, "Māori Presents," 7 August 1882, TNA, CO 209/241, no. 14080.

43 Edward Williams to Thomas William Lewis, 9 October 1882, ANZ, Taiwhanga's papers, N.O. 82/3178.

44 James Clendon to Thomas William Lewis, 27 September 1882, ANZ, Taiwhanga's papers, N.O. 82/3036.

45 *Ibid.*

46 Frederick Edward Manning to Thomas William Lewis, 2 October 1882, ANZ, Taiwhanga's papers, N.O. 82/3038.

47 *Ibid.*

48 "A Chapter in the History of New Zealand," in Royal Colonial Institute, *Report of Proceedings, 1882–1883*, 100.
49 *Ibid.*
50 *Ibid.*, 105.
51 *Ibid.*, 112.
52 *Ibid.*, 115.
53 *Ibid.*, 120.
54 *Ibid.*, 115.
55 *Ibid.*, 121.
56 "Sydney Taiwhanga," *Wanganui Herald*, 11 April 1883.
57 "Sydney Taiwhanga," *Marlborough Express*, 23 August 1883.
58 Hirini Taiwhanga to Frederick Chesson, 26 November 1883, BodL, MS Brit. Emp. s. 22 G99/1–6.
59 Hirini Taiwhanga to Frederick Chesson, 30 July 1883, BodL, MS Brit. Emp. s. 22 G98/74.
60 Hirini Taiwhanga to Frederick Chesson, 18 April 1883, BodL, MS Brit. Emp. s. 22 G98/68.
61 Taiwhanga to Chesson, 30 July 1883.
62 Hirini Taiwhanga to Frederick Chesson, 29 December 1882, BodL, MS Brit. Emp. s. 22 G98/62.
63 Taiwhanga to Chesson, 30 July 1883.
64 Hirini Taiwhanga to Frederick Chesson, 6 May 1885, BodL, MS Brit. Emp. s. 18 C143/192.
65 John Bryce to Sir William Jervois, governor of New Zealand, 11 January 1884, BodL, MS Brit. Emp. s. 22 G99/1–12.
66 Colonial Office minutes, "Translation of the Memorial of Māori Chiefs," 5 July 1884, TNA, CO 209/244, no. 11376.
67 Frederick Chesson to Edward Stanley, 15th earl of Derby, 30 May 1884, BodL, MS Brit. Emp. s. 22 G99/1–18.
68 Orange, *The Treaty of Waitangi*, 202–205.
69 "Section 71," in New Zealand, *The New Zealand Constitution Act: Together with Correspondence between the Secretary of State for the Colonies and the Governor-in-Chief of New Zealand in Explanation Thereof* (Wellington: R. Stokes, 1853).
70 Michael Belgrave, *Dancing with the King: The Rise and Fall of the King Country, 1864–1885* (Auckland: Auckland University Press, 2017), 340–342.
71 Susan Zaeske, *Signatures of Citizenship: Petitioning, Antislavery, and Women's Political Identity* (Chapel Hill: University of North Carolina Press, 2003), 1–2.
72 Richard Huzzey and Henry Miller, "Petitions, Parliament and Political Culture: Petitioning the House of Commons, 1780–1918," *Past & Present* 248, no. 1 (2020): 123–164 (149–150), DOI: 10.1093/pastj/gtz061.
73 James Curlewis to Thomas Upington, 4 November 1884, in British House of Commons, *Further Correspondence Respecting the Affairs of the Transvaal and Adjacent Territories, February 1885* (London: Eyre and Spottiswoode, 1885), 44.

74 Bryce to Jervois, 11 January 1884.

75 Glen Sean Coulthard, *Red Skin, White Masks: Rejecting the Colonial Politics of Recognition* (Minneapolis: University of Minnesota Press, 2014); Audra Simpson, *Mohawk Interruptus: Political Life across the Borders of Settler States* (Durham, NC: Duke University Press, 2014).

76 Charles Reed, *Royal Tourists, Colonial Subjects and the Making of a British World, 1860–1911* (Manchester: Manchester University Press, 2017), 169.

77 Zoë Laidlaw, "Indigenous Interlocutors: Networks of Imperial Protest and Humanitarianism in the Mid-Nineteenth Century," in Jane Carey and Jane Lydon (eds), *Indigenous Networks: Mobility, Connections and Exchange* (New York: Routledge, 2014), 114–139.

9

Humanitarian interference in indigenous delegations: New Zealand, 1884

On 31 May 1884, just two years after Hirini Taiwhanga's petition to Queen Victoria was rebuffed by the Colonial Office, another Māori delegation arrived in England to try again. Learning from Taiwhanga's experience of being dismissed as unrepresentative of Māori opinion, this new delegation was headed by some of the most important political leaders of the time: King Tāwhiao, leader of the Waikato iwi; Te Whēoro, member of the New Zealand House of Representatives; Tōpia Tūroa, chief of the Ngāti Patutokotoko hapū; and Hōri Rōpiha, a chief from the Hawkes Bay area. The delegation also brought Wiremu Pātara Te Tuhi, an assistant and secretary, and George Skidmore, an interpreter. Unlike Taiwhanga's 1882 delegation, Tāwhiao's 1884 delegation has received extensive scholarly attention. Charles Reed and Michael Belgrave have recently presented thorough examinations of the mission, balancing attention to the British government's political response to the delegates' petition with attention to the British public's reception of the Māori visitors. Both scholars conclude that the delegation's political mission was undermined by the British public's perception of the delegates as exotic imperial oddities rather than serious political agents, pointing particularly to newspaper coverage that reveals public fascination with the Māori's appearance and behaviour and almost complete disregard for their actual petition. Given that imperial citizenship as a claims-based identifier depended on claims of belonging being recognized by members of the British community, the process through which Tāwhiao's delegation were recognized as imperial spectacles but not as imperial citizens is revealing of the limitations of imperial citizenship for Indigenous subjects of the Empire.

Of course, the British public had no direct impact on the imperial government's response to the delegation's political demands. The newspaper evidence used by Reed and Belgrave indicates that the British public had little interest in Māori political demands, but "the British public" did not attend the delegation's meetings with the Colonial Office, and neither did it draft the Colonial Office's letters to the delegation. Nevertheless, British public apathy to Māori politics did have an indirect impact on the British government's response, most prominently via the mediating influence of the Māori's British allies. Lacking the experience and social networks necessary for navigating the British political system, Tāwhiao's delegation leaned upon friends and supporters to guide them through the process of obtaining audiences with the Colonial Office and Queen Victoria. Key among these supporters was the Aborigines' Protection Society (APS), which coordinated extensively with the Colonial Office to arrange official meetings and liaise between the delegates and the British government. Individual friends of the delegates also played important roles, with prominent figures such as the politician Sir John Gorst and the explorer and author James Henry Kerry-Nicholls applying pressure to the Colonial Office in support of the delegation. By acting as mediators, these allies shaped the delegation's interactions with the British government. In doing so, however, they injected themes from within British public discourse about the Māori delegates into every interaction between the two.

This chapter examines the impact that one particularly passionate ally, a philanthropist named Charlotte Weale, had on the Tāwhiao delegation's interactions with the British government. You may recall Weale as the woman who interfered with Hirini Taiwhanga's 1882 delegation by throwing away one of the gifts they intended to present to Queen Victoria. She reappears as the focus of this chapter not only because she was one of Tāwhiao's most ardent supporters while he was in Britain, but also because she left behind the most extensive archive of first-hand interactions with Tāwhiao's delegation in existence. She wrote over forty letters to the APS containing more than 30,000 words describing her personal conversations with the delegates and reflecting on her hopes and fears for their future. Crucially, Weale shared the British public's essential disinterest in Māori politics, and used her influence over the delegation to steer it in a direction she considered to be more important. Believing that the political side of their mission was largely hopeless, Weale determined that "they sh[oul]d receive pleasant invitations to one house and another so as to get into good intercourse with people and see the best side of English life."[1] Such visits, she believed, would help them "to be industrious and to become more educated and to give up all uncivilized and communistic habits and so to encourage good family life," as well as "to acknowledge the doctrine and discipline of the church."[2] Weale thus felt that it was more important to civilize the delegates than to support their political demands, and she actively set out to undermine their political mission and manipulate them to satisfy her own desire to civilize imperial savages. Through tracing Weale's efforts to manipulate Tāwhiao's delegation, this chapter demonstrates that Indigenous claims to imperial citizenship were challenged not only by Indigenous peoples' governmental and settler opponents, as detailed in other chapters of this book, but also by their closest humanitarian allies, who dictated the limited terms upon which they were willing to recognize the inclusion of Indigenous peoples within the British community.

Context of the petition

Decades of colonial violence, tracing back to the Treaty of Waitangi in 1840, provided the context for Tāwhiao's visit to Britain in 1884. Tāwhiao cited the Taranaki War of 1860–1861 and the Waikato War of 1863–1864 as part of the historical background for his visit, both of which ended in the New Zealand government confiscating large swaths of Māori land.[3] Tāwhiao also cited the creation of Native Land Courts in 1865, which placed the authority to sell Māori land in the hands of white judges who abused their authority to alienate that land.[4] But the direct spark for the delegation was the New Zealand government's attempts to survey and settle a piece of Māori land called Kāwhia in 1883.[5]

As the leader of the Kīngitanga, or Māori King movement, Tāwhiao was the elected leader of a select group of Māori nations, or iwi, from the central regions of New Zealand's North Island, who came together to resist colonial encroachment. After the Waikato War of 1860–1864, the New Zealand government expelled Tāwhiao and his followers from their lands and they retreated into the "King Country," where they proclaimed independence. Tāwhiao's stronghold in the King Country was the coastal harbour of Kāwhia, but in 1880 the New Zealand government began surveying Kāwhia with the intention of breaking up the Kingitanga.[6] Throughout 1883 Tāwhiao destroyed surveyors' beacons and petitioned the New Zealand government to assert his sovereignty over the King Country, but the surveying continued.[7] Tāwhiao therefore arranged the 1884 delegation to the British government as a last resort to retain his claim to Kāwhia and the King Country. He demanded the New Zealand government disband the Native Land Courts, return all land alienated through the Courts, return all taxes paid by Māori for the operation of the Courts, and cease all government operations in the King Country.[8]

Tāwhiao as a bronze spectacle

On 17 August 2015, a bronze bust of Tāwhiao was gifted to the Waikato Museum in honour of the 150th anniversary of the city of Hamilton, which is nearby the historical site of Kāwhia. The bust was created in the

1980s by Hamilton-born artist Gary Schofield, who explained that he saw Tāwhiao as a symbol of non-violent resistance, reconciliation, and restitution.[9] However, Schofield's piece was only the second bronze bust made of Tāwhiao. The first was made in London by a sculptor named Frederick Stanly Sheldon during Tāwhiao's visit in 1884, and has since disappeared from the archival record, along with a host of photographs and portraits of the king from the same trip.[10] Unlike that made of him a century later, the 1884 bust was no celebration of Tāwhiao or the resistance politics he represented. On the contrary, it was largely extorted out of an indignant Tāwhaio, who adamantly refused to have a bust made of himself and only did so under pressure from London humanitarians who claimed to have his best interests at heart. The lost bust of King Tāwhiao therefore offers a fitting starting place for exploring the subversion of Māori imperial citizenship by humanitarians at the heart of the Empire.

Tāwhiao was approached by at least three people with a proposal to commemorate his visit with a bronze bust. The first was an artist named Henry Charles Sepping Wright, who painted a life-sized portrait of Tāwhiao that has not been documented since the Colonial and Indian Exhibition in 1886. The second was Sir John Gorst, a retired resident magistrate from New Zealand turned British MP who tried his best to support Tāwhiao while he was in London. And the third was Charlotte Weale. Tāwhiao rebuffed all of them, for a variety of reasons. On one hand, he said that having multiple sketches and oil paintings made of him was enough. Newspapers reported Tāwhiao growing restless and frustrated sitting still for hours while his portraits were painted,[11] so it is possible that he simply did not want to go through such an annoying process again. Tawhaio also said that if the Queen did not wish to look at his living body, then she clearly had no interest in looking at his metal body either, indicating that the decision not to have a bust made was informed by bitterness at being rebuffed by the British monarchy. More than anything, however, Tāwhiao was self-conscious that a bust would be used to mock him after he returned home. According to Weale, Tāwhiao

> asserts a bust is a dreadful notion and that his disfigured eye from his wounds some years ago gives [*sic*] him (he spoke the English words) "crosseye looking" and he feels the prince and the great gentlemen will be able to go and look at the bust when complete "and make sport of this seventy years old stranger and that a bust is not like a painting it lasts forever and so his tribe will be mocked by the English when they discourse as to his native appearance."[12]

Thus, for Tāwhiao, having a bust made of him was not only a tedious insult to his desire to appear before the Queen in person, but also represented the reduction of his person from a political agent into an object of fascination and ridicule.

Despite Tāwhiao's reluctance, the bust was ultimately cast largely because of the nagging insistence of Charlotte Weale, who did everything she could to manipulate him. Weale tried reasoning with Tāwhiao, telling him that having a bust cast "was an honour conferred on him" that would buttress his reputation in England.[13] She also pressured Tāwhiao emotionally, telling him that having the bust cast "was the first thing I had asked of him,"[14] implying that he owed it to her in return for all of her assistance navigating London. When such efforts were insufficient, Weale finally resorted to essentially tricking Tāwhiao. She told Frederick Chesson, the secretary of the APS, to come over in the morning after Tawhaio had "a good night's sleep" so that he would "be in a more pleasant mood," and then put him in a cab without telling him where it was headed in the hope that "he will be got to go."[15] Ground down by Weale's nagging and tricked into a cab to the artist's studio, Tāwhiao eventually agreed to sit for the bust.

Weale left no written record explaining why exactly she was so determined to have a bust cast of Tāwhiao, but there are various clues within her correspondence with the APS pointing towards a voyeuristic desire to treat the Māori mission like a museum exhibit, just as Tāwhiao had feared. First, she repeatedly expressed her desire for and satisfaction with photos of the Māori delegates. When Chesson first told Weale that photos had been taken of the delegation, she immediately wrote back that "I should like to get the photographs you spoke of," not just for her own enjoyment, but "to show to the Wilsons and others who I am now seeing."[16] Chesson duly promised to obtain two copies for her, but they were not enough. Two months later, she asked "to have two more photos of the group, besides I mean the ones you are already getting for me, as I am going to give one to Liddon and Mrs Grace."[17] After four more months had passed, Weale yet again requested another "two of the large photos of the group."[18] Her ravenous hunger for photos of the Māori delegates, not just for her own viewing but also for showing off to her friends, suggests her motives for having a bronze bust. Whereas Tāwhiao's concern that "a bust is not like a painting it lasts forever" led him to worry that it would enable Britons to ridicule the Māori for generations, Weale probably found that very permanency appealing, as she would always be able to look at it and show it off to her friends. There are other possible motivations for making this bust, such as to conduct a phrenological study of Tāwhiao's head, though Weale made no allusions to such a desire.

Weale's efforts to turn Tāwhiao into a permanent piece of art was only one small piece of a much larger pattern in British responses to the Māori delegation. Charles Reed and Michael Belgrave both argue that "while Tāwhiao came to London with a political purpose in mind, metropolitan Britons treated his visit largely as a colonial spectacle, reflecting a limited interest in the politics and policies of Britain's empire," with the press working particularly hard to report on "Tāwhiao as celebrity rather than Tāwhiao as political leader and critic of colonisation."[19] Interestingly, however, neither Reed nor Belgrave identifies humanitarians such as Weale as contributors to this trend of "specticalization." On the contrary, Reed represents humanitarians as the Māori's lone supporters who worked to challenge the antagonism and apathy of the British public, while Belgrave represents Weale as a faithful Māori ally whose only major flaw was an overbearing concern for their spiritual welfare.[20]

An alternative and more insightful perspective is provided by the analyses of Gwilym Colenso and Brian Willan of the APS's response to African delegations in the late nineteenth and early twentieth centuries. Colenso and Willan point out that the APS was frequently unwilling to anger the Colonial Office by providing overt political support to African delegations, and occasionally actively opposed African delegations whose political objectives did not align with its own.[21] Moreover, by hosting special breakfasts and meetings for African delegations, the APS contributed to the "ceremonial diversion from the concrete objectives and real political mission of the delegations" identified by Reed and Belgrave.[22] Upon first glance, Weale's fascination with creating and showing off a bust of Tāwhiao may not seem to align with such a negative and pessimistic assessment of humanitarian responses to Indigenous delegations. However, when placed within the entire context of her relationships and interactions with Tāwhiao's delegation, it becomes clear that turning him into a sculpture was part of a larger effort by Weale to chisel away his political goals and mould him into an appropriately civilized figurine of a loyal British subject. To do this, Weale combined her efforts to cast Tāwhiao's bust with a quest to control the interpretation and translation of his voice and mediate his access to Queen Victoria.

Controlling Tāwhiao's interpreter

Besides showing off artwork of the delegates to her friends, Weale's primary concern was that the APS should place the Māori under the control of someone able to guide them towards civility and Christianity. Prior to their arrival, Weale told the APS on multiple occasions that "the Māories are folks that need guiding and being 'looked after,'"[23] insisting that the APS needed to find them "a sensible young man, firm yet kind, with tact and a little knowledge of the world, as servant."[24] Her list of the desirable characteristics of such a guide is revealing of her condescension towards the Māori, as well as her lack of interest in supporting their political objectives. The guide needed to be:

> The best sort of Christian gentlemen … pleasant and with zeal and kindness is the sort we need to go and escort the Māories … to chat with them and draw out their ideas and answer their questions and so inform their minds on subjects interesting to them. Patience wh[ich] is begotten of … and a strong head wh[ich] will not be overwearied by their endless talk over small matters and a good temper wh[ich] will not be worried by their versatility and unpunctuality, is what is required … if you c[oul]d find amongst those who belong to the Aborigines Protection Society [someone] to take the Māories in hand when they arrive, it w[oul]d be a benediction and a relief to my mind.[25]

Weale's image of the ideal guide reflected the type of control that she wanted to exert over the Māori group. Unconcerned with Tāwhiao's own interests in interviewing the Secretary of State for the Colonies, Lord Derby (Edward Stanley) and Queen Victoria, she was instead focused on "informing their minds," and her method of achieving that goal was to choose a suitable interpreter.

Weale was particularly concerned about George Skidmore, the mixed-race son of a whaling captain whom Tāwhiao brought as an interpreter. She fretted over the bad influence such a "halfcaste" would have on the Māori envoys, telling the APS that "often the halfcastes are less intelligent and less moral than the natives. I often wonder ab[ou]t this man as the halfcastes are usually the children of sin and shame."[26] Weale therefore tried to discredit Skidmore as an interpreter, telling the APS that "Skidmore did not translate correctly my few words."[27] And Weale was not alone: the Colonial Office also dismissed Skidmore from the moment of his arrival. Lord Derby's assistant, F. Fuller, wrote that Skidmore was "a rough sort of sea-faring man, a half-caste, once I believe in the whaling trade. He w[oul]d be quite insufficient as an interpreter in any matters requiring political knowledge or nicety."[28] That Tāwhiao brought Skidmore in the first place indicates that the Māori envoys had sufficient confidence in his capacity to translate, but Weale's disregard for Skidmore's skill as an interpreter is consistent with Gwilym Colenso's findings from African delegations, in which the Colonial Office distrusted white interpreters but entirely ignored Black interpreters.[29] Weale's disdain for his mixed-race heritage also reflects contemporary attitudes towards racial hybridity. Māori "half-castes" became a particularly significant concern for British observers throughout the nineteenth century. Their ability to move between Māori and British societies and thrive in both – without abandoning one for the other – seriously challenged stadial theory and the premise of cultural assimilation, and so British anthropologists throughout the century conducted extensive research to define Māori half-castes as a stable racial category and to locate its place in the imperial hierarchy.[30] Skidmore's dismissal as translator probably resulted from a combination of Weale's and Fuller's comments with these broader attitudes towards racial hybridity.

When an opportunity arose to hire a missionary as translator and guide, Weale did her best to make sure the APS took him on board. Only seven days after Tāwhiao had arrived the APS received a letter from George William Rusden, noted author of the 1883 *History of New Zealand*, introducing them to a missionary from New Zealand named Frederick Hamilton Spencer. Rusden informed the APS that Spencer "desires I believe to have an opportunity of seeing Tāwhiao and his friends, and as Mr Spencer is himself a native of New Zealand [i.e. born in New Zealand, not Indigenous] it would seem very natural that Tāwhiao should be glad to see one born under the Southern sky and acquainted with the Māori language."[31] The APS gladly arranged a meeting between Spencer and the Māori, and subsequently asked him to act as their interpreter and guide. Spencer replied that "I shall do all I can for the Māories and give all my services, i.e., within reasonable limits," but required remuneration: "being only a curate my purse is rather slender and if at any time I am wanted to go out with them, perhaps the bare travelling costs might be defrayed, as then I would not feel it pressing, for a shilling is a shilling to me at present and it is just as well to acknowledge it freely.[32] The APS did not have the funds to pay for Spencer's services, but when Weale learned of the situation she wrote that "I fancy you had best secure Mr Spencer's services and I'll try and beg donations from some others,"[33] and she commenced posting checks to the APS "toward providing the Māories with Mr Spencer as chaplain and interpreter."[34] Weale worked through her religious and philanthropic network to obtain donations from at least ten prominent families, including the suffragette Sophia Fry and the pacifist Priscilla Peckover, and in total she sent the APS over £60. These donations enabled the APS to hire Spencer for the duration of the Māori visit, and Weale celebrated that "they are supplied well with Mr Spencer and I am thankful to you for arranging that matter and hope his intercourse with them may prove a real blessing to them."[35]

It is worth noting that the Māori delegation was not short of such funds if they had wanted to hire Spencer themselves. They had raised around £4,000 in New Zealand to cover their costs, and the delegates themselves were moderately wealthy.[36] Indeed, Weale and the APS did not inform Tāwhiao that they were paying Spencer, allowing him to believe that Spencer was volunteering his time.[37] Weale and the APS were thereby able to obscure their attempts to manipulate the delegation by secretly paying a third party to exert influence over the Māori while allowing them to believe that Spencer was offering assistance of his own free will.

However, despite her efforts to obtain his services, Weale's satisfaction with Spencer quickly dissipated. To begin with, Spencer's style of translating by unravelling Māori idioms and rephrasing Māori statements to make sense in English bothered Weale no end. She had a voyeuristic desire to listen to the exoticism of Māori speech patterns, and she felt that when Spencer rephrased Māori into English he destroyed "all the beauty and peculiarity of their phraseology."[38] Transforming one culture's ways of speaking into another is, of course, a crucial element of translation, without which intercultural communication would be impossible. Weale's impatience with this translation therefore reveals her desire to hear Māori *voices* but not listen to their *ideas*. Spencer also failed to fulfil Weale's plan to Christianize and socialize the Māori envoys. She complained to the APS that "more and more do I trouble that Mr Spencer did not fufil his duty by their souls,"[39] and that he "hindered the Māories from caring to be introduced by me to people."[40]

But more than anything, Weale despised how Spencer "disparages the Colonial Office and the English."[41] She complained that Spencer supported the Māori in demanding imperial intervention, which she deemed "ridiculous," and alleged that by doing so "Mr Spencer has tried to set the Māories ag[ains]t you and ag[ains]t me and ag[ains]t the Colonial Office and authorities in this country."[42] Instead of supporting the Māori political mission, she believed that Spencer should "talk to them of the fairness wh[ich] Lord Derby and others will exercise in dealing with their difficulties and above all that our heavenly father loves them and will bless them."[43] Spencer's failure to live up to Weale's vision for how he should have managed the Māori delegation pushed her to ask the APS to replace him. She wrote that "more and more do I wish that you c[oul]d get some one speaking Māori" to take over from Spencer as translator, but no one else could be found.[44]

Weale's defensiveness at Spencer and the Māori disparaging the justice of the British government and people shows how the presence of victims of colonization could challenge British identities as humanitarians and benevolent bestowers of civilization. Weale experienced the Māori visit as a challenge to her perceptions of race and Empire and saw it as the duty of Spencer and herself to convince the Māori of British honour and justice. Her reaction underlines the fact that the delegation was not just a site of Indigenous resistance against colonialism in New Zealand, but also a "contact zone" right in the heart of the Empire. Mary Louise Pratt coined the term contact zone "to refer to social spaces where cultures meet, clash, and grapple with each other, often in context of highly asymmetrical relations of power, such as colonialism."[45] The concept of the contact zone is typically mobilized in colonial regions, as a place that existed out on imperial frontiers.[46] But the clash between Tāwhiao's and Weale's visions of Māori–British relations demonstrates that Indigenous delegations could bring the colonial contact zone directly into the metropole. Crucially, this was a contact zone in which British humanitarian identities were incompatible with, and unable to comprehend, the claims to imperial citizenship put forward by Māori delegates, claims that were premised upon the inhumanity of the British Empire.

A meeting with the Crown

Weale's conviction that shaping the Māori delegates into respectable gentlemen was more important than their political mission culminated in one final act of sabotage in the final week of their stay in England. An integral element of the delegation was to arrange a meeting between the delegates and Queen Victoria. For Tāwhiao, the Treaty of Waitangi established a reciprocal relationship between the Queen and his people, and he made a clear distinction between petitioning "the Queen's representatives" such as the governor and the Colonial Office, who were "too much occupied with [their] work ... to relieve the Māoris of their grievances," and petitioning the Queen.[47] Tāwhiao knew that the British government was aware of Māori suffering, but he believed that "this is the first time the Queen has seen or heard any of these great grievances amongst the Māoris and the Europeans, and I think perhaps the Queen will be very sorry that her wards in the Treaty of Waitangi have been trampled upon."[48] Obtaining a personal audience with the Queen was therefore the most important objective of the Māori delegation. For Charlotte Weale, however, obtaining an audience with the Queen was less important than learning the respectable manners of behaviour in elite society. This divergence of priorities led to conflict when the Māori delegates wanted to pursue all possible avenues to obtaining a royal audience, pushing Weale to interfere in their efforts to communicate with the Queen.

The conflict began with the initial refusal of Queen Victoria and Albert, Prince of Wales, to meet the Māoris. When the delegates submitted their formal request for audiences with both royals on 29 July, New Zealand's Agent General, Frederick Dillon Bell, responded by vociferously lobbying the Colonial Office to refuse the request. Colonial Office minutes indicate that "Sir F. Bell is very averse to their seeing H.R.H. [Her Royal Highness] not merely on political grounds, but because Tāwhiao is not of sufficiently good character to be given an interview."[49] Friends of the delegation challenged Bell on their behalf, with Sir George Grey vouching that Te Wheoro "is greatly respected by both races inhabiting New Zealand," and J. H. Kerry-Nicholls vouching that Tāwhiao "has of recent years acquired the good opinion and friendship of the colonists, and from my personal knowledge of his character, I believe that a more loyal or kindlier man does not exist."[50] But the Colonial Office remained convinced by Bell's propaganda, contending that "even Major Te Wheoro, good man as he is, may be led by injudicious advisors to assume an insolent tone ... I could certainly not ask the Queen to see him."[51]

The Colonial Office's official answer to the delegation was that "H.M. has left London to seek repose and is unable to grant any interviews at present,"[52] but the delegates suspected that political interests in the Colonial Office played a part in the Queen's refusal to see them, and they decided to write a letter directly to the Queen asking her personally for a meeting.[53] Weale thought it a terrible idea, however. She told the delegates that "an epistle thus sent w[oul]d damage their cause and be a very ungentlemanly course to pursue, that great men were always able to wait and only little nobodies w[oul]d approach Her Majesty."[54] As a consequence, they sent a request for reconsideration to the Colonial Office instead of to the Queen, who replied that the royals had already given their answer.[55] It is impossible to know if a different outcome could have developed without Weale's intervention, but it is significant that Weale was more interested in impressing upon the delegates British social norms of gentility than supporting their political objectives. There are no records of Tāwhiao's thoughts on the matter, but it is likely that he considered it more humiliating to be refused a meeting than to obtain a meeting in an ungentlemanly way. Weale's refusal to allow the Māori's write their letter because it was ungentlemanly lends some support to Douglas Lorimer's argument that Indigenous envoys were restrained by the need to conform to metropolitan expectations. Indeed, in reference to Black anti-slavery campaigners in Britain in the mid-nineteenth century, Lorimer argues that Black campaigners were only granted credibility and respect to the extent that they could "conform to conventions of correct behaviour."[56] Weale's refusal to allow the Māori to act like "little nobodies" shows that the same class-based discourses that Lorimer identified in anti-slavery campaigners could also be restrictive for Indigenous delegates.

Conclusion

Charlotte Weale's efforts to manipulate Tāwhiao into casting a bust of him, to assert control over the delegation through choosing an interpreter, and to dictate how the delegates could and could not communicate with the Queen, provide a useful window into British responses to Indigenous claims upon imperial citizenship. Previous scholarship has tended to categorize and differentiate governmental, humanitarian, and public responses to Indigenous delegations. In terms of government responses, Neil Parsons and Gwilym Colenso argue that the Colonial Office manipulated Indigenous delegations through its control over approved interpreters, its control over funding, and its control over meetings with the Crown.[57] Humanitarian responses have been studied by Brian Willan and Zoë Laidlaw, both of whom argue that the relationship between the APS and Indigenous delegates only entrenched colonial power structures, with educated and civilized Indigenous delegates valued primarily as proof that Indigeneity could be effectively erased through education and civilization, requiring Indigenous peoples to adhere to European standards of civilization if they were to be recognized as worthy of protection.[58] Meanwhile, Charles Reed and Michael Belgrave demonstrate that public responses to Indigenous delegations were grounded in fascination with the spectacle of Indigenous otherness alongside a complete disregard for Indigenous politics.[59]

Differentiating between governmental efforts at control, humanitarian obsession with civilization, and public disregard for Indigenous politics is useful to an extent for disaggregating the many cultural barriers preventing Indigenous claims upon imperial citizenship from being recognized in the imperial centre. At the same time, however, categorizing these various responses leads to an oversimplified model of British politics in which Indigenous delegations could leverage discrete government, humanitarian, and public bodies against one another. This simplicity obscures the reality that each audience experienced all three responses, intermingling concerns about controlling delegations and civilizing delegates with chronic disinterest in actually listening to Indigenous voices. Charlotte Weale captures this very complexity, demonstrating how one person simultaneously balanced the public's voyeuristic desire to turn Tāwhiao into a silent bust, a humanitarian desire to educate Tāwhiao, and a governmental desire to control Tāwhiao's access to Queen Victoria. By recognizing that all three responses could overlap within a single person, this chapter highlights the scale of the difficulty facing Indigenous delegations. With efforts to control, assimilate, and ignore them coming from all directions, there was little they could effectively accomplish by pitting government, humanitarian, and public audiences against one another.

Weale's refusal to recognize Tāwhiao's delegation as political agents underscores the inherent limitation of challenging settler colonialism through imperial citizenship, inasmuch as the success of claiming rights through imperial citizenship depended on its being recognized as a source of rights by the very Empire that took those rights away in the first place. Indigenous scholars Glen Coulthard and Audra Simpson strongly critique any strategy for decolonization that requires recognition of Indigenous rights by colonial authorities precisely because colonial authorities will only ever recognize Indigenous rights as subordinate to their own.[60] This structural inability of the imperial government to recognize Indigenous rights without compromising the very nature of an imperial system founded upon the subordination of Indigenous peoples is what truly differentiates the Indigenous and settler claims upon imperial citizenship explored throughout this book. In terms of political outcomes, the citizenship claims by settlers such as Philip Carpenter, William Akerman, and David Carley appear on first glance to be just as unsuccessful as those by Taiwhanga and Tāwhiao. In terms of reception and recognition, however, settler citizenship claims were largely recognized as legitimate even though they were ultimately rejected, rendering imperial citizenship most beneficial to those who needed it least.

Notes

1 Charlotte Weale to Frederick Chesson, 4 June 1884, Oxford, Bodleian Libraries (BodL), MSS Brit. Emp. s. 22 G99/1–21.
2 Charlotte Weale to Frederick Chesson, 14 July 1884, BodL, MS Brit. Emp. s. 22 G99/1–26.
3 Tāwhiao to Frederick Chesson, 22 March 1884, BodL, MS Brit. Emp. s. 22 G99/1–8.
4 *Ibid.*
5 *Ibid.*
6 Michael Belgrave, *Dancing with the King: The Rise and Fall of the King Country, 1864–1885* (Auckland: Auckland University Press, 2017), 36.
7 *Ibid.*, 283–288.
8 Tāwhiao to Chesson, 22 March 1884.
9 Andrew McRae, "Kingi Tawhiao Bust for Museum," Radio New Zealand, 17 August 2015, www.rnz.co.nz/news/te-manu-korihi/281637/kingi-tawhiao-bust-for-museum (accessed 20 March 2025).
10 Roger Blackley, "King Tāwhiao's Big O.E.," *Turnbull Library Record*, 1 January 2012, https://paperspast.natlib.govt.nz/periodicals/TLR20120101.2.9 (accessed 20 March 2025).
11 "Painting Tāwhiao's Portrait," *New Zealand Herald*, 1 November 1884.
12 Charlotte Weale to Frederick Chesson, 15 August 1884, BodL, MS Brit. Emp. s. 18 C149/147.
13 *Ibid.*
14 *Ibid.*
15 *Ibid.*
16 Weale to Chesson, 14 July 1884.
17 Charlotte Weale to Frederick Chesson, 25 August 1884, BodL, MS Brit. Emp. s. 18 C149/151.
18 Charlotte Weale to Frederick Chesson, 30 December 1884, BodL, MS Brit. Emp. s. 18 C149/154.
19 Charles Reed, *Royal Tourists, Colonial Subjects and the Making of a British World, 1860–1911* (Manchester: Manchester University Press, 2017), 168; Belgrave, *Dancing in King Country*, 321.
20 Reed, *Royal Tourists*, 167; Belgrave, *Dancing with the King*, 318–319.
21 Gwilym Colenso, "Breaking with the Old Pattern of Control: African Deputations to Britain from Southern Africa in the Late Nineteenth and Early Twentieth Centuries," *South African Historical Journal* 69, no. 4 (2017): 501–547, DOI: 10.1080/02582473.2017.1398777; Brian Willan, "The Anti-Slavery and Aborigines' Protection Society and the South African Natives' Land Act

of 1913," *The Journal of African History* 20, no. 1 (1979): 83–102, DOI: 10.1017/S002185370001673X.
22 Colenso, "Breaking with the Old Pattern," 532.
23 Charlotte Weale to Frederick Chesson, 22 September 1883, BodL, MS Brit. Emp. S. 22 G99/1–1.
24 Charlotte Weale to Frederick Chesson, n.d., BodL, MS Brit. Emp. s. 18 C149/342–343.
25 *Ibid.*
26 Weale to Chesson, 14 July 1884.
27 Weale to Chesson, 25 August 1884.
28 Colonial Office, "Major Te Wheoro," 18 September 1884, The National Archives, London (TNA), CO 209/244, no. 12930.
29 Colenso, "Breaking with the Old Pattern," 523–524.
30 Hope Marie Reilly, "Race, Gender, and British Anthropology in Nineteenth Century New Zealand" (MA thesis, College of Charleston, 2017), 1–20.
31 George William Rusden to Frederick Chesson, 6 June 1884, BodL, MS Brit. Emp. s. 18 C146/23.
32 Frederick Spencer to Frederick Chesson, 6 July 1884, BodL, MS Brit. Emp. s. 18 C147/213.
33 Charlotte Weale to Frederick Chesson, n.d., BodL, MS Brit. Emp. s. 22 G99/1–19.
34 Charlotte Weale to Frederick Chesson, 4 July 1884, BodL, MS Brit. Emp. s. 22 G99/1–25.
35 Charlotte Weale to Frederick Chesson, 8 July 1884, BodL, MS Brit. Emp. s. 22 G99/1–27.
36 Belgrave, *Dancing with the King*, 308.
37 Charlotte Weale to Frederick Chesson, 17 August 1884, BodL, MS Brit. Emp. s. 22 G99/1–35.
38 Charlotte Weale to Frederick Chesson, 18 August 1884, BodL, MS Brit. Emp. s. 18 C149/149.
39 Weale to Chesson, 17 August 1884.
40 Charlotte Weale to Frederick Chesson, 20 September 1884, BodL, MS Brit. Emp. s. 18 C149/152.
41 Charlotte Weale to Frederick Chesson, 12 August 1884, BodL, MS Brit. Emp. s. 18 C149/143.
42 Weale to Chesson, 25 August 1884.
43 Weale to Chesson, 18 August 1884.
44 *Ibid.*
45 Mary Louise Pratt, "Arts of the Contact Zone," *Profession* (1991): 33–40 (34).
46 For instance, see Sarah Carter, " 'The Faithful Children of the Great Mother Are Starving': Queen Victoria in Contact Zone Dialogues in Western Canada," in Sarah Carter and Maria Nugent (eds), *Mistress of Everything: Queen Victoria in Indigenous Worlds* (Manchester: Manchester University Press, 2017), 78–99; Sharika D. Crawford and Ana Isabel Márquez-Pérez, "A Contact Zone: The Turtle Commons of the Western Caribbean," *International Journal of*

Maritime History 28, no. 1 (2016): 64–80, DOI: 10.1177/0843871415624095; and Christian Moser, "Walking in the Contact Zone: Georg Forster and the Peripatetic Mode of Exploration (1768–1777)," in Frédéric Regard (ed.), *British Narratives of Exploration: Case Studies of the Self and Other* (London: Pickering and Chatto, 2009), 97–106.

47 Tāwhiao to Chesson, 22 March 1884.

48 *Ibid.*

49 Colonial Office minutes, "Audience with HM or Prince of Wales," 13 August 1884, TNA, CO 209/244, no. 13837.

50 Sir George Grey to Edward Stanley, 15th earl of Derby, 19 March 1884, TNA, CO 209/244, no. 12930; J. H. Kerry-Nicholls to the earl of Derby, 13 August 1884, TNA, CO 209/244, no. 13992.

51 Colonial Office minutes, "Major Te Wheoro," 19 March 1884, TNA, CO 209/244, no. 12930.

52 Colonial Office minutes, "Audience for Māori Chiefs with HM," 13 August 1884, TNA, CO 209/244, no. 13992.

53 Weale to Chesson, 12 August 1884.

54 *Ibid.*

55 Colonial Office, "Audience with HM or Prince of Wales."

56 Douglas Lorimer, *Colour, Class, and the Victorians: English Attitudes to the Negro in the Mid-Nineteenth Century* (Leicester: Leicester University Press, 1978), 52.

57 Neil Parsons, " 'No Longer Rare Birds in London': Zulu, Ndebele, Gaza, and Swazi Envoys to England, 1882–1894," in Gretchen Gerzina and Neil Parsons (eds), *Black Victorians, Black Victoriana* (New Brunswick: Rutgers University Press, 2003), 112–13; Colenso, "Breaking With the Old Pattern," 501–514.

58 Willan, "The Anti-Slavery and Aborigines' Protection Society," 87; Zoë Laidlaw, *Protecting the Empire's Humanity: Thomas Hodgkin and British Colonial Activism 1830–1870* (Cambridge: Cambridge University Press, 2021), 239.

59 Reed, *Royal Tourists*, 174; Belgrave, *Dancing with the King*, 321.

60 Glen Sean Coulthard, *Red Skin, White Masks: Rejecting the Colonial Politics of Recognition* (Minneapolis: University of Minnesota Press, 2014); Audra Simpson, *Mohawk Interruptus: Political Life across the Borders of Settler States* (Durham, NC: Duke University Press, 2014).

Conclusion

This book opened by posing two guiding questions about the interconnections between imperial authority, colonial self-government, and settler power structures. And so, to conclude, I would like to revisit each of these questions in turn and reflect on the answers provided by the nine case studies examined over the course of the book. The first question related to perceptions of imperial authority, asking: how did the rise of settler self-government impact local understandings of, and relationships with, imperial authority? A useful way to begin answering this question is to take stock of the various ways that the individuals in this book hoped to make use of imperial authority, wherein three overarching patterns emerged across all nine chapters. One pattern included individuals lacking political self-determination who looked to the imperial government to establish self-governing institutions. Two chapters (1 and 3) covered settlers living under direct imperial administration in British Columbia and Western Australia who longed for responsible government as their birthright as British men, while another two chapters (8 and 9) addressed Māori leaders who demanded fulfilment of the self-government promises in the Treaty of Waitangi. In the minds of imperial subjects such as these, the imperial government's provision of responsible institutions to some settler colonies while withholding them from Indigenous nations and other settler colonies underscored the power of the imperial government over the destiny of the colonies and emphasized the importance of currying imperial favour and working through imperial infrastructure to obtain reform.

In terms of settler societies in British Columbia and Western Australia, the disjunction between granting self-government to some colonies and not to others connects to arguments by Lisa Ford and Angela Woollacott that settler territorial sovereignty and self-government were constructed collaboratively and relationally as settlers observed political developments in other colonies.[1] However, Ford and Woollacott both focus on the intercolonial transmission of knowledge via newspapers and mobile agents moving between colonies, elaborating a model of imperial power based upon the existence of colony-to-colony connections and networks. This model provides an important corrective to an older overemphasis on colony–metropole relations, but in some ways it is an overcorrection. In my case studies of British Columbia and Western Australia, knowledge of the development of self-governing institutions in other colonies certainly gave settlers inspiration and some leverage, but the power nevertheless remained decidedly in the metropole. Responsible government was instituted in these colonies decades after knowledge reached them of successful self-government campaigns elsewhere, precisely because the metropole was unwilling to concede it. This was partly to do with demographic differences between colonies, with British Columbia and Western Australia less populous and thus less capable of generating sufficient public servants to operate a government. But even then, it was the Colonial Office that decided that demographic size was a prerequisite for democracy.

The centrality of the imperial government's control over trajectories of colonial government is sometimes lost in historical narratives that the Colonial Office wanted to shed colonies as quickly as possible, implying that their inhabitants simply had to meet a few basic criteria and then would be handed the keys to their colony. But that was not the experience of the individuals in Chapters 1 and 3. On the contrary, settlers in both colonies faced politicians nominated by the imperial government who were absolutely unwilling to relinquish their positions, and it was only through the exertion of imperial authority that their stonewalling could be overturned. In British Columbia, this required promising politicians lucrative postings elsewhere, while in Western Australia it amounted to threatening to partition the colony, dividing it in two. These cases demonstrate that the earlier rise of self-government in some colonies may have strengthened later campaigns for it in other colonies, but that these early victories simultaneously entrenched the power of the imperial government as "kingmaker." Settlers continued to have to work through rather than against imperial authority in order to obtain democratic institutions, highlighting the continuing importance of colony–metropole relations in the late nineteenth century.

The idea of the imperial government as "kingmaker" of colonial democracies also influenced those Māori who travelled to London to demand a parliament of their own. Not only had they witnessed Britain granting New Zealand self-government, they would also have been aware that the Zulu King Cetshwayo had travelled to London in 1882 and successfully petitioned to be reinstated as King (albeit in a very constrained manner). Moreover, Britain had already promised to recognize Māori self-determination in the Treaty of Waitangi and pledged itself to maintaining that promise in the New Zealand Constitution. These events would have impressed upon many Māori people that Britain had the power to create for them a separate parliament. Recent historians have puzzled over the decision to send a Māori delegation to London when such a strategy was certainly futile, yet such puzzlement is built upon a teleological stance that ignores what it would have been like to live in the late nineteenth century. The colony of New Zealand was self-governing only because, just a few years earlier, Britain had decreed it to be so, and it was not so unreasonable to think that Britain could amend that decree. After all, another case study from this book articulated this very idea in 1875 in reference to self-government in Canada: "The same government which gave or confined powers can take them away ... The Queen has power to call these Stewards to account for their stewardship; and if unfaithful, she can deprive them, and give it to others."[2] We now know this to be untrue, that Britain would be unwilling to grant Māori self-determination against the desires of the New Zealand government, but people at the time did not know that. This is why it is so crucial to appreciate the perceived importance of imperial authority to contemporaries. By attending to perceptions that it was necessary to work through imperial power to obtain self-determination, this book humanizes and rationalizes efforts to invoke imperial authority that today appear futile or counterintuitive.

The second pattern in perceived relationships to imperial authority consists of those who hoped that the imperial government could overrule or undermine the political decisions of responsible settler democracies. In other words, while the first pattern covers the use of imperial authority to build self-government, this second used imperial authority to constrain it. Two chapters (5 and 7) related to minority groups (English settlers in Quebec, and Black Africans in the Cape Colony) who experienced persecution at the hands of majority groups, and who consequently looked to the imperial government to protect their minority rights. Two other chapters (4 and 6) related to anti-war activists who hoped that imperial authorities could control the warmongering tendencies of settler governments in New Zealand and the Cape Colony. In all of these cases, imperial authority took on an increased importance following the rise of settler self-governments because it promised a means of governance untouched by local prejudices and political squabbles.

Those cases from New Zealand and the Cape Colony of appealing to imperial authority to avoid warfare are perhaps not unsurprising given that the imperial government excluded control over foreign affairs from those colonies' responsible constitutions. What is interesting, however, is the fact that settlers in these cases did not seek to use imperial military resources to fight colonial wars for them, which is a common theme across colonial historiography. Instead, these settlers wanted the imperial government to use their control over foreign affairs to end colonial wars that they believed jeopardized settler lives and property. Such wars were supported by the majority of their fellow colonists, but the individuals in these chapters believed that they understood something that others did not, and that democracy had essentially descended into mob rule. In these cases, the capacity of such misinformed governance by responsible governments increased the importance and significance of imperial authority as a guarantee that warfare would be in the hands of those with cooler heads on their shoulders.

On the other hand, those cases from Canada and Natal dealing with resistance to the introduction or operation of responsible government are entirely at odds with established historical narratives. Mythological national histories of these (and other) colonies hold that virtually everyone demanded the right to self-government in opposition to imperial authoritarianism. Even more recent critical histories, which question many of the whitewashed and gendered narratives within national mythologies, give little mention of those who preferred to remain under authoritarian rule. These anti-responsible perspectives provide crucial nuance to depictions of settler societies that have remained far too simplistic and homogeneous. More than that, they provide context for understanding the continuity of attachment to the British Empire following the dawn of self-government, for they demonstrate that the Empire was still associated with formal political power. Rather than simply connoting cultural association and heritage, the idea of imperial sovereignty gave people hope that a higher power existed that could unilaterally solve local problems and could act as a court of appeal when needed. Only by recognizing the power of that hope can we comprehend why settlers continued to profess their loyalty to an Empire that many denounced as tyrannical.

Moving beyond the realm of perception and belief, the second question raised at the beginning of this book related to real-world impact, asking: what was the relationship between imperial authority and the settler power structures that took shape in the years leading up to and following the cession of self-government? The *intentions* of the many petitioners in this book were varied and diverse, ranging from settlers fighting to secure control over Zulu land and society in Natal, to Māori fighting to resist settler dispossession in New Zealand. But these intentions are largely irrelevant in terms of impact given that the imperial government refused to intervene in nearly all of the issues surveyed in this book. It is therefore difficult to say that imperial authority had any direct impact at all.

Yet failure is itself impactful, because every success is contingent on failure. Antoinette Burton reminds us that "the very character of imperial power was shaped by its challengers and by the trouble they made for its stewards,"[3] meaning that it was only through pushing against Empire that Empire was forced to define and defend its borders. This principle is equally applicable to the failed appeals to imperial power examined in this book, because the oppressive and genocidal power structures in settler colonies of the late nineteenth and twentieth century were contingent upon the imperial government's disavowal of responsibility for policing colonial administration. This is the essence of Zoë Laidlaw's argument that imperial administrators became complicit in settler colonialism when they remained silent in the face of settler violence, creating a "series of silences" that allowed such violence to proliferate and become normalized.[4] However, as this book has shown, disavowal was seldom the sole responsibility of administrators in Britain.

On the contrary, imperial disavowal was disaggregated across a conglomeration of people from both sides of the metropole–colony divide. Settler government officials such as prime ministers, attorney generals, and ministers of native affairs played a major role in sabotaging claims upon imperial authority in Chapters 2, 4, 7, and 8. Settler civilians such as newspaper editors and townspeople at public meetings opposed imperial petitions in Chapters 5 and 6. Governors, as representatives of the Colonial Office in the colonies, asserted a heavy hand in their covering letters of petitions and their investigations of Indigenous rights abuses in Chapters 3, 4, and 7. In Britain, the complicity of Colonial Office officials was combined with that of newspaper editors, philanthropists, and the royal family themselves in Chapters 5, 8, and 9. This disaggregated conglomeration of complicity supports the assertion by Corey Snelgrove, Rita Dhamoon, and Jeff Corntassel that a host of contingent and conditional elements afforded settler colonialism the opportunity to become hegemonic.[5] The imperial government's ultimate decision not to intervene in the events covered in this book was contingent upon the combined actions of all of these people, some of whom purposefully worked to sabotage claims on imperial authority and some of whom were simply uninterested in Indigenous–settler relations.

Recognizing that this broad culture of imperial disavowal extended beyond administrators in the Colonial Office is important, because it underscores the intentionality of imperial complicity. In every chapter of this book, the imperial government was presented with at least two different points of view, and it consistently believed and supported the views of settler governments. This pattern shows that disavowal did not occur in a fit of absence of mind, but was a deliberate choice in the face of opposing perspectives and plausible alternative plans of action. The relationship between imperial authority and settler colonial power structures was thus not simply disavowal, but effectively amounted to endorsement.

These two overarching findings, that some people in the colonies perceived imperial authority to take on an increased importance as a guarantor of rights following settler self-government at the same time as others in the colonies and the metropole were working to sabotage imperial intervention, offer a new perspective on ongoing debates about the futures of the British World and settler colonial studies approaches to colonial history. The British World school is nearing its fourth decade as a formal subdiscipline (if the first British World conference at the Institute of Commonwealth Studies in 1998 is taken as its starting point) and continues to inform myriad new papers, monographs, and edited collections.[6] Nevertheless, critics have identified numerous limitations to the British World framework. Many of these limitations are debatable. For instance, Dan Kennedy, Rachel Bright, and Andrew Dilley are sceptical of the British World's ambiguity over who exactly counts as "British" and which exact territories fell within this "World," and express concerns that it "begs for definitional clarity" so that "many different and distinct phenomena are collapsed together without precision."[7] Yet most British World scholars see this ambiguity as a strength rather than a weakness, and neither Kennedy nor Bright and Dilley offer any counterpoints indicating why their preference for precision is better than ambiguity. Indeed, as historians from Ann Laura Stoler and Frederick Cooper to Andrew Porter have argued for decades, imperial history must always be somewhat fluid, whether because historical identifiers such as "civilized" or "coloured" were open to constant negotiation and interpretation or because scholarly categories such as "formal" and "informal" empire are overlapping and abstract.[8]

A more convincing critique of the British World school holds that it fails to attend to power structures, and I entirely agree. [9] From Simon Potter's contention that the imperial press shaped culture but not politics to John Darwin's insistence that Britishness entailed loyalty to British institutions but not to the British government, British World approaches have consistently ignored power struggles between colonial and imperial authorities.[10] This ignorance is often somewhat justified by the sources that historians tend to use. For example, many British World scholars lean upon powerful polemicists such as Charles Dilke and Joseph Chamberlain to access what late Victorians understood as the proper relationship between the various nodes of the British World, and such analyses find that Dilke clearly saw Greater Britain as a *cultural* rather than a *political* unit while Chamberlain never achieved popular support for an imperial federation.[11] Yet the polemics of "great men" such as Chamberlain and Dilke do not necessarily represent the perspectives of colonial inhabitants themselves, and it is these on-the-ground perspectives on the proper relationship between colonial and imperial power that have remained understudied. To address this issue, I have borrowed settler colonial studies' analytical framework of imperialism and colonialism as overlapping power structures and applied it to the expressions of imperial belonging articulated by the individuals in this book.

By doing so, I have been able to identify relationships between cultural connectivity within the British World and subjectivity to settler and imperial power. My findings across all chapters reveal that continued connection to the British World was *not* detached from subjectivity to imperial power, but that adherence to cultural ideals of British subjecthood were closely entangled with visions of colonial subjection to imperial power.

More importantly, visions of colonial subjection to imperial power nearly always revolved around policing racial hierarchies and controlling access to land. John Akerman invoked imperial power to control Zulu marital practices and land rights. Philip Carpenter looked to the Empire to assert the rights of settler populations to access and control Mohawk land. John Tengo Jabavu and Hirini Taiwhanga called on imperial networks to undermine settler discourses of racialized credibility. All of these cases show that the interconnected networks of the British World, far from simply transferring ideas across imperial spaces, were directly utilized to maintain and challenge the unbalanced racialized power structures within settler societies. Thus, by applying a settler colonial studies analysis of imperial and colonial power to a British World analysis of identity and connectivity, this book offers one possible means of writing power into the British World.

Settler colonial studies as a distinct field of study is around the same age as the British World school, tracing back to Patrick Wolfe's theoretical framework laid out in 1994 (although based on previous and chronically undercited Indigenous scholarship),[12] and it too continues to inspire countless monographs and articles.[13] Just as with the British World school, settler colonial studies has been subject to significant criticism in recent years, although some critiques are more substantial than others. One of the most common refrains is that settler colonial studies remarginalizes Indigeneity by focusing on settler violence instead of Indigenous resistance.[14] But J. Kēhaulani Kauanui argues that such claims are ignorant of the wide variety of settler colonial scholarship that does centre Indigenous agency, while Alice Te Punga Somerville and Shino Konishi point out that settler colonial studies provides valuable analytical tools for contextualizing Indigenous agency as long as Indigeneity and settler colonialism are not treated as mutually exclusive fields of study.[15] This is precisely the model I adopted in the case studies of John Tengo Jabavu, Hirini Taiwhanga, and Tāwhao, where I converged structures of settler government control and Indigenous agency to challenge and subvert those structures into a single frame.

A more problematic critique of settler colonial studies is that it succumbs to what Alissa Macoun and Elizabeth Strakosch term "colonial fatalism," in which excessive emphasis on structure produces representations of settler colonialism as inevitable. This critique is specifically directed towards the impact of scholarship on activism in the present. According to Macoun and Strakosch (among other Indigenous scholars), settler colonial studies' analysis of oppression as a deep-rooted historical structure precludes efforts at decolonization so that "the role of political activists is to wait for the structurally determined future, and at most to prepare others for its arrival."[16] Yet the colonial fatalism critique also applies to the study of the past. Historians have been quite correct to identify the development of responsible government in the colonies as a pivotal moment in the construction of settler power structures and have usefully theorized settler and imperial sovereignty as oppositional. In the process, however, historians have too readily assumed that the advent of self-government and the oppositionality of settler and imperial sovereignty inevitably led to the settler colonial nation states that took shape in the early twentieth century and remain with us today.

On the contrary, this book reveals that there was no inevitability to how settler and imperial sovereignties would reconcile between 1860 and 1890. Instead, I have demonstrated that colonial inhabitants continued attempting to negotiate the terms of settler–imperial power relations for decades after self-government first arose in the 1850s. By arguing that people in the colonies articulated hybrid imperial/colonial subjectivities long after the dawn of settler self-government, this book presents a novel interpretation of the origins of settler colonial sovereignty that is better suited to the ambiguity and open-endedness of the period. Combining British World approaches to continuities of imperial interconnectivity with settler colonial studies approaches to conceptualizing settler and imperial sovereignty therefore offers one means of ameliorating the colonial fatalism issues within settler colonial studies scholarship.

Notes

1 Lisa Ford, *Settler Sovereignty: Jurisdiction and Indigenous People in America and Australia, 1788–1836* (Cambridge, MA: Harvard University Press, 2010), 4; Angela Woollacott, *Settler Society in the Australian Colonies: Self-Government and Imperial Culture* (Oxford: Oxford University Press, 2015), 103–104.

2 Philip Carpenter to Frederick Chesson, 1 January 1876, Oxford, Bodleian Libraries, MS Brit. Emp. s. 22 G83b/1–9.

3 Antoinette Burton, *The Trouble with Empire: Challenges to Modern British Imperialism* (Oxford: Oxford University Press, 2015), 1.

4 Zoë Laidlaw, "Imperial Complicity: Indigenous Dispossession in British History and History Writing," in Catherine Hall, Nicholas Draper, and Keith McClelland (eds), *Emancipation and the Remaking of the British Imperial World* (Manchester: Manchester University Press, 2014), 131–148.

5 Corey Snelgrove, Rita Dhamoon, and Jeff Corntassel, "Unsettling Settler Colonialism: The Discourse and Politics of Settlers, and Solidarity with Indigenous Nations," *Decolonization: Indigeneity, Education & Society* 3, no. 2 (2014): 1–32, https://jps.library.utoronto.ca/index.php/des/article/view/21166/17970 (accessed 11 March 2025).

6 For examples, see Jatinder Mann and Iain Johnston-White (eds), *Revisiting the British World: New Voices and Perspectives* (Bristol: Peter Lang, 2022); Jeremy Black, *Geographies of an Imperial Power: The British World, 1688–1815* (Bloomington: Indiana University Press, 2018); Peter Denney, Bruce Buchan, David Ellison, and Karen Crawley (eds), *Sound, Space and Civility in the British World, 1700–1850* (London: Routledge, 2019); Géraldine Vaughan, "A Global Network: Ultra-Protestant Societies throughout the British World," in Géraldine Vaughan (ed.), *Anti-Catholicism and British Identities in Britain, Canada and Australia, 1880s–1920s* (Cham: Palgrave Macmillan, 2022), 31–71; David Thackeray, "Selling the Empire? Marketing and the Demise of the British World, c. 1920–1960," *The Journal of Imperial and Commonwealth History* 48, no. 4 (2020): 679–705, DOI: 10.1080/03086534.2020.1741837; Hugh Morrison, *Protestant Children, Missions and Education in the British World* (Leiden: Brill, 2021); and Leigh Muffet, "The Cape of Good Hope Colony and the British World Turned Upside-Down, 1806–1836," *The Journal of Imperial and Commonwealth History* (2022): 1–35, DOI: 10.1080/03086534.2022.2086205.

7 Rachel Bright and Andrew Dilley, "After the British World," *The Historical Journal* 60, no. 2 (2017): 547–568 (554–557), DOI: 10.1017/S0018246X16000510; Dane Kennedy, *The Imperial History Wars: Debating the British Empire* (London: Bloomsbury Academic, 2018), 75–77.

8 Andrew Porter, *European Imperialism, 1860–1914* (Basingstoke: Macmillan, 1994), 1–13; Frederick Cooper and Ann Laura Stoler, *Tensions of Empire: Colonial Cultures in a Bourgeois World* (Berkeley: University of California Press, 1997), 6–11.

9 Bright and Dilley, "After the British World," 562–563; Tamson Pietsch, "Rethinking the British World," *Journal of British Studies* 52, no. 2 (2013): 441–463 (446), DOI: 10.1017/jbr.2013.53; Gary Magee and Andrew Thompson, *Empire and Globalisation: Networks of People, Goods and Capital in the British World, c. 1850–1914* (Cambridge: Cambridge University Press, 2010), 25–26; Kennedy, *The Imperial History Wars*, 78–80.

10 Simon Potter, *News and the British World: The Emergence of an Imperial Press System, 1876–1922* (Oxford: Clarendon Press, 2003), 58–62; John Darwin, *The Empire Project: The Rise and Fall of the British World-System, 1830–1970* (Cambridge: Cambridge University Press, 2009), 147.

11 For instance, see Daniel Gorman, *Imperial Citizenship: Empire and the Question of Belonging* (Manchester: Manchester University Press, 2007); and Duncan Bell, *The Idea of Greater Britain: Empire and the Future of World Order, 1860–1900* (Princeton: Princeton University Press, 2007).

12 J. Kēhaulani Kauanui, "False Dilemmas and Settler Colonial Studies: Response to Lorenzo Veracini, 'Is Settler Colonial Studies Even Useful?,'" *Postcolonial Studies* 24, no. 2 (2021): 290–296, DOI: 10.1080/13688790.2020.1857023.

13 For examples, see Philip Steer, *Settler Colonialism in Victorian Literature: Economics and Political Identity in the Networks of Empire* (Cambridge: Cambridge University Press, 2020); Cole Harris, *A Bounded Land: Reflections on Settler Colonialism in Canada* (Vancouver: University of British Columbia Press, 2021); Natsu Taylor Saito, *Settler Colonialism, Race, and the Law: Why Structural Racism Persists* (New York: NYU Press, 2020); T. J. Tallie, *Queering Colonial Natal: Indigeneity and the Violence of Belonging in Southern Africa* (Minneapolis: University of Minnesota Press, 2019); Lisa Slater, *Anxieties of Belonging in Settler Colonialism: Australia, Race and Place* (New York: Routledge, 2018); and Adam Dahl, *Empire of the People: Settler Colonialism and the Foundations of Modern Democratic Thought* (Lawrence: University Press of Kansas, 2018).

14 For instance, see Kennedy, *The Imperial History Wars*, 83.

15 Kauanui, "False Dilemmas and Settler Colonial Studies," 292–293; Alice Te Punga Somerville, "OMG Settler Colonial Studies: Response to Lorenzo Veracini's 'Is Settler Colonial Studies Even Useful?,'" *Postcolonial Studies* 24, no. 2 (2021): 278–282, DOI: 10.1080/13688790.2020.1854980; Shino Konishi, "First Nations Scholars, Settler Colonial Studies, and Indigenous History," *Australian Historical Studies* 50, no. 3 (2019): 285–304, DOI: 10.1080/1031461X.2019.1620300.

16 Alissa Macoun and Elizabeth Strakosch, "The Ethical Demands of Settler Colonial Theory," *Settler Colonial Studies* 3, no. 3 (2013): 426–443 (435), DOI: 10.1080/2201473X.2013.810695. See also Snelgrove *et al.*, "Unsettling Settler Colonialism," 8–9; and Konishi, "First Nations Scholars," 291–292.

Bibliography

Primary material

Unpublished

Anglican Diocese of Perth Archives, Perth, Australia

Yearbooks. 200900055001.

Archives New Zealand, Wellington, New Zealand

Taiwhanga's papers.

Bodleian Libraries, Oxford, United Kingdom

Aborigines' Protection Society papers. Frederick Chesson files. MSS Brit. Emp. s. 18 C123–149.
Anti-Slavery Society papers. Territorial files. MSS Brit. Emp. s. 22 G83–99.

Lambeth Palace Library, London, United Kingdom

Edward White Benson papers.

Library and Archives Canada, Ottawa, Canada.

Department of Indian Affairs files. RG10.

State Library of Western Australia, Perth, Australia

Bishop Henry Hutton Parry papers. ACC.

The National Archives, London, United Kingdom

Canada Original Correspondence. CO 42.
Cape of Good Hope Original Correspondence. CO 48.
Colonial Office papers.
Natal Original Correspondence. CO 179.
New Zealand Original Correspondence. CO 209.

Vancouver Island Original Correspondence. CO 305.
Western Australia Original Correspondence. CO 18.

University of KwaZulu-Natal Libraries, Durban, South Africa

Killie Campbell Collections, Papers of Sir John Ackerman

Wellington City Libraries, Wellington, New Zealand

Octavius Hadfield Papers. 50008.

Published

Akerman, John. *Native Government in Natal*. London: 17 King William Street, 1877.

Browne, Harold. *The Case of the War in New Zealand from Authentic Documents*. Cambridge: Deighton, Bell, 1860.

Busby, James. *Remarks upon a Pamphlet Entitled "The Taranaki Question, by Sir William Martin, D.C.L., Late Chief Justice of New Zealand."* Auckland: Philip Kunst, 1860.

Green, William Sebright. "British Columbia." In *British America, with Two Maps*. London: Kegan Paul, Trench, Trübner, 1900.

Gribble, John Brown. *Dark Deeds in a Sunny Land; or, Blacks and Whites in North-West Australia*. Nedlands: University of Western Australia Press, 1987.

Hadfield, Octavius. *A Sequel to "One of England's Little Wars": Being an Account of the Real Origin of the War in New Zealand, Its Present Stage, and the Future Prospects of the Colony*. London: Williams and Norgate, 1861.

Harvey, Arthur, ed. *The Year Book and Almanac of Canada for 1869: Being an Annual Statistical Abstract for the Dominion, and a Record of Legislation and of Public Men in British North America*. Montreal: Montreal Printing and Publishing Company, 1869.

Jones, John James. *The Emigrants' Guide: Being a Statement Culled from Reliable Sources, as to the Relative Merits of the Dominion of Canada, New South Wales, Victoria, South Australia, Queensland, Western Australia, New Zealand, Tasmania, Cape of Good Hope, Natal, United States of America, etc., with Their Wages, Cost of Living, and Other Necessary Information for Those Seeking New Homes*. London: The International Employment & Emigration Agency, 1880.

Lambton, John, earl of Durham. *The Report and Despatches of the Earl of Durham, Her Majesty's High Commissioner and Governor-General of British North America*. London: Ridgways, 1839.

Maclean, John. *A Compendium of Kafir Laws and Customs: Including Genealogical Tables of Kafir Chiefs and Various Tribal Census Returns*. Mount Coke: Wesleyan Mission Press, 1858.

Martin, William. *Remarks on "Notes Published for the New Zealand Government" on Sir William Martin's Pamphlet Entitled The Taranaki Question*. London: W. H. Dalton, 1861.

Martin, William. *The Taranaki Question*. Auckland: The Melanesian Press, 1860.

Mayne, Richard Charles. *Four Years in British Columbia*. London: John Murray, 1862.

New Zealand. *Extracts of Letters from New Zealand on the War Question, with an Article from the New Zealand Spectator of November 3rd 1860, and a Copy of the Native Offenders' Bill.* London: F. J. Wilson, 1861.

Protestant Defence Alliance. *The Indians of the Lake of Two Mountains and the Seminary of St Sulpice.* Montreal: Witness Printing House, 1876.

Royal Colonial Institute. *Report of Proceedings, 1882–1883.*

Todd, Alpheus. *Parliamentary Government in the British Colonies.* 2nd edn. London: Longmans, Green, 1894.

Cape of Good Hope

Commission and Instructions to Major-General Sir Charles Warren, K.C.M.G., as Special Commissioner to Bechuanaland, November 1884. London: Eyre and Spottiswoode, 1884.

Cape of Good Hope Commission on Native Laws and Customs, *Report and Proceedings: With Appendices of the Government Commission on Native Laws and Customs. Presented to Both Houses of Parliament by His Excellency the Governor, January, 1883.* Cape Town: W. A. Richards and Sons, 1883.

Statues of the Cape of Good Hope, 1652–1886. Cape Town: W. A. Richards and Sons, 1887.

Statutes of the Cape of Good Hope Passed by the Seventh Parliament during Sessions 1884–1888. W. A. Richards and Sons, 1889.

British Columbia

Debate on the Subject of Confederation with Canada: Reprinted from the Government Gazette Extraordinary of March, 1870. Victoria: William H. Cullin, 1912.

Journals of the Legislative Council of British Columbia from the 15th February to the 23rd April, 1870. Victoria: Government Printing Office, 1870.

British House of Commons

Commission and Instructions to Major-General Sir Charles Warren, K.C.M.G., as Special Commissioner to Bechuanaland, November 1884 (London: Eyre and Spottiswoode, 1884).

Correspondence Relating to the Proposal to Establish Responsible Government in Natal, Presented to Both Houses of Parliament by Command of Her Majesty, July 1891. London: Eyre and Spottiswoode, 1891.

Correspondence Respecting Native Affairs in New Zealand, and the Imprisonment of Certain Māories, Presented to Both Houses of Parliament by Command of Her Majesty August 1882. London: Eyre and Spottiswoode, 1882.

Further Correspondence Respecting the Affairs of the Transvaal and Adjacent Territories, October 1884. London: Eyre and Spottiswoode, 1884.

Further Correspondence Respecting the Affairs of the Transvaal and Adjacent Territories, December 1884. London: Eyre and Spottiswoode, 1885.

Further Correspondence Respecting the Affairs of the Transvaal and Adjacent Territories, February 1885. London: Eyre and Spottiswoode, 1885.

Further Correspondence Respecting the Affairs of the Transvaal and Adjacent Territories, May 1885. London: Eyre and Spottiswoode, 1885.
Further Correspondence Respecting the Affairs of the Transvaal and Adjacent Territories, August 1885. London: Eyre and Spottiswoode, 1885.

New Zealand

Appendix to the Journals of the House of Representatives. 1876.
Appendix to the Journals of the House of Representatives. 1878.
The New Zealand Constitution Act: Together with Correspondence between the Secretary of State for the Colonies and the Governor-in-Chief of New Zealand in Explanation Thereof (Wellington: R. Stokes, 1853).

Periodicals

The Aborigines' Friend (London).
Belfast News-Letter.
British Colonist (Victoria, British Columbia).
Cape Argus (Cape Town).
Cape Times (Cape Town).
Daily News (London).
Daily News (Perth).
Graham's Town Journal (Cape Colony).
Illustrated London News.
Marlborough Express (New Zealand).
Montreal Daily Witness.
Montreal Gazette.
Montreal Herald.
Montreal Star.
Morning Chronicle (London).
Natal Witness (Pietermaritzburg).
New Zealand Gazette.
New Zealand Herald.
Thames Advertiser (Ontario).
The Standard (London).
The Times.
Toronto Globe.
Wanganui Herald (New Zealand).

Secondary material

Allbrook, Malcolm. "'A Disguised and Unquestionable Form of Slavery': Aboriginal Labour on the Nineteenth-Century Pearling Fleet in North-West Australia." *Australian Journal of Biography and History* 6 (2022): 79–101, DOI: 10.22459/AJBH.06.2022.04.
Allbrook, Malcolm. *Henry Prinsep's Empire: Framing a Distant Colony*. Canberra: Australian National University Press, 2014.
Banerjee, Sukanya. *Becoming Imperial Citizens: Indians in the Late-Victorian Empire*. Durham, NC: Duke University Press, 2010.

Banner, Stuart. *Possessing the Pacific: Land, Settlers, and Indigenous People from Australia to Alaska*. Cambridge, MA: Harvard University Press, 2007.

Bannet, Eve Tavor. *Empire of Letters: Letter Manuals and Transatlantic Correspondence, 1688–1820*. Cambridge: Cambridge University Press, 2005.

Barnes, Felicity. *Selling Britishness: Commodity Culture, the Dominions, and Empire*. Montreal: McGill-Queen's University Press, 2022.

Baxby, Derrick. "Smallpox Vaccine: Ahead of Its Time." *Interdisciplinary Science Reviews* 26, no. 2 (2001): 125–138, DOI: 10.1179/isr.2001.26.2.125.

Belgrave, Michael. *Dancing with the King: The Rise and Fall of the King Country, 1864–1885*. Auckland: Auckland University Press, 2017.

Belich, James. *The New Zealand Wars and the Victorian Interpretation of Racial Conflict*. Auckland: Auckland University Press, 1986.

Belich, James. *Replenishing the Earth: The Settler Revolution and the Rise of the Anglo-World, 1783–1939*. Oxford: Oxford University Press, 2011.

Bell, Duncan. *The Idea of Greater Britain: Empire and the Future of World Order, 1860–1900*. Princeton: Princeton University Press, 2007.

Bell, Duncan. *Reordering the World: Essays on Liberalism and Empire*. Princeton: Princeton University Press, 2016.

Bell, Rachael. "'Texts and Translations': Ruth Ross and the Treaty of Waitangi." *New Zealand Journal of History* 43, no. 1 (2009): 39–58, www.nzjh.auckland.ac.nz/docs/2009/NZJH_43_1_03.pdf (accessed 11 March 2025).

Bennett, Alison. "Diplomatic Gifts: Rethinking Colonial Politics in Uganda through Objects." *History in Africa* 45 (2018): 193–220, DOI: 10.1017/hia.2018.5.

Benton, Lauren. *A Search for Sovereignty: Law and Geography in European Empires, 1400–1900*. Cambridge: Cambridge University Press, 2009.

Benton, Lauren, and Lisa Ford. *Rage for Order: The British Empire and the Origins of International Law*. Cambridge, MA: Harvard University Press, 2016.

Benton, Lauren, and Richard Ross, eds. *Legal Pluralism and Empires, 1500–1850*. New York: New York University Press, 2013.

Biedermann, Zoltán, Anne Gerritsen, and Giorgio Riello, eds. *Global Gifts: The Material Culture of Diplomacy in Early Modern Eurasia*. Cambridge: Cambridge University Press, 2017.

Bierbach, Jeremy. *Frontiers of Equality in the Development of EU and US Citizenship*. The Hague: TMC Asser Press, 2017.

Black, Jeremy. *Geographies of an Imperial Power: The British World, 1688–1815*. Bloomington: Indiana University Press, 2018.

Blackley, Roger. "King Tāwhiao's Big O.E.." *Turnbull Library Record*, 1 January 2012, https://paperspast.natlib.govt.nz/periodicals/TLR20120101.2.9 (accessed 20 March 2025).

Boyd, Robert. *The Coming of the Spirit of Pestilence: Introduced Infectious Diseases and Population Decline among Northwest Coast Indians, 1774–1874*. Vancouver/Seattle: University of British Columbia Press/University of Washington Press, 1999.

Brantlinger, Patrick. *Dark Vanishings: Discourse on the Extinction of Primitive Races, 1800–1930*. Ithaca: Cornell University Press, 2003.

Brealey, Kenneth. "Travels from Point Ellice: Peter O'Reilly and the Indian Reserve System in British Columbia." *The British Columbian Quarterly* 115, no. 6 (1997): 181–236.

Bright, Rachel, and Andrew Dilley. "After the British World." *The Historical Journal* 60, no. 2 (2017): 547–568, DOI: 10.1017/S0018246X16000510.

Buckner, Phillip. "The Creation of the Dominion of Canada, 1860–1901." In Phillip Buckner, ed., *Canada and the British Empire*. Oxford: Oxford University Press, 2010.

Burton, Antoinette. *The Trouble with Empire: Challenges to Modern British Imperialism*. Oxford: Oxford University Press, 2015.

Byrd, Jodi. *The Transit of Empire: Indigenous Critiques of Colonialism*. Minneapolis: University of Minnesota Press, 2011.

Carey, Hilary. *Empire of Hell: Religion and the Campaign to End Convict Transportation in the British Empire, 1788–1875*. Cambridge: Cambridge University Press, 2019.

Carey, Hilary. *God's Empire: Religion and Colonialism in the British World, c. 1801–1908*. Cambridge: Cambridge University Press, 2011.

Carter, Sarah, and Maria Nugent, eds. *Mistress of Everything: Queen Victoria in Indigenous Worlds*. Manchester: Manchester University Press, 2017.

Cavanagh, Allison. "Letters to the Editor as a Tool of Citizenship." In Allison Cavanagh and John Steel, eds, *Letters to the Editor: Comparative and Historical Perspectives*. Cham: Palgrave Macmillan, 2019.

Cavanaugh, Edward, and Lorenzo Veracini, eds. *The Routledge Handbook of the History of Settler Colonialism*. Oxford: Routledge, 2017.

Christopher, A. J. "South African Petitions to the House of Commons, 1833–1914: Grievances, Protests, Advice and Information." *Historia* 63, no. 1 (2018): 1–23, DOI: 10.17159/2309-8392/2018/v63n1a1.

Christopher, Anthony. "South African Petitions to the House of Commons, 1833–1914: Grievances, Protests, Advice and Information." *Historia* 63, no. 1 (2018): 1–23, DOI: 10.17159/2309-8392/2018/v63n1a1.

Cochrane, Peter. *Colonial Ambition: Foundations of Australian Democracy*. Melbourne: Melbourne University Press, 2006.

Colenso, Gwilym. "Breaking with the Old Pattern of Control: African Deputations to Britain from Southern Africa in the Late Nineteenth and Early Twentieth Centuries." *South African Historical Journal* 69, no. 4 (2017): 501–547, DOI: 10.1080/02582473.2017.1398777.

Cooper, Frederick. *Citizenship, Inequality, and Difference: Historical Perspectives*. Princeton: Princeton University Press, 2018.

Cooper, Frederick, and Ann Laura Stoler. *Tensions of Empire: Colonial Cultures in a Bourgeois World*. Berkeley: University of California Press, 1997.

Coulthard, Glen. *Red Skin, White Masks: Rejecting the Colonial Politics of Recognition*. Minneapolis: University of Minnesota Press, 2014.

Crawford, Sharika D., and Ana Isabel Márquez-Pérez. "A Contact Zone: The Turtle Commons of the Western Caribbean." *International Journal of Maritime History* 28, no. 1 (2016): 64–80, DOI: 10.1177/0843871415624095.

Cruickshank, Joanna, and Patricia Grimshaw. "Indigenous Land Loss, Justice and Race: Ann Bon and the Contradictions of Settler Humanitarianism." In Zoë Laidlaw and Alan Lester, eds, *Indigenous Communities and Settler Colonialism: Land Holding, Loss and Survival in an Interconnected World*. Cham: Palgrave Macmillan, 2015.

Cumming, Catherine. "The Hokianga Dog Tax Uprising." *Counterfutures* 11 (2021): 18–33, DOI: 10.26686/cf.v11.7351.

Cunliffe, Emily. "Whales and Whale Bone Technology in New Zealand Prehistory." MA thesis, University of Otago, 2014.

Curthoys, Ann. "The Dog that Didn't Bark: The Durham Report, Indigenous Dispossession, and Self-Government for Britain's Settler Colonies." In Karen Dubinsky, Adele Perry, and Henry Yu, eds, *Within and without the Nation: Canadian History as Transnational History*. Toronto: University of Toronto Press, 2015.

Curthoys, Ann, and Jeremy Martens. "Serious Collisions: Settlers, Indigenous People, and Imperial Policy in Western Australia and Natal." *Journal of Australian Colonial History* 15 (2013): 121–144.

Curthoys, Ann, and Jessie Mitchell. "Bring This Paper to the Good Governor: Aboriginal Petitioning in Britain's Australia Colonies." In Saliha Belmessous, ed., *Native Claims: Indigenous Law against Empire, 1500–1920*. Oxford: Oxford University Press, 2011.

Curthoys, Ann, and Jessie Mitchell. *Taking Liberty: Indigenous Rights and Settler Self-Government in Colonial Australia, 1830–1890*. Cambridge: Cambridge University Press, 2018.

Dahl, Adam. *Empire of the People: Settler Colonialism and the Foundations of Modern Democratic Thought* (Lawrence: University Press of Kansas, 2018).

Dalziel, Raewyn. "Southern Islands: New Zealand and Polynesia." In Andrew Porter and William Roger Louis, eds, *The Oxford History of the British Empire*, Vol. III, *The Nineteenth Century*. Oxford: Oxford University Press, 1999.

Darwin, John. *The Empire Project: The Rise and Fall of the British World-System, 1830–1970*. Cambridge: Cambridge University Press, 2009.

Davenport, T. R. H. *The Afrikaner Bond: The History of a South African Political Party, 1880–1911*. Oxford: Oxford University Press, 1966.

Davenport, T. R. H. "The Responsible Government Issue in Natal, 1880–1882." *Butterworths South African Law Review* (1957): 84–133.

Davenport, T. R. H., and Christopher Saunders. *South Africa: A Modern History*. London: Palgrave Macmillan, 2000.

De Costa, Ravi. "Identity, Authority, and the Moral Worlds of Indigenous Petitions." *Comparative Studies in Society and History* 48, no. 3 (2006): 669–698, DOI: 10.1017/S0010417506000260.

De Zwart, Pim. "Cape Colony Price Index, 1835–1910." International Institute of Social History, www.iisg.nl/hpw/data.php#southafrica (accessed 11 March 2025).

Denney, Peter, Bruce Buchan, David Ellison, and Karen Crawley, eds. *Sound, Space and Civility in the British World, 1700–1850*. London: Routledge, 2019.

Denoon, Donald. "Understanding Settler Societies." *Historical Studies* 18, no. 73 (1979): 511–527, DOI: 10.1080/10314617908595611.

Douglas, Heather, and Mark Finnane. *Indigenous Crime and Settler Law: White Sovereignty after Empire*. New York: Palgrave Macmillan, 2012.

Du Plessis, Willemien, and Juanita Pienaar. "The More Things Change, the More They Stay the Same: The Story of Communal Land Tenure in South Africa." *Fundamina* 16, no. 1 (2010): 73–89, https://journals.co.za/doi/pdf/10.10520/EJC34404 (accessed 11 March 2025).

Edgecombe, D. R. "The Non-Racial Franchise in Cape Politics, 1853–1910." *African Historical Review* 10, nos 1–2 (1978): 21–37, DOI: 10.1080/00232087885310031.

Elbourne, Elizabeth. *Empire, Kinship and Violence: Family Histories, Indigenous Rights and the Making of Settler Colonialism, 1770–1842*. Cambridge: Cambridge University Press, 2023.

Elbourne, Elizabeth. “Indigenous Peoples and Imperial Networks in the Early Nineteenth Century: The Politics of Knowledge.” In Phillip Buckner and Douglas Francis, eds, *Rediscovering the British World*. Calgary: University of Calgary Press, 2005.

Elbourne, Elizabeth. “The Sin of the Settler: The 1835–36 Select Committee on Aborigines and Debates over Virtue and Conquest in the Early Nineteenth-Century British White Settler Empire.” *Journal of Colonialism and Colonial History* 4, no. 3 (2003), DOI: 10.1353/cch.2004.0003.

Evans, Julie, Patricia Grimshaw, and David Phillips. *Equal Subjects, Unequal Rights: Indigenous People in British Settler Colonies, 1830–1910*. Manchester: Manchester University Press, 2003.

Ewing, Cindy. “The Right to Petition in the Anticolonial Struggle at the United Nations.” In Erez Manela and Heather Streets-Salter, eds, *The Anticolonial Transnational: Imaginaries, Mobilities, and Networks in the Struggle against Empire*. Cambridge: Cambridge University Press, 2023.

Eyford, Ryan. “Quarantined within a New Colonial Order: The 1876–1877 Lake Winnipeg Smallpox Epidemic.” *Journal of the Canadian Historical Association* 17, no. 1 (2006): 55–78, DOI: 10.7202/016102ar.

Fennario, Tom. “Mohawk Land Dispute Unresolved 3 Decades after Siege of Kanehsatake,” *APTN News*, 11 July 2020, www.aptnnews.ca/national-news/siegekanehsatake30th/ (accessed 18 March 2025).

Festa, Lynn. “Humanity without Feathers.” *Humanity: An International Journal of Human Rights, Humanitarianism, and Development* 1, no. 1 (2010): 3–27, DOI: 10.1353/hum.2010.0007.

Fisher, Robin. “Joseph Trutch and Indian Land Policy.” In J. Friesen and H. K. Ralston, eds, *Historical Essays on British Columbia*. Ottawa: The Carleton Library, 1980.

Forbes, James. “‘A Deplorable Speech’: The Liberal Party vs Anti-Catholicism during the Alexander Mackenzie Administration, 1873–1878.” *Journal of the Canadian Historical Association* 28, no. 1 (2017): 193–216, DOI: 10.7202/1050899ar.

Ford, Lisa. *Settler Sovereignty: Jurisdiction and Indigenous People in America and Australia, 1788–1836*. Cambridge, MA: Harvard University Press, 2010.

Fuka, Lauren. “Object Monday: Māori Kete Baskets,” Maxwell Museum of Anthropology, 10 May 2021, https://maxwellmuseum.unm.edu/maxwell-at-home/objects/object-monday-m%C4%81ori-kete-baskets (accessed 19 March 2025).

Galbraith, John. “The Pamphlet Campaign on the Boer War.” *The Journal of Modern History* 24, no. 2 (1952): 111–126.

Gentry, Kynan. *History, Heritage, and Colonialism: Historical Consciousness, Britishness, and Cultural Identity in New Zealand, 1870–1940*. Manchester: Manchester University Press, 2015.

Gill, Rebecca. *Calculating Compassion: Humanity and Relief in War, Britain 1870–1914*. Manchester: Manchester University Press, 2013.

Gorman, Daniel. *Imperial Citizenship: Empire and the Question of Belonging*. Manchester: Manchester University Press, 2007.

Greer, Allan. “1837–38: Rebellion Reconsidered.” *The Canadian Historical Review* 76, no. 1 (1995): 1–18, www.muse.jhu.edu/article/574662 (accessed 11 March 2025).

Guy, Jeff. *The Heretic: A Study of the life of John William Colenso, 1814–1883*. Johannesburg: Ravan Press, 1983.

Guy, Jeff. *Theophilus Shepstone and the Forging of Natal: African Autonomy and Settler Colonialism in the Making of Traditional Authority*. Scottsville: University of KwaZulu-Natal Press, 2013.

Habermas, Jürgen. *The Structural Transformation of the Public Sphere: An Inquiry into a Category of Bourgeois Society*. Cambridge, MA: MIT Press, 1989.

Hackett, Paul. "Averting Disaster: The Hudson's Bay Company and Smallpox in Western Canada during the Late Eighteenth and Early Nineteenth Centuries." *Bulletin of the History of Medicine* 78, no. 3 (2004): 757–609, www.jstor.org/stable/44448061 (accessed 11 March 2025).

Haig-Brown, Celia, and Daniel Nock, eds, *With Good Intentions: Euro-Canadian and Aboriginal Relations in Colonial Canada* (Vancouver: University of British Columbia Press, 2005).

Hardwick, Joseph. *Prayer, Providence and Empire: Special Worship in the British World, 1783–1919*. Manchester: Manchester University Press, 2021.

Harrington, Jack. *The Uses of Imperial Citizenship: The British and French Empires*. Lanham: Rowman & Littlefield, 2020.

Harris, Cole. *A Bounded Land: Reflections on Settler Colonialism in Canada*. Vancouver: University of British Columbia Press, 2021.

Harris, Cole. *Making Native Space: Colonialism, Resistance, and Reserves in British Columbia*. Vancouver: University of British Columbia Press, 2002.

Harris, John. *One Blood: 200 Years of Aboriginal Encounter with Christianity: A Story of Hope*. Sutherland: Albatross Books, 1990.

Hastings, Paula. *Dominion over Palm and Pine: A History of Canadian Aspirations in the British Caribbean*. Montreal: McGill-Queen's University Press, 2022.

Heartfield, James. *The Aborigines' Protection Society: Humanitarian Imperialism in Australia, New Zealand, Fiji, Canada, South Africa, and the Congo, 1836–1909*. New York: Columbia University Press, 2011.

Henare, Amiria. "Taonga Mäori: Encompassing Rights and Property in New Zealand." In Amiria Henare, Martin Holbraad, and Sari Wastell, eds, *Thinking through Things: Theorising Artefacts Ethnographically*. London: Routledge, 2006.

Hendrickson, James E., ed. *Journals of the Colonial Legislatures of the Colonies of Vancouver Island and British Columbia, 1851–1871*, Vol. V. Victoria: Provincial Archives of British Columbia, 1980.

Herd, Norman. *The Bent Pine: The Trial of Chief Langalibalele*. Johannesburg: Ravan Press, 1976.

Hickford, Mark. *Lords of the Land: Indigenous Property Rights and the Jurisprudence of Empire*. Oxford: Oxford University Press, 2011.

Hildebrandt, Paula, and Sybille Peters. "Introduction." In Paula Hildebrandt, Kerstin Evert, Sibylle Peters, Mirjam Schaub, Kathrin Wildner, and Gesa Ziemer, eds. *Performing Citizenship: Bodies, Agencies, Limitations*. Cham: Palgrave Macmillan, 2019.

Hill, Robert. *Voice of the Vanishing Minority: Robert Sellar and the Huntingdon Gleaner, 1863–1919*. Montreal: McGill-Queen's University Press, 1998.

Hunt, Su-Jane. "The Gribble Affair: A Study in Colonial Politics." In John Brown Gribble, *Dark Deeds in a Sunny Land; or, Blacks and Whites in North-West Australia*. Nedlands: University of Western Australia Press, 1987.

Hutchinson, Sam. *Settlers, War, and Empire in the Press: Unsettling News in Australia and Britain, 1863–1902*. London: Palgrave Macmillan, 2018.

Huzzey, Richard. *Freedom Burning: Anti-Slavery and Empire in Victorian Britain*. Ithaca: Cornell University Press, 2012.

Huzzey, Richard, and Henry Miller. "Colonial Petitions, Colonial Petitioners, and the Imperial Parliament, ca. 1780–1918." *Journal of British Studies* 61, no. 2 (2022): 261–289, DOI: 10.1017/jbr.2021.185.

Huzzey, Richard, and Henry Miller. "Petitions, Parliament and Political Culture: Petitioning the House of Commons, 1780–1918." *Past & Present* 248, no. 1 (2020): 123–164, DOI: 10.1093/pastj/gtz061.

Hyam, Ronald, and Ged Martin. *Reappraisals in British Imperial History*. London: Macmillan, 1975.

Ishiguro, Laura. *Nothing to Write Home About: British Family Correspondence and the Settler Colonial Everyday in British Columbia*. Vancouver: University of British Columbia Press, 2019.

Isin, Engin. *Citizens without Frontiers*. New York: Continuum International, 2012.

Isin, Engin. "Theorizing Acts of Citizenship." In Engin Isin and Greg Nielsen, eds, *Acts of Citizenship*. London: Palgrave Macmillan, 2008.

Ivey, Jacob. " 'The Same Effort and the Same Death': The Memory of the Langalibalele Incident of 1873." In Katherine Haldane Grenier and Amanda R. Mushal, eds, *Cultures of Memory in the Nineteenth Century: Consuming Commemoration*. Cham: Palgrave Macmillan, 2020.

Jackson, Stephen. *Religious Education and the Anglo-World: The Impact of Empire, Britishness, and Decolonization in Australia, Canada, and New Zealand*. Boston, MA: Brill, 2020.

Karatani, Rieko. *Defining British Citizenship: Empire, Commonwealth and Modern Britain*. London: Routledge, 2022.

Kauanui, J. Kēhaulani. "False Dilemmas and Settler Colonial Studies: Response to Lorenzo Veracini, 'Is Settler Colonial Studies Even Useful?'" *Postcolonial Studies* 24, no. 2 (2021): 290–296, DOI: 10.1080/13688790.2020.1857023.

Keane, Basil. "Pounamu – Jade or Greenstone – Symbols of Chieftainship." *Te Ara – the Encyclopedia of New Zealand*. Ministry for Culture and Heritage Te Manatu Taonga, 12 June 2006, https://teara.govt.nz/en/pounamu-jade-or-greenstone/page-5 (accessed 11 March 2025).

Kennedy, Dane. *The Imperial History Wars: Debating the British Empire*. London: Bloomsbury Academic, 2018.

Kennedy, William Matthew. *The Imperial Commonwealth: Australia and the Project of Empire, 1867–1914*. Manchester: University of Manchester Press, 2023.

Kidambi, Prashant. "The Petition as Event: Colonial Bombay, circa 1889–1914." *Modern Asian Studies* 53, no. 1 (2019): 203–239, DOI: 10.1017/S0026749X17000555.

Konishi, Shino. "First Nations Scholars, Settler Colonial Studies, and Indigenous History." *Australian Historical Studies* 50, no. 3 (2019): 285–304, DOI: 10.1080/1031461X.2019.1620300.

Korieh, Chima. "'May It Please Your Honor': Letters of Petition as Historical Evidence in an African Colonial Context." *History in Africa* 37 (2010): 83–106, DOI: 10.1353/hia.2010.0034.

Laband, John. "British Boundary Adjustments and the uSuthu-Mandlakazi Conflict in Zululand, 1879–1904." *South African Historical Journal* 30 (1994): 33–60, DOI: 10.1080/02582479408671781.

Laband, John. *Rope of Sand: The Rise and Fall of the Zulu Kingdom in the Nineteenth Century*. Johannesburg: Jonathan Ball, 1995.

Laidlaw, Zoë. "'Aunt Anna's Report': The Buxton Women and the Aborigines Select Committee, 1835–37." *The Journal of Imperial and Commonwealth History* 32, no. 2 (2004): 1–28, DOI: 10.1080/0308653041000170038I.

Laidlaw, Zoë. "Breaking Britannia's Bounds? Law, Settlers, and Space in Britain's Imperial Historiography." *The Historical Journal* 55, no. 3 (2012): 807–830, DOI: 10.1017/S0018246X12000313.

Laidlaw, Zoë. "Imperial Complicity: Indigenous Dispossession in British History and History Writing." In Catherine Hall, Nicholas Draper, and Keith McClelland, eds, *Emancipation and the Remaking of the British Imperial World*. Manchester: Manchester University Press, 2014.

Laidlaw, Zoë. "Indigenous Interlocutors: Networks of Imperial Protest and Humanitarianism in the Mid-Nineteenth Century." In Jane Carey and Jane Lydon, eds, *Indigenous Networks: Mobility, Connections and Exchange*. New York: Routledge, 2014.

Laidlaw, Zoë. *Protecting the Empire's Humanity: Thomas Hodgkin and British Colonial Activism 1830–1870*. Cambridge: Cambridge University Press, 2021.

Laidlaw, Zoë, and Alan Lester, eds, *Indigenous Communities and Settler Colonialism: Land Holding, Loss and Survival in an Interconnected World*. London: Palgrave Macmillan, 2015.

Lake, Marilyn, and Henry Reynolds. *Drawing the Global Colour Line: White Men's Countries and the International Challenge of Racial Equality*. Cambridge: Cambridge University Press, 2008.

Lambert, John. "The Responsible Government Question in Natal, 1856–1893." *Kleio* 7, no. 1 (1975): 22–39, DOI: 10.1080/00232087585310021.

Lester, Alan. "British Settler Discourse and the Circuits of Empire." *History Workshop Journal* 54, no. 1 (2002): 24–48, DOI: 10.1093/hwj/54.1.24.

Lester, Alan. "Colonial Settlers and the Metropole: Racial Discourse in the Early 19th-Century Cape Colony, Australia and New Zealand." *Landscape Research* 27, no. 1 (2002): 39–49, DOI: 10.1080/01426390220110757

Lester, Alan. "Humanitarians and White Settlers in the Nineteenth Century." In Norman Etherington, ed., *Missions and Empire*. Oxford: Oxford University Press, 2005.

Lester, Alan. *Imperial Networks: Creating Identities in Nineteenth-Century South Africa and Britain*. New York: Routledge, 2001.

Lester, Alan. "Race and Citizenship." In Martin Hewitt, ed., *The Victorian World*. London: Routledge, 2012.

Lester, Alan, and Fae Dussart. *Colonization and the Origins of Humanitarian Governance: Protecting Aborigines across the Nineteenth-Century British Empire*. Cambridge: Cambridge University Press, 2014.

Lester, Alan, Kate Boehme, and Peter Mitchell. *Ruling the World: Freedom, Civilisation and Liberalism in the Nineteenth-Century British Empire*. Cambridge: Cambridge University Press, 2021.

Levine, Philippa, ed. *Gender and Empire*. Oxford: Oxford University Press, 2004.

Lorimer, Douglas. *Colour, Class, and the Victorians: English Attitudes to the Negro in the Mid-Nineteenth Century*. Leicester: Leicester University Press, 1978.

Lutz, John, and Keith Carlson. "The Smallpox Chiefs: Bioterrorism and the Exercise of Power in the Pacific Northwest." *Western Historical Quarterly* 55, no. 2 (2024): 87–104, DOI: 10.1093/whq/whae001.

Lydon, Jane. *The Flash of Recognition: Photography and the Emergence of Indigenous Rights*. Sydney: University of New South Wales Press, 2013.

Lydon, Jane. *Imperial Emotions: The Politics of Empathy across the British Empire*. Cambridge: Cambridge University Press, 2020.

Lyons, Scott Richard. *X-Marks: Native Signatures of Assent*. Minneapolis: University of Minnesota Press, 2010.

Macdonald, Charlotte. "Woolwich to Wellington: From Settler Colony to Garrisoned Sovereignty." *New Zealand Journal of History* 53, no. 1 (2019): 50–76, https://muse.jhu.edu/pub/426/article/883327 (accessed 11 March 2025).

MacLeod, Roderick. "Dougall, John Redpath." In *Dictionary of Canadian Biography*. Toronto: University of Toronto Press, 2021.

Macoun, Alissa, and Elizabeth Strakosch. "The Ethical Demands of Settler Colonial Theory." *Settler Colonial Studies* 3, no. 3 (2013): 426–443, DOI: 10.1080/2201473X.2013.810695.

Magee, Gary, and Andrew Thompson. *Empire and Globalisation: Networks of People, Goods and Capital in the British World, c. 1850–1914*. Cambridge: Cambridge University Press, 2010.

Major, Andrea. "British Humanitarian Political Economy and Famine in India, 1838–1842." *Journal of British Studies* 59, no. 2 (2020): 221–244, DOI: 10.1017/jbr.2019.293.

Mann, Jatinder. "The Evolution of Commonwealth Citizenship, 1945–1948 in Canada, Britain and Australia." *Commonwealth & Comparative Politics* 50, no. 3 (2012): 293–313, DOI: 10.1080/14662043.2012.692923.

Mann, Jatinder, and Iain Johnston-White, eds, *Revisiting the British World: New Voices and Perspectives*. Bristol: Peter Lang, 2022.

Marshall, Daniel. *Those who Fell from the Sky: A History of the Cowichan Peoples*. Duncan: Cowichan Tribes, 1999.

Martin, John. "Refusal of Assent: A Hidden Element of Constitutional History in New Zealand." *Victoria University of Wellington Law Review* 41, no. 1 (2010): 51–84, DOI: 10.26686/vuwlr.v41i1.5245.

Matsumoto-Best, Saho. *Britain and the Papacy in the Age of Revolution*. London: The Boydell Press, 2003.

McClendon, Thomas V. *White Chief, Black Lords: Shepstone and the Colonial State in Natal, South Africa, 1845–1878*. Rochester, NY: Boydell & Brewer, 2010.

McClintock, Anne. *Imperial Leather: Race, Gender, and Sexuality in the Colonial Contest*. New York: Routledge, 1995.

McCracken, J. L. *The Cape Parliament, 1854–1910*. Oxford: Clarendon Press, 1967.

McDonald, Jared. *Khoesan and Imperial Citizenship in Nineteenth Century South Africa*. New York: Routledge, 2023.

McHugh, Paul, and Lisa Ford. "Settler Sovereignty and the Shapeshifting Crown." In Lisa Ford and Tim Rowse, eds, *Between Indigenous and Settler Governance*. London: Taylor & Francis, 2012.

McIndoe, Andrew. "A Pluralistic Imperialism? Britain's Understanding of Sovereignty at the Signing of the Treaty of Waitangi." *Auckland University Law Review* 21 (2015): 60–85, www.nzlii.org/nz/journals/AukULawRw/2015/5.pdf (accessed 11 March 2025).

McLisky, Claire. "'Due Observance of Justice, and the Protection of Their Rights': Philanthropy, Humanitarianism and Moral Purpose in the Aborigines Protection Society circa 1837 and Its Portrayal in Australian Historiography, 1883–2003." *Limina: A Journal of Historical and Cultural Studies* 11 (2005): 57–66, DOI: 10.3316/informit.225751412200669.

McRae, Andrew. "King Tawhiao Bust for Museum." Radio New Zealand, 17 August 2015, www.rnz.co.nz/news/te-manu-korihi/281637/kingi-tawhiao-bust-for-museum (accessed 20 March 2025).

Melville, Fred. *The Postage Stamps of the Cape of Good Hope, with Mafeking and Vryburg*. London: The Melville Stamp Books, 1913.

Midgley, Clare, ed. *Gender and Imperialism*. Manchester: Manchester University Press, 1998.

Miller, J. R. "Anti-Catholic Thought in Victorian Canada." *Canadian Historical Review* 66, no. 4 (December 1985): 474–494, DOI: 10.3138/CHR-066-04-03.

Miller, J. R. "Anti-Catholicism in Canada: From the British Conquest to the Great War." In Terrence Murphy and Gerald Stortz, eds, *Creed and Culture: The Place of English-Speaking Catholics in Canadian Society, 1750–1930*. Montreal: McGill-Queen's University Press, 1993.

Miller, J. R. *Equal Rights: The Jesuits' Estates Act Controversy*. Montreal: McGill-Queen's University Press, 1979.

Miller, J. R. *Reflections on Native–Newcomer Relations: Selected Essays*. Toronto: University of Toronto Press, 2004.

Mitcham, John. *Race and Imperial Defence in the British World, 1870–1914*. Cambridge: Cambridge University Press, 2016.

Mkhize, Khwezi. "'To See Us as We See Ourselves': John Tengo Jabavu and the Politics of the Black Periodical." *Journal of Southern African Studies* 44, no. 3 (2018): 413–430, DOI: 10.1080/03057070.2018.1462993.

Mohr, Thomas. "A British Empire Court: A Brief Appraisal of the History of the Judicial Committee of the Privy Council." In Anthony McElligott, Liam Chambers, Ciara Breathnach, and Catherine Lawless, eds, *Power in History: From Medieval Ireland to the Post-Modern World*. Dublin: Irish Academic Press, 2011.

Moreton-Robinson, Aileen, ed. *Sovereign Subjects: Indigenous Sovereignty Matters*. Crows Nest: Allen & Unwin, 2007.

Morgan, Cecilia. *Building Better Britains? Settler Societies in the British World, 1783–1920*. Toronto: University of Toronto Press, 2016.

Morgan, Cecilia. *Travellers through Empire: Indigenous Voyages from Early Canada*. Montreal: McGill-Queen's University Press, 2017.

Morin, Karen, and Lawrence Berg. "Gendering Resistance: British Colonial Narratives of Wartime New Zealand." *Journal of Historical Geography* 27, no. 2 (2001): 196–222, DOI: 10.1006/jhge.2000.0299.

Morrison, Hugh. *Protestant Children, Missions and Education in the British World*. Leiden: Brill, 2021.

Moser, Christian. "Walking in the Contact Zone: Georg Forster and the Peripatetic Mode of Exploration (1768–1777)." In Frédéric Regard, ed., *British Narratives of Exploration: Case Studies of the Self and Other*. London: Pickering and Chatto, 2009.

Muffet, Leigh. "The Cape of Good Hope Colony and the British World Turned Upside-Down, 1806–1836." *The Journal of Imperial and Commonwealth History* (2022): 1–35, DOI: 10.1080/03086534.2022.2086205.

Muller, Hannah Weiss. *Subjects and Sovereign: Bonds of Belonging in the Eighteenth-Century British Empire*. Oxford: Oxford University Press, 2017.

Nahaboo, Zaki. "Rémy Ollier and Imperial Citizenship." *Interventions* 20, no. 5 (2018): 717–733, DOI: 10.1080/1369801X.2018.1487317.

Nettelbeck, Amanda. "Bracelets, Blankets and Badges of Distinction: Aboriginal Subjects and Queen Victoria's Gifts in Canada and Australia." In Sarah Carter and Maria Nugent, eds, *Mistress of Everything: Queen Victoria in Indigenous Worlds*. Manchester: Manchester University Press, 2017.

Nettelbeck, Amanda. *Indigenous Rights and Colonial Subjecthood: Protection and Reform in the Nineteenth-Century British Empire*. Cambridge: Cambridge University Press, 2019.

Nettelbeck, Amanda. "'We Are Sure of Your Sympathy': Indigenous Uses of the Politics of Protection in Nineteenth-Century Australia and Canada." *Journal of Colonialism and Colonial History* 17, no. 1 (2016), DOI: 10.1353/cch.2016.0009.

Nettelbeck, Amanda, Russell Smandych, Louis A. Knafla, and Robert Foster. *Fragile Settlements: Aboriginal Peoples, Law, and Resistance in South-West Australia and Prairie Canada*. Vancouver: University of British Columbia Press, 2016.

Nicholson, Amber. "Hau: Giving Voices to the Ancestors." *The Journal of the Polynesian Society* 128, no. 2 (2019): 137–162, DOI: 10.15286/jps.128.2.137-162.

Nunn, Neil. "Toxic Encounters, Settler Logics of Elimination, and the Future of a Continent." *Antipode* 50, no. 5 (2018): 1330–1348, DOI: 10.1111/anti.12403.

Nyika, Farai, and Johan Fourie. "Black Disenfranchisement in the Cape Colony, c. 1887–1909: Challenging the Numbers." *Journal of Southern African Studies* 46, no. 3 (2020): 455–469, DOI: 10.1080/03057070.2020.1741177.

Orange, Claudia. "Taiwhanga, Hirini Rāwiri." In *Dictionary of New Zealand Biography*, 1993, https://teara.govt.nz/en/biographies/2t4/taiwhanga-hirini-rawiri (accessed 11 March 2025).

Orange, Claudia. *The Treaty of Waitangi*. Wellington: Allen & Unwin, 1987.

Parsons, Neil. " 'No Longer Rare Birds in London': Zulu, Ndebele, Gaza, and Swazi Envoys to England, 1882–1894." In Gretchen Gerzina and Neil Parsons, eds, *Black Victorians, Black Victoriana*. New Brunswick: Rutgers University Press, 2003.

Perry, Adele. *Colonial Relations: The Douglas-Connolly Family and the Nineteenth-Century Imperial World*. Cambridge: Cambridge University Press, 2015.

Pickles, Katie, and Catharine Coleborne, eds. *New Zealand's Empire*. Manchester: Manchester University Press, 2016.

Pietsch, Tamson. "Rethinking the British World." *Journal of British Studies* 52, no. 2 (2013): 441–463, DOI: 10.1017/jbr.2013.53.

Porter, Andrew. *European Imperialism, 1860–1914*. Basingstoke: Macmillan, 1994.

Porter, Andrew. *Religion versus Empire? British Protestant Missionaries and Overseas Expansion, 1700–1914*. Manchester: Manchester University Press, 2004.

Potter, Simon. *News and the British World: The Emergence of an Imperial Press System, 1876–1922*. Oxford: Clarendon Press, 2003.

Pratt, Mary Louise. "Arts of the Contact Zone." *Profession* (1991): 33–40.

Price, Richard. *Empire and Indigeneity: Histories and Legacies*. London: Routledge, 2021.

Puketapu-Hetet, Erenora. *Māori Weaving*. Auckland: Pitman, 1989.

Reed, Charles. *Royal Tourists, Colonial Subjects and the Making of a British World, 1860–1911*. Manchester: Manchester University Press, 2017.

Reid, Darren. "The Aborigines' Protection Society as an Anticolonial Network: Rethinking the APS 'from the Bottom Up' through Letters Written by Black South

Africans, 1883–87." *Journal of Colonialism and Colonial History* 22, no. 2 (2021), DOI: 10.1353/cch.2021.0028.

Reid, Darren. "Shadrach Boyce Mama and the 'Kaffir Depot': Navigating Imperial Networks to Agitate against the Forced Removal of Xhosa Women and Children from Cape Town, May–December 1879." *South African Historical Journal* 72, no. 4 (2020): 561–578, DOI: 10.1080/02582473.2020.1827018.

Reilly, Hope Marie. "Race, Gender, and British Anthropology in Nineteenth Century New ealand." MA thesis, College of Charleston, 2017.

Reynolds, Henry. *This Whispering in Our Hearts*. St Leonards: Allen & Unwin, 1998.

Reynolds, Henry. *This Whispering in Our Hearts Revisited*. Sydney: University of New South Wales Press, 2018.

Sage, Walter. "The Critical Period of British Columbia History, 1866–1871." *Pacific Historical Review* 1, no. 4 (1932): 424–443, DOI: 10.2307/3633112.

Saito, Natsu Taylor. *Settler Colonialism, Race, and the Law: Why Structural Racism Persists*. New York: NYU Press, 2020.

Sampson, Jane. "British Authority or 'Mere Theory'? Colonial Law and Native People on Vancouver Island." *Western Legal History* 39 (1998): 39–63.

Schnurr, Matthew A. "Cotton as Calamitous Commodity: The Politics of Agricultural Failure in Natal and Zululand, 1844–1933." *Canadian Journal of African Studies* 47, no. 1 (2013): 115–132, DOI: 10.1080/00083968.2013.771423.

Schreuder, Deryck. *Gladstone and Kruger: Liberal Government & Colonial "Home Rule" 1880–85*. London: Routledge, 1969.

Sillery, Anthony. *The Bechuanaland Protectorate*. Oxford: Oxford University Press, 1952.

Simpson, Audra. *Mohawk Interruptus: Political Life across the Borders of Settler States*. Durham, NC: Duke University Press, 2014.

Slater, Lisa. *Anxieties of Belonging in Settler Colonialism: Australia, Race and Place*. New York: Routledge, 2018.

Snelgrove, Corey, Rita Dhamoon, and Jeff Corntassel. "Unsettling Settler Colonialism: The Discourse and Politics of Settlers, and Solidarity with Indigenous Nations." *Decolonization: Indigeneity, Education & Society* 3, no. 2 (2014): 1–32, https://jps.library.utoronto.ca/index.php/des/article/view/21166/17970 (accessed 11 March 2025).

Somerville, Alice Te Punga. "OMG Settler Colonial Studies: Response to Lorenzo Veracini's 'Is Settler Colonial Studies Even Useful?'" *Postcolonial Studies* 24, no. 2 (2021): 278–282, DOI: 10.1080/13688790.2020.1854980.

Ste Croix, Lorne. "Penny, Edward Goff." In *Dictionary of Canadian Biography*. Toronto: University of Toronto Press, 1982.

Steer, Philip. *Settler Colonialism in Victorian Literature: Economics and Political Identity in the Networks of Empire*. Cambridge: Cambridge University Press, 2020.

Stevenson, Garth. *Community Besieged: The Anglophone Minority and the Politics of Quebec*. Montreal: McGill-Queen's University Press, 1999.

Storey, Kenton. "Colonial Humanitarian? Thomas Gore Browne and the Taranaki War, 1860–61." *Journal of British Studies* 53, no. 1 (2014): 111–135, DOI: 10.1017/jbr.2013.210.

Storey, Kenton. *Settler Anxiety at the Outposts of Empire: Colonial Relations, Humanitarian Discourses, and the Imperial Press*. Vancouver: University of British Columbia Press, 2016.

Swain, Harry. *Oka: A Political Crisis and Its Legacy.* Vancouver: Douglas & McIntyre, 2010.

Tallie, T. J. *Queering Colonial Natal: Indigeneity and the Violence of Belonging in Southern Africa.* Minneapolis: University of Minnesota Press, 2019.

Tcherkézoff, Serge. "On Cloth, Gifts and Nudity: Regarding Some European Misunderstandings during Early Encounters in Polynesia." In Chloë Colchester, ed., *Clothing the Pacific.* Oxford: Berg, 2003.

Thackeray, David. "Selling the Empire? Marketing and the Demise of the British World, c. 1920–1960." *The Journal of Imperial and Commonwealth History* 48, no. 4 (2020): 679–705, DOI: 10.1080/03086534.2020.1741837.

Thomas, Nicholas. *Entangled Objects: Exchange, Material Culture, and Colonialism in the Pacific.* Cambridge, MA: Harvard University Press, 1991.

Thompson, Andrew. "The Languages of Loyalism in Southern Africa, c. 1870–1939." *The English Historical Review* 118, no. 477 (2003): 617–650, www.jstor.org/stable/3489288 (accessed 11 March 2025).

Thompson, John. *A Brief History of the Land Dispute at Kanesatake [Oka] from Contact to 1961.* Ottawa: Treaties and Historical Research Centre, 1991.

Thompson, Paul. "The Natal Militia: Defence of the Colony, 1893–1910." *Journal of Natal and Zulu History* 29, no. 1 (2011): 20–65, DOI: 10.1080/02590123.2011.11964164.

Trapido, Stanley. "'The Friends of the Natives': Merchants, Peasants and the Political and Ideological Structure of Liberalism in the Cape, 1854–1910." In Shula Marks and Anthony Atmore, eds, *Economy and Society in Pre-Industrial South Africa.* London: Longman, 1980.

Trapido, Stanley. "The Origins of the Cape Franchise Qualifications of 1853." *The Journal of African History* 5, no. 1 (1964): 37–54, DOI: 10.1017/S0021853700004497.

Travers, Robert. "Indian Petitioning and Colonial State-Formation in Eighteenth-Century Bengal." *Modern Asian Studies* 53, no. 1 (2019): 89–122, DOI: 10.1017/S0026749X17000841.

Van Rijn, Kiran. "'Lo! The Poor Indian!' Colonial Responses to the 1862–63 Smallpox Epidemic in British Columbia and Vancouver Island." *Canadian Bulletin of Medical History* 23, no. 2 (2006): 541–560, DOI: 10.3138/cbmh.23.2.541.

Vaughan, Géraldine. *Anti-Catholicism and British Identities in Britain, Canada and Australia, 1880s–1920s.* Histories of the Sacred and Secular, 1700–2000. Cham: Palgrave Macmillan, 2022.

Vaughan, Géraldine. "'Britishers and Protestants': Protestantism and Imperial British Identities in Britain, Canada and Australia from the 1880s to the 1920s." *Studies in Church History* 54 (2018): 359–373, DOI: 10.1017/stc.2017.20.

Veracini, Lorenzo. "Containment, Elimination, Endogeneity: Settler Colonialism in the Global Present." *Rethinking Marxism* 31, no. 1 (2019): 118–140, DOI: 10.1080/08935696.2019.1577611.

Veracini, Lorenzo. *Settler Colonialism: A Theoretical Overview.* Cham: Palgrave Macmillan, 2010.

Visser, Beaurel. "African Resistance to the Parliamentary Voters' Registration Act." *Journal of Southern African Studies* 48, no. 6 (2022): 975–991, DOI: 10.1080/03057070.2023.2167392.

Waitangi Tribunal. *The Taranaki Report: Kaupapa Tuatahi.* Wellington, NZ: Legislation Direct, 1996.

Waite, P. B. "White, Thomas." In *Dictionary of Canadian Biography*. Toronto: University of Toronto Press, 1982.

Weaver, John. *The Great Land Rush and the Making of the Modern World, 1650–1900*. Montreal: McGill-Queen's University Press, 2003.

Welsh, David. *The Roots of Segregation: Native Policy in Colonial Natal, 1845–1910*. Oxford: Oxford University Press, 1971.

Willan, Brian. "The Anti-Slavery and Aborigines' Protection Society and the South African Natives' Land Act of 1913." *The Journal of African History* 20, no. 1 (1979): 83–102, DOI: 10.1017/S002185370001673X.

Wilson, Jon, and Andrew Dilley. "The Incoherence of Empire; or, the Pitfalls of Ignoring Sovereignty in the History of the British Empire." *Transactions of the Royal Historical Society* 1 (2023): 191–217, DOI: 10.1017/S0080440123000063.

Wolfe, Patrick. "Settler Colonialism and the Elimination of the Native." *Journal of Genocide Research* 8, no. 4 (2006): 387–409, DOI: 10.1080/14623520601056240.

Wolffe, John. "Anti-Catholicism and the British Empire, 1815–1914." In Hilary Carey, ed., *Empires of Religion*. London: Palgrave Macmillan, 2008.

Woollacott, Angela. *Gender and Empire*. New York: Palgrave Macmillan, 2006.

Woollacott, Angela. *Settler Society in the Australian Colonies: Self-Government and Imperial Culture*. Oxford: Oxford University Press, 2015.

Zaeske, Susan. *Signatures of Citizenship: Petitioning, Antislavery, and Women's Political Identity*. Chapel Hill: University of North Carolina Press, 2003.

Index

EU authorised representative for GPSR:
Easy Access System Europe, Mustamäe tee 50,
10621 Tallinn, Estonia
gpsr.requests@easproject.com

www.ingramcontent.com/pod-product-compliance
Lightning Source LLC
Jackson TN
JSHW060720021225
95051JS00027B/32
9781526181626